DEATH, GENDER AND SEXUALITY IN CONTEMPORARY ADOLESCENT LITERATURE

Children's Literature and Culture
Jack Zipes, *Series Editor*

Little Women and the
Feminist Imagination
Criticism, Controversy, Personal Essays
edited by Janice M. Alberghene and
Beverly Lyon Clark

The Presence of the Past
*Memory, Heritage, and Childhood
in Postwar Britain*
by Valerie Krips

The Case of Peter Rabbit
*Changing Conditions of Literature
for Children*
by Margaret Mackey

The Feminine Subject in Children's
Literature
by Christine Wilkie-Stibbs

Ideologies of Identity in
Adolescent Fiction
by Robyn McCallum

Recycling Red Riding Hood
by Sandra Beckett

The Poetics of Childhood
by Roni Natov

Voices of the Other
*Children's Literature and the
Postcolonial Context*
edited by Roderick McGillis

Narrating Africa
George Henty and the Fiction of Empire
by Mawuena Kossi Logan

Reimagining Shakespeare for Children
and Young Adults
edited by Naomi J. Miller

Representing the Holocaust in
Youth Literature
by Lydia Kokkola

Translating for Children
by Riitta Oittinen

Beatrix Potter
Writing in Code
by M. Daphne Kutzer

Children's Films
History, Ideology, Pedagogy, Theory
by Ian Wojcik-Andrews

Utopian and Dystopian Writing for
Children and Young Adults
edited by Carrie Hintz and Elaine Ostry

Transcending Boundaries
*Writing for a Dual Audience of
Children and Adults*
edited by Sandra L. Beckett

The Making of the Modern Child
*Children's Literature and Childhood in the
Late Eighteenth Century*
by Andrew O'Malley

How Picturebooks Work
by Maria Nikolajeva and Carole Scott

Brown Gold
*Milestones of African American Children's
Picture Books, 1845-2002*
by Michelle H. Martin

Russell Hoban/Forty Years
Essays on His Writing for Children
by Alida Allison

Apartheid and Racism in South African
Children's Literature
by Donnarae MacCann and
Amadu Maddy

Empire's Children
*Empire and Imperialism in Classic British
Children's Books*
by M. Daphne Kutzer

Constructing the Canon of
Children's Literature
Beyond Library Walls and Ivory Towers
by Anne Lundin

Youth of Darkest England
*Working Class Children at the Heart of
Victorian Empire*
by Troy Boone

Ursula K. Leguin Beyond Genre
Literature for Children and Adults
by Mike Cadden

Twice-Told Children's Tales
edited by Betty Greenway

Diana Wynne Jones
The Fantastic Tradition and Children's Literature
by Farah Mendlesohn

Childhood and Children's Books in
Early Modern Europe, 1550-1800
edited by Andrea Immel and
Michael Witmore

Voracious Children
Who Eats Whom in Children's Literature
by Carolyn Daniel

National Character in South African
Children's Literature
by Elwyn Jenkins

Myth, Symbol, and Meaning in
Mary Poppins
The Governess as Provocateur
by Georgia Grilli

A Critical History of French Children's
Literature, Vol. 1 & 2
by Penny Brown

Once Upon a Time in a Different World
*Issues and Ideas in African American
Children's Literature*
by Neal A. Lester

The Gothic in Children's Literature
Haunting the Borders
Edited by Anna Jackson, Karen Coats,
and Roderick McGillis

Reading Victorian Schoolrooms
*Childhood and Education in
Nineteenth-Century Fiction*
by Elizabeth Gargano

Soon Come Home to This Island
West Indians in British Children's Literature
by Karen Sands-O'Connor

Boys in Children's Literature and
Popular Culture
*Masculinity, Abjection, and the
Fictional Child*
by Annette Wannamaker

Into the Closet
*Cross-dressing and the Gendered Body
in Children's Literature*
by Victoria Flanagan

Russian Children's Literature and Culture
edited by Marina Balina and
Larissa Rudova

The Outside Child In and Out of the Book
by Christine Wilkie-Stibbs

Representing Africa in Children's
Literature
Old and New Ways of Seeing
by Vivian Yenika-Agbaw

The Fantasy of Family
*Nineteenth-Century Children's Literature
and the Myth of the Domestic Ideal*
by Liz Thiel

From Nursery Rhymes to Nationhood
*Children's Literature and the Construction
of Canadian Identity*
by Elizabeth A. Galway

The Family in English Children's Literature
by Ann Alston

Enterprising Youth
*Social Values and Acculturation in
Nineteenth-Century American
Children's Literature*
by Monika Elbert

Constructing Adolescence in
Fantastic Realism
Alison Waller

Crossover Fiction
Global and Historical Perspectives
by Sandra L. Beckett

The Crossover Novel
*Contemporary Children's Fiction and Its
Adult Readership*
by Rachel Falconer

Shakespeare in Children's Literature
Gender and Cultural Capital
by Erica Hateley

Critical Approaches to Food in
Children's Literature
edited by Kara K. Keeling and
Scott T. Pollard

Death, Gender and Sexuality in
Contemporary Adolescent Literature
by Kathryn James

DEATH, GENDER AND SEXUALITY IN CONTEMPORARY ADOLESCENT LITERATURE

KATHRYN JAMES

Routledge
Taylor & Francis Group

NEW YORK AND LONDON

First published 2009
by Routledge
270 Madison Ave, New York NY 10016

Simultaneously published in the UK
by Routledge
2 Park Square, Milton Park, Abingdon, Oxon, OX14 4RN

Routledge is an imprint of the Taylor & Francis Group, an informa business

Transferred to Digital Printing 2010

© 2009 Taylor & Francis

Typeset in by Minion by IBT Global.

Library of Congress Cataloging in Publication Data
James, Kathryn.
    Death, gender, and sexuality in contemporary adolescent literature / Kathryn James.
        p. cm.—(Children's literature and culture ; 61)
    Includes bibliographical references and index.
    1. Young adult literature, American—History and criticism.   2. Death in literature.   3. Sex role in literature.   4. Sex in literature.   5. Teenagers—Books and reading.   I. Title.
    PS374.D34K38 2009
    810.9'9282—dc22
    2008026189

ISBN10: 0-415-96493-8 (hbk)
ISBN10: 0-415-88856-5 (pbk)
ISBN10: 0-203-88515-5 (ebk)

ISBN13: 978-0-415-96493-7 (hbk)
ISBN13: 978-0-415-88856-1 (pbk)
ISBN13: 978-0-203-88515-4 (ebk)

Contents

Series Editor's Foreword

Dedicated to furthering original research in children's literature and culture, the Children's Literature and Culture series includes monographs on individual authors and illustrators, historical examinations of different periods, literary analyses of genres, and comparative studies on literature and the mass media. The series is international in scope and is intended to encourage innovative research in children's literature with a focus on interdisciplinary methodology.

Children's literature and culture are understood in the broadest sense of the term children to encompass the period of childhood up through adolescence. Owing to the fact that the notion of childhood has changed so much since the origination of children's literature, this Routledge series is particularly concerned with transformations in children's culture and how they have affected the representation and socialization of children. While the emphasis of the series is on children's literature, all types of studies that deal with children's radio, film, television, and art are included in an endeavor to grasp the aesthetics and values of children's culture. Not only have there been momentous changes in children's culture in the last fifty years, but there have been radical shifts in the scholarship that deals with these changes. In this regard, the goal of the Children's Literature and Culture series is to enhance research in this field and, at the same time, point to new directions that bring together the best scholarly work throughout the world.

Jack Zipes

Acknowledgments

Death is often represented as a journey. Myth and folklore drawn from a diversity of cultures documents the flight of the dead soul across rivers and seas, through mazes of underground passages, along tunnels, and even up the sun's rays towards the sun itself. My own inquiry into the subject of death has been something of a journey too—a journey that would have been difficult, if not impossible, without the help, support, and encouragement of those whom I acknowledge here.

Special thanks must first go to Clare Bradford. Clare's generosity, guidance, and her unfailing faith not only in the project but in my ability to do it justice, have been invaluable. As this book began its life as a doctoral thesis, I am indebted to a number of people for providing advice, assistance, and information during the course of my degree, including Linda Bennett, Diana Hodge, Steve Smith, Tony Smith, Gerry Turcotte, Sascha Valewink, Paul Banks, Deb Mohring, Nadene Murphy, Jennifer Peck, Laurel Kerr, Matt Osborne, Cate Hayes, Jan Smith, Faye Wiffen, and Jude Wilks. At Deakin University, I owe thanks to: Research Services and the Faculty of Arts for the funding that allowed me to undertake the initial research; the library staff in the Off-Campus and Interlibrary Loans units; and my colleagues in the School of Communication and Creative Arts—in particular, Kate McInally and Liz Parsons. I am also grateful to: Elizabeth Braithwaite for her contribution to Chapter 5; Kerry Mallan and Roberta Seelinger Trites for their helpful comments regarding the project's transformation from dissertation to book; Liz Levine and Ryan Kenney for their assistance with all the fiddly bits of the production stage; Nick Nicholson at the National Gallery of Australia for his part in securing permission to use the front cover image; and, for their keen editorial eye, Jack Zipes and the ever-cheerful Erica Wetter.

Finally, my friends and family deserve to be recognised for their contribution, but here I especially thank Steve. His patience with, and willingness to be subjected to, the range of moods I experienced while working on this project—both as a thesis and as a book—is commendable. During this time, Steve has also acted as a sounding board, proofread and edited various drafts of my work, and made me endless cups of tea. For all this, and more, I am extremely appreciative, and it is with love and gratitude that I dedicate this book to him.

Portions of Chapter 2 and Chapter 3 were previously published in *Papers: Explorations into Children's Literature* (volume and issue numbers 19.1 and 16.2, respectively). Permission to reproduce this material has been granted by the editors. A revised and condensed version of Chapter 2 first appeared in "Other Contact Zones", volume seven of *New Talents 21C* (2007). Permission to reprint has been granted by the editor. Part of Chapter 4 was presented at the Australasian Children's Literature Association for Research (ACLAR) conference, Wellington, New Zealand, in June 2008.

Introduction
Beginning with Endings:
Death in Children's Literature

> Death loves to be represented.
> (Ariès, *Images* 1)

There is nothing more certain at the moment of our birth than the inevitability of our death. As human beings, we are arguably the only creatures able to reflect on this knowledge about our mortality, making death a topic unlike any other. Indeed, death is one of the few subjects that is of truly universal concern; throughout human history, this sense of ending has had an impact on the ways in which we order and give meaning to our lives, it has been central to many (if not all) of our religious beliefs and practices, and it has played a significant role in our mythology, art, literature, science, and philosophy. Arthur Schopenhauer argues, for instance, that death is "the true inspiring genius, or the muse of philosophy", because without it there would scarcely be any philosophising (249), while for Archibald MacLeish, death is "the perspective of every great picture ever painted and the underbeat of every measurable poem" (qtd. in Kearl, "Images"). The "foreground of life" is only possible with the "background of death", Michael Kearl claims, because death is omnipresent; it lies within our fantasies and dreams, language and metaphor, and is central to our thought systems and activities (*Endings* 3, 6). Much of what we call culture, then, comes together around the collective response to death (Bronfen and Goodwin 3), but it is only fairly recently that talking about it and studying it has become fashionable once again. During the last three or four decades, death has undergone something of a "revival", to use Tony Walter's term (*Revival* 1), with the result that in virtually all academic disciplines

1

today there now exists an abundance of critical inquiries into death, its relationship with culture, and the ways it is understood and represented.

Despite this resurgence of interest—and despite some theoretically sophisticated work emerging in other literary contexts—the field of children's literature is notable for its lack of scholarship in this area.[1] The frequency of death's appearance in books published for children has increased markedly in the period post-1970, yet academic analyses of the subject remain limited. Perhaps the very act of bringing "death" and "children" together is unsettling. Some critics argue, for instance, that death is not a suitable topic for either children or the novels that are produced for them: it is too morbid, too painful, or too likely to induce psychological harm, they claim. Others believe that exposing young people to graphic or violent depictions of death merely generates more violence; in becoming so familiar with death, they argue, children have lost the capacity to be shocked by it or to conceive of its finality. Without doubt, death can be a difficult subject to read and write about. As Philip A. Mellor and Chris Shilling's sociological study of death and modernity indicates, "the existential contradiction of being aware of the inevitability of death, while being unable to have certain knowledge of what death will entail" can be such a powerful threat to an individual's ontological security that confrontations with death (however abstract) are often avoided (421).

Nevertheless, for several reasons, representations of death in children's fiction can provide an unusually clear opportunity to understand some of the ways in which meaning is created and shared within a society. For one, any critical study of a culture's approaches and responses to death can expose some of the most fundamental features of its social life (Seale 211). As Philippe Ariès's studies illustrate (*Hour; Images; Western*), a culture's representations of death may be read collectively as a text to give insights into its social systems, death ethos, conceptions of selfhood, temporal orientation, and religious and secular attitudes. Secondly, children's literature may reflect these values with special clarity, both because of the vigilance with which it is monitored (Niall 5), and because it is intimately engaged in the socialisation of children. Childhood is viewed as "the crucial formative period in the life of a human being, the time for basic education about the nature of the world, how to live in it [. . .] what to believe, what and how to think", John Stephens points out. And the usual purpose of children's fiction, he adds, is to assist in this process, meaning that children are offered a network of ideological positions in these texts pertaining to "life" and how to "live it" (*Language* 8).

Indeed, the most pervasive themes in children's fiction are those of growth and development (Stephens, *Language*). Given that attention is predominantly focused on personal identity, the individual psyche, subjective development, and social- and self-awareness, it is a literature of *becoming*, so representations of death (the end of life) can have especial relevance. Lois Rauch Gibson and Laura M. Zaidman's appraisal of the articles submitted to the *Children's Literature Association Quarterly* Winter 1991–92 issue on death essentially illustrates this point: "[W]hen a character dies, another learns a little more about how to live—to appreciate the gift of life even while mourning. The dying instruct the living about true priorities and the worth of each individual's life" (233). Undoubtedly, this statement fails to take into account that "true priorities" and "worth" are not universal, but subjective and culturally specific. However, like the other essays in the journal, it is useful in revealing something about the critical angle that has dominated discussions of death in children's literature to date. As a group, these studies suggest that while there is a large secondary literature dealing with death, critical engagement with the subject has tended to be descriptive rather than analytical, preoccupied with death in a bibliographic or thematic sense, and largely focused on bibliotherapy (that is, dedicated to explaining how narratives featuring death help children to cope with grief).

It would be fair to say, then, that there has been little discussion of the social and cultural meanings of death, and insufficient examination of its function in discursive, ideological, and rhetorical forms, creating a clear sense of the work that remains to be done in the field. Of course, this book represents just a fraction of that work, particularly as its focus is so narrow. In examining representations of death only in adolescent literature, and only how they appear in relation to gender and sexuality, I do not engage with a number of other prominent meanings that death has for and within Western culture. At this point, it therefore becomes pertinent to ask: Why these texts in particular? And why gender/sexuality?

As I have argued, in the last thirty years or so, death's presence in books for children of all ages has increased markedly. However, its repeated appearance across a multitude of genres in the adolescent category suggests that it has an especially powerful appeal to teen audiences in particular. According to Roberta Seelinger Trites, death is the *sine qua non* of adolescent literature, "the defining factor that distinguishes it both from children's and adult literature" (*Disturbing* 118). Suggesting as much, the form/s that death takes does tend to differ between these two genres. Books for younger readers are generally aimed at introducing children to the concepts of death and grief, often by exploring the deaths of grandparents and pets. In these texts, learning about death "symbolizes a degree of separation from one's parents" (*Disturbing* 118–19). Those for pre-teen audiences are also likely to feature the deaths of loved ones (such as a parent, sibling, or friend), although depictions of the kind of graphic deaths that are such a staple of the horror genre are present here too. Where adolescent fictions are concerned, however, representations of death are as varied as they are numerous.

Trites also contends that the discourse surrounding death recurs in adolescent fiction with the consistency of the two other dominant discourses of the genre: "the establishment of an identity independent from one's parents and the exploration of sexuality". Death, sexuality, and authority are "mutually implicated" in these texts, she explains, because not only are sex and death "biological concepts that are linked inviolably", but depictions of those rites of passage which involve adolescents learning their place in the power structure, trying to understand death, and experiencing sexuality are often treated together (*Disturbing* x, 117, 122). I refer to Trites at length here because it is this premise that largely informs my discussion; that is, knowledge about carnality and its limits provides the agenda for much of the fiction that is written today for adolescent readers.

John Green's *Looking for Alaska* is a case in point. Trying to seek what a dying François Rabelais labelled the "Great Perhaps", the novel's protagonist, Miles Halter, leaves his safe, sheltered life in Florida for boarding school in Alabama. The narrative traces his journey from naïve, overprotected, and unpopular geek to mature, self-aware, daring, and articulate almost-adult. Along the way, Miles develops a penchant for insubordination to authority figures, cigarettes, and vodka; he learns about loyalty, love, orgasms, and loss; and he becomes a star pupil in his world religions class. As his fascination with famous last words suggests, the novel is largely concerned with philosophical questions about life and death. The separate threads of the story coalesce when his friend, Alaska Young—"the hottest girl in all of human history" (14)—dies in a car accident. Poignantly, for Miles, this occurs just after an intense make-out session during which Alaska tutors him in the art of kissing. "*We are all going,*" Miles thinks several weeks later, "and it applies to turtles and turtlenecks, Alaska the girl and Alaska the place, because nothing can last, not even the earth itself" (196, emphasis original).

In broad terms, then, gender and sexuality are the "lens" through which I explore death by examining: the trope of woman/death; the eroticising and sexualising of death; and the ways in which femininity and masculinity are constructed in association with these representations. As Elisabeth Bronfen and Sarah Webster Goodwin contend, representations of death "bring into play the binary tensions of gender constructs, as life/death engages permutations with masculinity/femininity and with fantasies of power" (20). Underpinning this examination is the supposition that an individual's notions of death and gender may be grounded in biology, yet they are also culturally constructed; that is, channelled to, formed by, and learned through the social structures, images, symbols, and rituals of a culture. The book is also informed by the understanding that the methods by which readers make meaning from texts are complex ones, but that by paying attention to the linguistic and narratological processes involved in their construction, it is possible to gauge how those texts function both ideologically and in relation to the culture from which they were produced (Stephens, *Language*).

There are a number of questions that may be asked in order to frame such a discussion: What are the discursive practices involved in the texts' constructions of death-gender-sexuality?, In what (gendered) ways do these representations of death instruct the living?, What are the "true priorities" (relating to gender and sexuality) inscribed within the text?, How are readers positioned to respond to these ideologies?, Do the texts conflate experiences of death with the theme of (gendered/sexual) growth and, if so, how?, In what way is the relationship between death and power manifested?, and finally, How do these representations (as a group) coalesce to produce particular patterns or themes?

Before I map out some directions for this discussion, I want to make some clarifications regarding the novels I have selected for the book, and the parameters that have influenced it. In the field of children's literature, it is recognised that the very terms used to define the genre and its readers are problematic. Indeed, notions of childhood and adolescence, and the features that can be said to characterise fictions produced for audiences in these age categories, have stimulated much debate.[2] Not only do the ways in which a culture defines adolescence vary greatly, for instance, it has been suggested that the terms "adolescent" and "young adult fiction" are themselves open to interpretation given that both can be seen as social constructs.[3] Claims have been made, moreover, that the adolescent fiction genre exists only to serve the purposes of a publisher-driven market.[4] My intention here is not to add to this dialogue, suffice it to say that due to this general lack of consensus, it is necessary to outline what the terms mean in the context of this book.

Although the boundaries defining young adult (or YA) fiction are notoriously fluid, I therefore take "adolescent literature" to mean those fictive texts which have an implied teenage audience; that is, books which either feature protagonists of secondary school age (twelve to eighteen years), or, it is reasonable to suppose, would be read by those in this age group. In using the term "contemporary", I am referring to those novels which have been published over the last two or three decades. Admittedly, YA fiction was well established as a literary genre in English-speaking countries by the late 1960s. However, the period from the mid-1980s to the present is a more useful one here, not least because it can be seen as "a golden age" in the publishing of teenage fiction (Scutter 2), but also because the years beyond the 1980s saw a paradigm shift in the ways that narratives of identity—and thus, to borrow a phrase of Stephens's, the "semiotics of class, ethnicities and gender" ("Always" vi)—were represented and problematised in children's literature.

Needless to say, it is beyond the scope of this book to examine each and every text that fits these parameters. My emphasis, therefore, is on the novels which speak the loudest to the themes and aims of the book. Due to its origins as a doctoral thesis focused on Australian literature, I have largely relied on texts produced and disseminated in Australia. However, with the exception of some parts of Chapter 2 (which is concerned with Australia and Australian national identity) and Chapter 5, I believe that what I have to say goes beyond the specificity of "local" criticism and thus has broad applicability to other Anglophone adolescent fictions.

To return, then, to the direction the study will take, I begin with an introductory chapter which provides some "points of departure." As this chapter demonstrates, due to the nature of the subject under inquiry, the theoretical approaches that inform this discussion as a whole are interdisciplinary rather than grounded in a specific theory. Drawing on a range of ideas from philosophy, discourse analysis, and literary and social theory, here I explore some of the ways that representations of death can be "read", and some of the intersections between mortality, gender, and sexuality. By bringing these ideas together with others concerning the sociology of death, this section also provides a cultural context for the study.

Death is a difficult topic to pin down; its meaning/s exist in "a kind of perpetual vacillation", to use Bronfen and Goodwin's term (19). The divisions between Chapters 2 to 5, which constitute the body of the book, may therefore seem somewhat artificial. Indeed, in arranging these sections according to recognised genres in the field of children's literature, I have merely followed a well-established practice. Nevertheless, a number of common patterns and themes emerge from this arrangement, suggesting not only that texts within genres share a variety of conventions (such as language, syntax, style, and narrative sequencing), but that they treat representations of death—particularly as they relate to gender and sexuality—in similar ways too.

Perhaps, as Stephens suggests, this is because there is a tendency for major genres in children's literature to be "endemically gendered in their character functions, events and outcomes" ("Gender" 17). This idea is, in fact, examined at length since the affinities of concern that can be traced through these genres work to frame the principal arguments of each chapter. Chapter 2, which is concerned with historical literature, uses Australia as an exemplary model to examine some of the ways in which a country's "national fictions" can shape the culture's "national experience, knowledge, awareness and responses to mortality" (Charmaz, Howarth, and Kellehear vii). A good part of this chapter is given over to texts which feature the deaths of iconic Australian figures (such as the convict, the bushranger, and the ANZAC soldier), or which focus on female experiences of death. As I argue here, by drawing upon a narrative tradition that is characterised by its habit of linking masculinity, death, and heroism with key moments in Australian history, these texts work to endorse a view of Australia's past that is gendered, masculinist, and selective. The treatment of death in these books illustrates some of the ways that the past continues to inform and shape meaning in the present too, a thesis that is also pertinent to another set of novels in this section which bring together the themes of Aboriginality and death. These fictions foreground ideas about relations between Indigenous and non-Indigenous Australians since their stories are largely centred on the discovery of evidence from the colonial period relating to the massacre of Aboriginal people. In this instance, what I propose is that, for the most part, the past is "managed" for readers by drawing upon the attitudes and ideologies of colonial discourse (Bradford, *Reading* 15).

Historical fiction for adolescents is usually overtly ideological as it tends to work towards imparting some moral, social or political lesson to its audience, often by fusing narratives about large-scale events with personal stories, and by mapping these lessons onto a linear developmental trajectory which values maturation as its endpoint (Stephens, *Language*). The genre of realism, which is the focus of Chapter 3, works in a similar way since its readers are positioned to accept personal growth as a value, and most importantly, to accept that growth as a consequence of coming into contact with various social issues and problems (including violence, teenage pregnancy, homosexuality, sexual abuse, suicide, death, and disease). The implication here is that these experiences teach protagonists (and, by extension, readers) about life and about how to "grow up". What I concentrate on in this section, then, is fictions which represent death as a significant event influencing the growth of the adolescent subject, arguing that this narrative pattern tends to have implications for how that subject formulates and perceives their own sense of (gendered and sexual) self. As a group, these texts also demonstrate some of the ways that death can be seen to operate as an instrument of power since the boundary which defines what it is to be male or female is often brutally demarcated by the corpse.

In fact, the intersection between death and power manifests itself clearly in these texts because the dominant concern of realism, like that of fantasy which I deal with in Chapter 4, is the nature and operation of power in human societies (Stephens, *Language* 287). Kathryn Hume describes fantasy as "the deliberate departure from the limits of what is usually accepted as real and normal [...] any departure from consensus reality" (21). The texts in this section therefore share a preoccupation not only with altered realities, but also, like those realist fictions discussed above, with boundaries and with limiting categories: "animate and inanimate, life and death, self and other" (Jackson 1–2). By focusing upon particular genres or characteristic features of fantasy, here I argue that the representations of death in these narratives are inclined to reaffirm hegemonic ideologies pertaining to gender and sexuality since, while they function to enable a transgression of those boundaries, at the same time, they generally work towards restoring them too. Similarly, this chapter also suggests that the presence of controversial themes and/or unconventional closures in a narrative offers no guarantee that corresponding ideologies are inscribed within the text.

A genre of fantasy that is not explored in Chapter 4 is that of post-disaster fiction; instead, it becomes the focus of Chapter 5. Death is a familiar theme in post-disaster narratives because they are set in an imagined future some time after the world—or a part of it—has been destroyed or irrevocably damaged by a cataclysmic disaster (Stephens, "Post-Disaster" 126). As a consequence, the novels in this largely adolescent genre have a tendency to be overtly didactic and ideologically explicit, functioning as cautionary tales, or acting as vehicles through which various social and ethical values can be explored. Discussions and choices relating to gender roles, power, and agency are characteristic, for instance, particularly as the protagonists of these texts often undergo a political and/or sexual awakening during the course of the narrative, but also because the work of rebuilding a new world from the remnants of the past inevitably involves making choices about which values and systems to preserve and which to discard. Of the arguments which are raised in this section, a number are concerned with the inclination of the post-disaster text to fall back on patriarchally gendered systems of meaning, and to position readers to view the future in terms of its return to a masculinist past. The genre's capacity to offer a space where the "normal" rules of gendered behaviour have changed is a focus too. Looking specifically at the female action hero paradigm, I argue here that there is a distinct uneasiness surrounding representations of the female as killer because, although these texts offer women new roles, they also tend to demonstrate that these roles are bound within a patriarchal framework.

The process of building up a general picture of the ways in which the various representations of death under study function in a discursive, narrative, and ideological sense occurs within each of Chapters 2 to 5. Thus, although I make general references in the Conclusion to the patterns or themes that emerge within the texts as a group, this final chapter is largely reserved for exploring the limitations of the study, looking at the implications these results have for the field of children's literature, and offering potential directions for further research.

Chapter One
Points of Departure:
Death, Culture, Representation

It is impossible to define death, as death stands for the final void, for that non-existence which, absurdly, gives existence to all being.

(Bauman 2)

Death is [...] necessarily constructed by a culture; it grounds the many ways a culture stabilizes and represents itself, and yet it always does so as a signifier with an incessantly receding, ungraspable signified, always pointing to other signifiers, other means of representing what finally is just absent.

(Bronfen and Goodwin 4)

It has been suggested that awareness of death is the origin of self-conscious-ness itself, yet perhaps the most obvious thing about death is that it is ulti-mately *unknowable*. Death is "always only represented" Elisabeth Bronfen and Sarah Webster Goodwin contend; "there is no knowing [it], no experienc-ing it and then returning to write about it, no intrinsic grounds for authority in the discourse surrounding it" (4). Indeed, the concept does not just defy imagination, Zygmunt Bauman argues, it is the archetypal contradiction in terms; death is "an absolute *nothing* and 'absolute nothing' makes no sense" (2, 15, emphasis original).

Reading Death

So how, then, *can* the impossible be defined, how can death be "read"? In Bronfen's view, narrative and visual representations of death can be read as

9

"symptoms" of a culture because they draw their material from "a common cultural image repertoire" (*Over* xi), while for Michael Kearl, death can be defined as a socially constructed idea: "The fears, hopes, and orientations people have regarding it are not instinctive, but rather are learned from such public symbols as the language, arts, and religious and funerary rituals of their culture" ("You Never" 22). Although the pairing of life with death does not occur by nature, semantics suggests that there can be no discussion of death without a reference to life—"death exists in a relationship to life [. . .] 'death' both is and is not a 'part' of life; it is a 'stage' of life (a part) and the negation of life altogether (is 'other')" (Schleifer, *Rhetoric* 5–6). Needless to say, because death "lies beyond the realm of images [that] the living body knows" (Burke 369), any reading becomes a complex process of negotiation between multiply-coded signs, symbols, and terms. A typical dictionary definition, for example, covers meanings which are corporeal, theological, representational, and mythological:

> **death** *n*. **1** the final cessation of vital functions in an organism; the ending of life. **2** the event that terminates life. **3 a** the fact or process of being killed or killing (*stone to death; fight to the death*). **b** the fact or state of being dead (*eyes closed in death; their deaths caused rioting*). **4 a** the destruction or permanent cessation of something (*was the death of our hopes*). **b** *colloq.* something terrible or appalling. **5** (usu. **Death**) a personification of death, esp. as a destructive power, usu. represented by a skeleton. **6** a lack of religious faith or spiritual life. (Hughes, Michell, and Ramson 284)

Death can be represented by: a coffin; cross; crow; devil; grave; grim reaper; hourglass; journey; river; scythe; skeleton; skull; tombstone; weeping willow; the colour black; and the colour white. Death figures prominently in everyday language too. There are: death-rattles, death-rolls, death rows, death seats, death squads, death-tolls, death-traps, death-warrants, death-watches, and death-wishes. A person can: catch their death, or have a dead heat (*draw*); be: at death's door, dead-and-alive (*slow*), dead and buried (*past; over*), a dead beat (*loser*), dead on their feet, deadpan, dead tired, dead to the world, a dead weight, or like death warmed up. *Dead* can be added to: boring, broke, and cold; or it can mean: defunct, exhausted, extinct, flat, or tedious. *Die* can also mean: disappear, fail, fizzle, founder, rot, sink, stall, or subside.[1]

For Bronfen and Goodwin, this indeterminacy is the crux in any representation of death: death occupies a double position as "anomalous, marginal, repressed, and at the same time masterful, central, everywhere manifest", while the corpse is a destabilising force: it is both "the here and the nowhere" (12, 19). Resembling itself (its own double), they argue, it suspends "stable categories of reference and position in time and space" (12). As Peter Schwenger contends, the corpse is "never wholly object", for it is "always also image—an image of otherness that is also, paradoxically, the image of self, image *as* self" (400, emphasis original). This analogy between the image and the corpse is one that has also been drawn by Maurice Blanchot. Blanchot sees the cadaver as "its own image" because it ceases to bear any relation with the world in which it still appears, except as an image—an "obscure possibility". In Blanchot's words, the corpse is "present in absence", it bears a likeness to itself, "like to an absolute degree, overwhelming and marvellous", and yet it is like *nothing* (258, emphasis added). Both the cadaver and the image are the "object's aftermath", he argues—"that which comes later, which is left over and allows us still to have the object at our command when there is nothing left of it" (260). In this sense, says Schwenger, the image is not "inadequate" to what it is supposed to represent; rather, it means that the image "surpasses representation" (408).

Blanchot is one amongst many scholars in the more recent Western philosophical tradition (including Georges Bataille, Jacques Derrida, Michel Foucault, Sigmund Freud, Martin Heidegger, and Maurice Merleau-Ponty) who have made a study of death. The subject of death has also been a preoccupation of contemporary social science. Jacques Choron (*Death; Modern*) has brought together Western views of death from Socrates to Descartes, Kearl (*Endings*) has provided a sociology of death and dying, and in the seminal *On Death and Dying*, Elizabeth Kübler-Ross has documented the subjective experiences of the dying. It is the work of Philippe Ariès (*Hour; Images; Western*), however, that provides some of the most valuable insights into the ways in which death can be read in Western culture. Ariès's comprehensive survey of death, which spans more than one thousand years, historicises death and its images in the Western world by examining death's relationship to cultural representation. Arguing that the image is "the richest and most direct means that man has of expressing himself [when] faced with the mystery of the end of life", Ariès suggests that, if all the images of death from this period are juxtaposed to form a sequence, they will create a "continuous film of a series of historical cultures" (*Images* 1). The primary changes that have occurred during the "death epochs" of Western civilisation, Ariès contends, may thus be mapped along a historical trajectory: Before the thirteenth century, death was characterised as tame, familiar, collective, and public, but from the medieval period onwards, death became progressively more individualised, medicalised, asocial, traumatic, and unfamiliar. According to Kearl's interpretation, these death epochs reveal how "cultural shifts in the relationship between individuals and social structure are measured by changes in conceptions of death", and the rituals and images that are associated with it (*Endings* 29). Ariès has been consistently criticised for the generalisation of his approach, for being overly descriptive with his interpretation, for suggesting that the West's relationship with death has moved from healthy to pathological, and for the masculinist terms and views that inform the study and its titles.[2] Nonetheless, as I have argued in the Introduction, the basic thesis which informs this vast study is of interest here because it suggests that a culture's representations of death may be read collectively as a text to give insights into a wide array of its functions, values, social order, and systems of meaning.

Reading death also refers to reading *of* death—to quote Garrett Stewart, the "one inevitably fictional matter in prose fiction" (*Death* 4). Stewart joins several others who have produced some theoretically sophisticated work in the last decade or so since the surge of interest in death has extended to the field of literary criticism, and specifically—although somewhat later—to analyses of children's literature.[3] As a summary of the main points in several of these texts reveals, much of the criticism on death in literature approaches the topic through theories concerned with language, narrative, representation, body politics, power, gender, and sexuality. Gerald Doherty, Ronald Schleifer ("Afterword"; *Rhetoric*), and Beth Ann Bassein all focus on narrative, rhetoric, and death, for example: Doherty by drawing on Jakobson's system of rhetoric to argue that representations of death in the English novel are configured in either a metaphoric or metonymic mode; Schleifer in the context of discourse theory; and Bassein by calling on literary tradition to demonstrate how Woman's transgression of accepted codes of behaviour has often resulted in her literal or symbolic death. The bond between story and mortality is Stewart's angle too; death, he argues, is "signatory to the very charter of fiction" (*Death* 51). For Bronfen (*Over*) and Kerry Mallan ("Fatal"), death is inexorably linked with femininity—eroticised, sexualised, and subject to close inspection. They, like Laura E. Tanner, examine the relationship between literary representations of death and the power dynamics of the gaze, suggesting, in Mallan's words, that Western culture has come to see the deaths of women as "fatal attractions calling a crowd of onlookers" ("Fatal" 175).

The diverse essays in Goodwin and Bronfen's edited collection *Death and Representation* (a number of which I have referred to above) are grouped together in a way which reveals similar resonances. Beginning with a section which looks at representations of death as texts, these studies collectively ask such questions as: "How does the psyche represent death? What forms does that representation take? How does the process take place? What are the purposes and meanings of such representations?" (Bronfen and Goodwin 10). The focus then turns to essays which take death and gender as their study by exploring the trope of woman/death, but also by examining the ways that femininity and masculinity intersect with death. Almost without exception, it is argued here, representations of death in Western culture are gendered, and especially gendered female: "death and femininity have formed two possible axes of negation and enigma in relation to masculine subjectivity and culture", Bronfen and Goodwin contend, because they appear in cultural discourses as "the blind spot the representational system seeks to refuse even as it constantly addresses it" (14, 15, 20). Lastly, several chapters which analyse selected representations of death within a historical moment are clustered together. Through the workings of power and ideology, these essays suggest that death can be located in history and defined as "a social and cultural phenomenon" (15).

Theorising Death

It would be reasonable to suggest that the affinities of concern that emerge from the analyses in *Death and Representation* may provide some key directions—or points of departure—for my own inquiry. It is these salient observations which I therefore now take up, and which can be summarised as following: death is both threat to and instrument of power; death is gendered; death is inextricably tied to sex/uality; death is the constructed Other; and death is physical (Bronfen and Goodwin 15, 20).

Death is Both Threat to and Instrument of Power

The importance of death to any theory of representation is clearest, Bronfen and Goodwin contend, by recalling that the term *representation* "comes to current critical usage from essentially two sources: politics and psychoanalysis", meanings which relate to each other chiefly through issues of power (4). Representations of death necessarily engage questions about power, they argue: "its locus, its authenticity, its sources, and how it is passed on" (5). To speak of power in a discursive sense—and particularly in relation to bodies—is unavoidably to speak of Foucault. Much of Foucault's theory is instrumental in revealing how power is installed into discourse, how it operates in relation to other discourses, and how it produces real material effects (McHoul and Grace 19, 21). For Foucault, "death is at once the locus and the instrument of power: that is, an independent power inheres in death itself, but other forms of power rely on death to disclose and enforce themselves" (Bronfen and Goodwin 5). As Bronfen and Goodwin explain: "Death—not in the abstract, but people dying and the processes by which they die—may signify by turns a monarch's sovereignty, a people's own power, and the primacy of biology over culture"; Foucault essentially asks "Who has the power over these deaths? [. . .] What do these deaths signify, what do they represent? What power can I/we exercise over them?"(5).

The Foucauldian concept of "biopower" is helpful in expanding on these ideas about death and political representation. It begins with the view that populations have an economic value—that they are a resource which aids in the production of strength, wealth, and power for the state: "biological existence [is] reflected in political existence", Foucault argues (*History* 142). In the chapter "Right of Death and Power over Life" in *The History of Sexuality*, Foucault historicises death and state power, arguing that in traditional modes of power, the privilege of sovereign power was the right to decide life and death; a right of seizure of things, time, bodies, and ultimately life itself. Since the classical age, however, these mechanisms of power have been transformed in the West, so that "this death that was based on the right of sovereign is now manifested as simply the reverse of the right of the social body to ensure, maintain, or develop its life" (*History* 136). Thus, "the ancient right to *take* life or *let* live is replaced by a power to *foster* life or *disallow* it to the point of death" (*History* 138, emphases original). For Foucault, this is the function of the bodies of knowledge and the administrative apparatus (social/human sciences, and the "policing" institutions which are concerned with criminal activity, health, and welfare) that have formed during this process: to watch, regulate, discipline, and control populations—to aid in "the administration of bodies and the calculated management of life" (*History* 140).

Very simply, then, biopower is the term used for the "numerous and diverse techniques for achieving the subjugations of bodies and the control of populations" (*History* 140). It is therefore not really death itself that is the issue for Foucault, but rather control over life because "it is over life, throughout its unfolding, that power establishes its dominion; death is power's limit, the moment that escapes it" (*History* 138). The mechanisms of power are "addressed to the body, to life", says Foucault, and the way that individuals and populations come to understand themselves, their behaviours, values, and aspirations are all produced by, and subject to, the forces of the apparatuses and technologies of this power (*History* 147). A culture's perception of what constitutes "healthy" and "normal", for instance, is created discursively through these institutions (thus making notions of normality powerful ideological tools). For Jean Baudrillard, the ultimate example of that which is abnormal and unhealthy is death, because death is "an incurable deviancy [. . .] nothing else is as offensive as this" (126). Our social survival depends on prohibiting, manipulating, and legislating death, Baudrillard argues—to ward off death "in order to evade the unbearable moment when flesh becomes nothing but flesh, and ceases to be a sign" (180). Like Foucault, Baudrillard sees death as an instrument of power: Death helps to divide and circulate power in culture because power is established over those divisions where the dissolution of unity between life and death (or the disruption of exchange) occurs. This is why "every death and all violence that escapes the State monopoly is subversive", he contends: It is "a prefiguration of the abolition of power" (hence the fascination wielded by "great" murderers, bandits, or outlaws) (175). Death, therefore, "ought never to be understood as the real event that effects a subject or a body", Baudrillard argues, "but as a *form* in which the determinacy of the subject and of value is lost" (5, emphasis original).

Death is Gendered

Any analysis of a representation of death therefore needs to determine not only how this representation claims to portray death, say Bronfen and Goodwin, but also (however suppressed) what else the representation in fact represents: "assertion of alternative power, self-referential metaphor, aggression against individuals or groups, formation of group identities and ideologies, and so forth" (20). With their destabilising, enigmatic nature, representations of death are inexorably associated, for example, with those of the (similarly) multiply-coded feminine body. Death and femininity have been discursively constructed as "the point of impossibility" within Western culture, Bronfen and Goodwin argue, because both are viewed as radically other to the norm (14). As Bronfen explains, Woman is "a symptom of death's presence, precisely because she is the site where the repressed anxiety about death re-emerges in a displaced, disfigured form"; over representations of the dead feminine body, "culture can repress and articulate its unconscious knowledge of death which it fails to foreclose even as it cannot express it directly" (*Over* xi, 215). Efrat Tseëlon makes a similar argument when she writes that Woman "serves the dual function of signifying a fear and the defence against [death] at the same time" (101). Drawing on Freudian psychoanalytic theory, Tseëlon argues that Woman and death share many characteristics. In the same way that the sight of the female body triggers male anxiety of castration, she contends, the sight of the dead body triggers anxiety of mortality. Thus, in the patriarchal cultural imagination, both are mysterious, ambiguous, unrepresentable, silent, and a threat to stability; both are the eternal Other; and both are a metaphor of disruption and transgression (113). As suggested by the conjunction between death, femininity, and aesthetisation, both have also become aligned with beauty in the West (Bronfen, *Over;* Tseëlon). Indeed, it is this association which doubly inscribes Woman as death, Tseëlon argues—she is a signifier for death (lack, castration), and her beauty is a veil for death (the illusion of wholeness):

> The aesthetisation of death and the beautification of the living are defensive strategies. They are designed to protect the person from realisation of some lack by creating an illusion of wholeness and immortality. Death is the lack or cut in the physical and the social body, while castration is a lack that creates the awareness of sexual difference. (117)

So how, then, does Western culture characterise or define the relationship between death and masculinity? According to Bronfen, it is the age-old discursive association between Woman and death that allows masculinity to be constructed as that which lacks death: "Woman is symptom for the hope of masculine wholeness and because her relation to death is seen as a relation to Otherness, she enacts precisely the fact that this relation is missing from the masculine" (*Over* 218). Death in war has also helped to define manhood as so many cultural commentators have pointed out. Stories about sacrifice, heroism, and the noble, manly endeavours of soldiers have been prominent ones in Western cultures, although, even here, the vulnerability and corporeality of the body can be ignored by placing "life" on the side of the masculine. As

Leigh Astbury argues, war memorials (which "act as surrogate grave sites for the bodies of the dead") can work to reconstruct "the unblemished beauty of the intact male body" by depicting the warrior as youthful, powerful, and graceful (72). War is constructed in this way as the "enemy of life", a term that is also frequently applied to those models of masculinity which threaten the hegemonic ideal represented by the warrior. The homosexual male is consistently associated with pathology and death, for instance—a link, Jonathan Dollimore contends, that is often imagined to include both suicidal and murderous impulses in which homosexuals court death, contract the AIDS virus, and then knowing of their impending death, willingly infect others through sexual contact (x).

Death is Inextricably Tied to Sex/uality

The relationship between "deviance" and mortality that is evident in such representations is one that reflects not only upon the homophobia of contemporary hegemonic society, but also on current concerns about sexually transmissible diseases. In a study of films that are not self-consciously about AIDS, but which reflect societal anxieties about the disease, Monica B. Pearl claims that AIDS is "the nexus and manifestation of what is traditionally and essentially terrifying about sex and death in Western society" (210–11). AIDS is itself only a representation, she asserts: The virus itself is meaningless; rather, cultural anxieties concerned with sex/uality, infection, mortality, and loss can be linked to—and arise from—the discourse on, and fear of, the virus. The idea that sex/uality can be threatening or lethal is not new, however. Images of the *femme fatale*, the vampire, the woman as monster, and the necrophile have acted again and again over time as pointers to the desires, preoccupations, and fears that characterise the West's relationship with sex and death. As Michele Aaron argues in *The Body's Perilous Pleasures*, the combination between pleasure (sexual expression) and danger (potential death) in Western culture is one that "seems always to leak out of society's unconscious into its perilous, if ostensibly innocent representations" ("Introduction" 10).

In the Judaeo-Christian narrative tradition, the figure of the female prostitute has always been a pervasive signifier of potential danger. Here, cultural anxiety is located in the "excessive" sexuality of the female, making the death of the prostitute a cure, a punishment, or a way to contain the threat she poses to the heterosex and the patriarchy. As Sander L. Gilman's examination of a variety of nineteenth-century images and texts featuring dead prostitutes suggests, the prostitute's death expiates her "sins against the male" (263). In this study, Gilman also sees death as that which "purge[s] the dead prostitute of her pollution" because "[t]he touching of the dead body is not merely a piteous gesture toward the 'fallen', it is a permitted touching of the female, a not contagious, not infecting touch, a control over the dead woman's body" (265). The prostitute's perversion in these texts (which is also associated with her relation to capital and the power of money) constructs her as an "enemy within the body politic", as corrupt and dangerous—hence the need to destroy her (Bronfen and Goodwin 18). It suggests, too, that it is at the site of the dead body that gender, sexuality, and power most clearly intersect.

Indeed, the argument that literal or symbolic death represents one of the ways that the "perverse" body can be removed from the sexual economy (and thus work to reinforce the heterosexual norm), is a theme I take up throughout this book. The conceptual foundation upon which I base this argument is drawn from Foucault's work on sexuality and body politics. For Foucault, sex and sexuality "together comprise a set of practices, behaviours, rules and knowledges" by which an individual produces itself and is produced as a "knowing"—ethical, social, and juridical—subject. In this way, sex/uality is tied up with meanings and power because subjects (and bodies) are written and regulated by, or are the product of, various institutional practices, ideologies, and discourses (Danaher, Schirato, and Webb 136). As Judith Butler explains, "the body is not 'sexed' in any significant sense prior to its determination within a discourse through which it becomes invested with an 'idea' of natural or essential sex"; instead, the body "gains meaning in discourse only in the context of power relations" (117). In Foucauldian terms, sexuality must therefore "not be thought of as a kind of natural given"—rather, it is:

> a great surface network in which the stimulation of bodies, the intensification of pleasures, the incitement to discourse, the formation of special knowledges, the strengthening of controls and resistances, are linked to one another, in accordance with a few major strategies of knowledge and power. (*History* 105–06)

It is through the transformation of sex into discourse, Foucault argues, that our epoch has "initiated sexual heterogeneities", expelling from "reality" the forms of sexuality "that are not amenable to the strict economy of reproduction" and thus creating a "norm" of sexual development (*History* 36, 37). In this way, "appropriate" sexual behaviours are defined, sexual irregularity is annexed to pathology, and alternative forms of non-reproductive sexuality are branded "perversions".

Although not always consciously articulated, throughout history the most fundamental taboos on human behaviour have been those concerned with death and sexual functions (McNay 41). Indeed, much of Bataille, Freud, and Julia Kristeva's work intersects around this idea. Freudian psychoanalytic theory hinges upon the notion that the psychic life of the subject is governed by two antagonistic biological or instinctual urges: one towards reproduction, and the other towards destruction. The first—libidinal energy (Eros)—embraces sexual and life-preserving instincts, while the second—the death drive (Thanatos)—represents the urge to dissolution (ultimately, non-existence). The two exist in a state of tension dominated by the death drive, Baudrillard explains, effectively making death the "price" for sexuality: "Eros is nothing but an immense detour taken by culture towards death, which subordinates everything to its own ends" (149). This unresolved tension between Thanatos and its adversary, Eros, is played out in Freud's *Civilization and its Discontents*. Here, Freud draws an analogy between the libidinal development of the individual and the evolution of Western civilisation by addressing the conflict between sexual needs and societal mores. Civilisation is "obeying the laws of economic necessity", he argues, "since a large amount of the psychical energy which it uses for its own purposes has to be withdrawn from sexuality" (*Civilization* 59). Restrictions and taboos (largely against incest) placed on the sexual subject work in conjunction with the laws and customs of culture, says Freud, to counteract the impulse towards destruction or aggression. This process—by which psychical energy is redirected from ego-desire (erotic attraction, sexual gratification) into cultural endeavours (such as art)—Freud calls "sublimation".

Theories concerning the social taboos of incest and murder form the cornerstone of Freud's research. Indeed, Freud argues that healthy psychosexual development—the ability to attain "normal" (heterosexual) adult sexuality—is dependent upon the successful repression of the desires and drives related to such restrictions. During one of several stages of development, he argues, the child must resolve the Oedipal complex (so-named after the myth of Oedipus, who killed his father and then married his mother). Very simply, this involves a rejection of the maternal/the mother, which occurs after the father intervenes to separate mother from child, followed by: for the male child, identification with the father (which begins initially with a longing to *be* the father *with* the mother); and for the female, a desire for the father which exists simultaneously with the desire to take her mother's place as the father's sex object. In each case, the path to becoming a gendered subject is dependant on the child relinquishing these desires for the parent and seeking other objects outside the family (Rivkin and Ryan, "Strangers" 122). Also crucial to this stage of development is the formation of the super-ego, the part of the mind that is associated with moral and ethical restraints and acts as a "conscience" by maintaining the prohibition of such taboos. The super-ego is "representative of our relation to our parents", Freud claims, but it retains the character of the father because it develops after the father's prohibition of the (incestuous) dyadic relationship between mother and child ("Ego" 36). This prohibition—which can be perceived as "the obstacle to a realization of [the] Oedipus wishes" ("Ego" 34)—is termed "the Law of the father" by Freudian psychoanalysts, and is a symbolic embodiment of "all the higher authority to be later encountered" (Eagleton 136).

In contrast to Freud, Bataille sees death and sexuality in the same cyclical revolution of continuity—as exchanged in the same cycle: "they exchange their energies and excite one another" (Baudrillard 155). Like Foucault, Bataille claims that a sexed, gendered subject "is constituted through the taboos and prohibitions that shape a cultural system" (Krzywinska 190). However, in Bataille's view, the framework of the law that shapes the subject (the processes of socialisation) is associated with the expulsion of the "accursed share"—that portion of the self that is bodily and material: forbidden eroticism (incest), excrement, and death (the return to material nature of human life) (Rivkin and Ryan, "Class" 337). As Paul Hegarty explains, death is central to this notion of repugnance because it is "the (primordial) object of disgust" (58). Humans have a horror of "all that threatens their unitary existence", he argues; excretions, filth, loss of control through drunkenness, eroticism, and all such disgusts are caught up within taboos (58). According to Bataille, at the same time that humanity pushes death away, however, it is drawn towards it: In trying to exclude what is horrifying, this exclusion creates the necessity and/or desire to approach what threatens (this double movement between repulsion or exclusion, and attraction or intrusion, is what Bataille terms "abjection") (Hegarty 61, 62). For Bataille, then, an "aura of death is what denotes passion" (20) since the essence of eroticism is to be found in "the inextricable confusion of sexual pleasure and taboo": the taboo "never makes an appearance without suggesting sexual pleasure" and "nor does the pleasure without evoking the taboo" (108).

In *Powers of Horror*, Kristeva makes a similar claim to Bataille by arguing that erotic pleasure emerges as a symbolic response to the uncontainable threat of mortality: The erotic is both a reaction to the threat of castration, she argues, and an attempt to sustain life itself in the face of death (Tanner 24). Like Bataille, Kristeva's notion of abjection is founded on ideas about the taboo and implicated in the construction of the sexual subject. Drawing on Lacanian psychoanalytic phases and realms, Kristeva argues that abjection is first experienced at the point of separation from the mother when the child enters the symbolic order, a realm which marks the threshold of the acquisition of language and "proper" sociality. During this process of becoming an autonomous being (a stable self) and claiming the body as its own, she contends, the child must disavow or *abject* the "improper", "unclean" and thus disorderly aspects of its corporeal existence. Yet the attempt to expel what is improper or unclean is never truly successful, says Kristeva; these "antisocial" elements always hover at the border of the subject's identity, threatening the apparent unity of the subject with disruption and possible dissolution (Grosz, "Body"). It is the subject's "recognition of this impossibility", Elizabeth Grosz argues, which provokes the sensation and attitude that Kristeva calls "abjection" ("Body" 87).

Kristeva correlates those objects which generate abjection with various social and individual taboos against food, waste, and the signs of sexual difference (bodily fluids, excrement, menstrual blood, incest, the corpse, decay, infection, disease, etc). According to Grosz, the subject's reaction to these abjects is visceral: "it is usually expressed in retching, vomiting, spasms, choking—in brief, in disgust". These reactions signal what the "rational consciousness cannot accept" (Grosz, "Body" 89) because, says Barbara Creed,

> [t]he place of the abject is where meaning collapses, the place where *I am not*. The abject threatens life, it must be radically excluded from the place of the living subject, propelled away from the body and deposited on the other side of an imaginary border which separates the self from that which threatens the self. ("Horror" 252–53, emphasis added)

For Kristeva, the corpse is the "utmost of abjection", the definitive border, that "most sickening of wastes" which "encroaches upon everything"; it is "death infecting life". The corpse threatens to break down the very boundary between subject and object, and thus between meaning and meaninglessness, she contends, and so it does not signify death, but instead all that is "thrust aside in order to live" (3, 4). Thus, Kristeva explains, confronting the abject does not just threaten the subject with losing part of itself, but with losing its "whole life": "It is no longer I who expel. 'I' is expelled" (4). In this sense, she argues, the "erotization of abjection, and perhaps any abjection to the extent that it is already eroticized" is therefore "an attempt at stopping the hemorrhage: a threshold before death, a halt or a respite" (55).

Death is the Constructed Other

Bataille, Freud, and Kristeva each suggest that the connection between death and sexuality is pervasive in Western culture. And yet, as Dollimore argues in *Death, Desire and Loss in Western Culture*, it is one that is both manifest and concealed, allowing it to be recognised and registered at the same time that it is not "seen" (xii). According to Bronfen, representations of death function in psychoanalytic terms like a symptom (a repression that fails): The knowledge of death (a threat to the health of the psyche) is repressed, yet so strong in its desire for articulation that it cannot be. As a consequence, the psychic apparatus compromises by representing "this dangerous and fascinating thing by virtue of a substitution [. . .] by obliquely pointing to that which threatens to disturb the order". Narrative or aesthetic representations of death encourage repression of "the knowledge of the reality of death precisely because here death occurs *at* someone else's body and *as* an image". There is death, Bronfen contends, "but it is not my own" (*Over* x, emphases original). In Kristevan terms, then, death can be seen as Other—what the subject has disavowed by excluding or abjecting that which "does not respect borders, positions, rules" (4).

The concept of otherness is critical to understandings of narratives about the "living dead" (angels, ghosts, vampires, cyber-beings, zombies). Concerned with limits, with the blurring or the violation of the boundaries between life and death, representations of the "undead" (those who are technically dead but still animate) essentially question what it is to be mortal, but can also point to deep-seated cultural anxieties regarding death and difference. Studies suggest that a wide variety of shifting meanings are located in aesthetic representations of the living dead. The undead can: stand for a crisis of subjectivity; function to demonise those who threaten the stability of the cultural order; point to that which must be defeated in order for ideals and social cohesion to be maintained; or work to challenge the notion of death's permanence. Rather than being presented as the predictable outcome of historical or biographical events, in these latter instances, death engages with the political economy of immortalism that is prevalent in contemporary popular culture (Kearl, "You Never"; Kellehear). Their presence can also reveal much about fears relating to gender and sexuality. Judith Halberstam argues, for example, that the monsters of contemporary horror literature tend to "show clearly the markings of deviant sexualities and gendering" (4), while Stacy Gillis suggests that in accounts of the disembodied female body of cyberpunk, Woman is often "simultaneously figured as excess and lack", as "sexualised and as [site] of activity" (12, 16).

Angela Connolly approaches such liminal figures in psychoanalytic terms, arguing that encounters with the abject beings of horror and terror have both an individual and a collective function in Western culture, and that they represent ways of dealing with "limits, differences, evil and death" (410). Connolly differentiates between uncanny horror, where the monster represents the return of the repressed; abject horror, in which the monster can be seen as all that lies outside the symbolic order; and sublime terror, where the monster is at the same time abject and subjectivised. According to Connolly, uncanny horror and its attendant images of the monster (the werewolf, the vampire, and the mummy) on the one hand offer the spectator "the possibility of an unconscious participation in guilty pleasures through the identification with the monster and its subjectivity", but, on the other, suggest "the super-egoical pleasure of control over and repression of the monster as the dark shadow double of the ego consciousness" (419). By contrast, she contends, the monsters of abject horror (the zombie, the devil, the alien) are devoid of subjectivity and psychic reality: they are "faceless, speechless and [possess] a kind of mechanical quality that identifies [them] as utterly inhuman", and thus they are "incapable of producing any change in psychic structure or in the dominant cultural ideology" (419–20). In the final category, sublime terror, Connolly sees the erosion of boundaries and the encounters with the abject Other as bringing about "an 'unlimiting' of the imagination, an increase in consciousness and a capacity to accept ethical guilt about our abject desires". Here, the monsters can be neither repressed nor foreclosed. Rather, the solution becomes a recognition that "the perverse and psychotic desires of the monster are a mirror image of our own perverse desires and the perversity of our own community and culture, based as they are on mechanisms of sacrifice and of scapegoating" (419–20).

Death is Physical

Death is an abstract concept, but it is also a physical event involving "real" bodies. The body is both the vehicle through which an individual experiences life and the dictator of the material limits of these same experiences. Academic interest in the body and its sociology has grown substantially in recent years, yet understandings of the body continue to be marked by uncertainties. Contemporary sociological approaches to human embodiment not only question knowledge about what the body *is* as well as its ultimate limitations, but also explore the complex relationship between physical and social death by arguing that the two processes do not necessarily correspond (Seale; Shilling; B. Turner). The definition of death also poses a particular problem as arguments over the ethics of abortion, euthanasia, and, more recently, stem cell research, become increasingly urgent. Death is, on the one hand, the permanent end of all life functions, but on the other, an endless debate. As Baudrillard argues: "Neither life nor death can any longer be assigned a given *end*: there is therefore no punctuality nor any possible *definition* of death" (159, emphases original). Irrespective of advances in modern medical technology, however, the fact remains that bodies are mortal; death is still a biological inevitability, and, as Chris Shilling points out, it is only in the context of the body's inevitable death that its full social importance can be understood (175). To quote Clive Seale:

> Embodiment dictates basic parameters for the construction of culture, the key problem for which is contained in the fact that bodies eventually die. On the one hand this threatens to make life meaningless, but on the other it is a basic motivation for social and cultural activity, which involves a continual defence against death. (1)

The Sociology of Death

The meanings a culture creates for death are, therefore, very much "a sociological problem" (Kearl, *Endings* 58). Yet, for much of the twentieth century, analyses of death and inquiries into the nature of mortality were defined by demography and pathology (Prior; Walter, "Sociologists")—"visible only through an objective and scientific language" which spoke of "mortality, disease and causation", rather than "attitudes, sentiment and awareness" (Prior 11). The reduction of death to a mere physical or statistical event reveals much about the epistemological and ontological precepts of this period; this approach has been challenged, however, in recent sociological studies. As Philip A. Mellor indicates when he argues that death "is one of the very small number of universal parameters within which both individual and social life is constructed" (27), generally speaking, sociologists are now of the view that the subject of death—

an inescapable facet of the human condition—is central to any understanding of the development, functioning, and structure of human society.

Contrary to past arguments on the reluctance of Western communities to talk about death, it is now usually accepted that death is not a taboo subject in modern society (Kearl, *Endings;* Mellor; Walter, *Revival,* "Sociologists", "Sociology"). In fact, the resurgence of interest in the subject has meant that a number of discursive regimes and a vast body of literature—both of academic and popular interest—devoted to human mortality now exists. Tony Walter's *The Revival of Death,* which uses theories of modernity and postmodernity to examine this resurgence of interest in death, is one such example. A sociological approach to death and dying in Western society, it places this revival in a historical context, identifying some themes and tensions characteristic to the death culture of the modern era. By examining the ways in which public discourses shape attitudes towards death and dying, Walter demonstrates how an individual's experiences of the dying process are intrinsically linked with cultures and social institutions.

Walter places cultural responses to death (proceeding from approximately the fifteenth century) into three categories or ideal types.[4] Beginning with traditional responses to death and moving on to modern and then to "neo-modern", he organises death in such a way that identifies consistencies within each type that relate to: bodily context; social context; authority; coping; the journey; and values. According to Walter, the traditional language of death is religious, communal, and quick and frequent, while modern experiences of death are hidden, and are typified by the domination of the public sphere over the private—authority in this era, he argues, is assigned to the doctor and the hospital, and the patient is objectified as a case or a site of disease. The neo-modern strand came into existence, Walter explains, because of the suppression of private experiences of death by medical discourse and bureaucratic practices; the revival of death challenges modern notions and "attempts to intertwine public discourse and private experience" rather than viewing them as separate to each other (*Revival* 39, 46). Neo-modern responses to death are thus classified by two disparate themes: "postmodern" and "late-modern". In the postmodern strand, "private experience invades and fragments public discourse", while in the late-modern strand, "expert discourse manipulates private experience" (*Revival* 39). The two exist together in tension and in a reflexive state which feeds back into the experiences of death and the practices that a society has associated with it (which in turn generate new—or revived—ways of approaching death).

Although Walter's social structure of death sees the private and the public intertwined, he nevertheless concludes that the authority associated with death now rests with the self, and that the meaning of death is created interpersonally. Dying, death rituals, and mourning have become very much an individual process, he contends—the logical conclusion of Western individualism whereby living "my own way" has extended to "dying/mourning my own way" too (*Revival*). Like Mellor, then, Walter argues that meaning in contemporary society is becoming increasingly privatised. For Mellor, this means that "any attempts to construct meaning around death [will be] inherently fragile" (21). Walter's idea of the revivalist's modern death also exposes this fragility; it is one in which meaning is *taken* from tradition, ritual, and religion, but is not *rooted* in them, reflecting the fragmented, disconnected and disposable aspects of postmodern society (*Revival* 188). Anne Hunsaker Hawkins identifies similar trends in "Constructing Death: Three Pathographies about Dying" (pathographies being personal narratives of illness and death told by a parent, spouse, relative, etc.). Despite the similarities in authorial background and circumstances, in each of these instances, death is apt to generate a plurality of meanings. All produce markedly different formulations of the experience too. As Hawkins contends, it seems that the tendency to ignore death has been replaced with the tendency to generate a plurality of concepts about it. Furthermore, all models invariably construct notions of a "good death", an ideology which, Hawkins argues, is prevalent in the pathographies of contemporary society: "Today's popular books describing the illness and death of a loved one suggest not that a new *ars moriendi* shaped by the death and dying movement is underway, but that we are still very much in search of a model for the 'good death'" (303).[5]

In the age of social sciences, Walter argues, surveys are conducted into how people die and grieve which "identify those styles that have greater and lesser personal costs, and these results [are then] fed back into popular consciousness" (*Revival* 199). Such constructions inevitably contribute to ideas of good or right deaths, says Hawkins—ideas which ultimately become mythic expectations. As medicine continues to contribute to longer life spans, a typical death today is prolonged, and signified by old age, cancer, or heart disease. Untypical deaths (and thus distressing or "bad") are those that are sudden, involve children or young people, or are construed as senseless. Using Walter's theory, a neo-modern construction of the good death is an aware and pain-free death which is characterised by an ability to finish personal psychological business, and also a death which does not carry culturally negative values (e.g. a suicide, drug overdose, murder, or car accident caused by speed or driver intoxication), while a "bad" death would constitute one in which the dying person was isolated, in denial, and unable to exercise control over both the manner in which they die and the arrangements for disposal of their body after death. For Walter, the catch-phrases of the neo-modern death are "expression of emotion, personal growth, sharing, autonomy, and informed choice", while the most heinous sins are "social isolation and psychological denial" (*Revival* 59).

In Walter's view, creating narratives from the experiences of death, and paying more attention to the emotional and psychological aspects of dying and grieving is part of the humanising of death, dying, and bereavement in the last 40 years ("Sociologists" 285). Hawkins suggests that these narratives about death organise the experience into a coherent pattern which gives the event a specific meaning. By identifying different paradigms of these experiences, Hawkins, like Walter, formulates several ideal types (such as ritual death, victorious death, one's own death, easy death, meaningful death, graceful death, and heroic death), each of which contribute to notions of the "good" or "right" death. Above all, her study suggests that, in a society which values individuality and emphasises pluralism, and in the absence of the *ars moriendi* common to Western culture in past times, death is constructed in terms of the personal and the individual—as an "experience that can be possessed by or assimilated into the personality" (317). It would seem, then, that the impetus behind the structuring, ritualising, ordering, and narrativising of the experience of death—paradoxically—is to come to *know* it, to create sense and meaning out of something which is not only unknowable but, as Hawkins points out, quite simply the end of life (318).

Although Walter demonstrates that death and dying are now popular subjects of discussion, the ideology associated with death in contemporary Western society nevertheless often implies that, in theory, death is preventable. In this sense, death is constructed in terms of failure, as a "morality tale" which is, moreover, medically endorsed (Kellehear and Anderson 8, 9) so that death becomes no more than "an extreme example of disease" (Seale 77). As Baudrillard so succinctly argues, today "*it is not normal to be dead*" (126, emphases original). Death can then be seen as a product of risk—with an accompanying ideal of the risk-avoiding individual who is "subject to exhortations to prolong life and avoid death by engaging with [a] widespread social value of healthy, safe behaviour" (Seale 82). The political implications of these statements are vast, particularly in light of Linda Singer's argument that "[c]oncerns about health can be used to justify any number of interventions into the lives of bodies and the forms of exchange in which they move" (30). At the same time, death can conversely engage with a rhetoric characterised by blame and responsibility, in which fault rests not with the individual but with other social agencies. Ironically, during a period when death is constructed more and more as an individual experience, and bodies as the province of the self, there is a social tendency to release individuals from responsibility for their actions; the blame for death can then be laid elsewhere—the system, society as a collective whole, the situation, the institution, or even another person.

Death is also systematically represented in Western cultures as something to be feared—in particular, when it is associated with, or occurs as a result of, violence and pain. Here, death can be seen as "an enemy to be conquered", an attitude which, it is claimed, results from the West's "activist approach" to life, and its recent technological ability to control biological processes (Veatch qtd. in Hawkins 302). For Kearl, the perception that death can be controlled is behind the "immortalist ethos" pervading American culture.

This notion, Kearl argues, which has also left its mark on the culture of other Western nations, underlies the obsession with youth, cultural "gerontophobia", demands for a risk-free life, the fight against disease, the expansion of the cosmetic and surgical rejuvenation industry, and the prevalence of immortalist themes in popular culture ("You Never" 192).

Conclusion

From this critical overview, it is reasonable to conclude not only that death gives "meaning" to life, but that the central force behind social organisation is the fact of human mortality and the knowledge of living with this awareness (Seale).[6] As Kearl contends, the ways in which a culture defines and orientates itself towards death dictates to a large extent "how their social institutions, symbolic systems and cognitive schema coalesce into distinctive, meaningful cultural wholes" ("You Never" 184). Yet, by asking such questions as: How does an individual cope with dying, or define their own death?; and How does an institution control suffering, or facilitate a person to die in a manner of their own choosing?, it would seem that much of the sociology of death (particularly in an age where the typical death is a prolonged one) is concerned with the dying process per se—the hospice environment, palliative care, psychological profiling, and counselling. Walter suggests as much when he argues that sociology's role in helping to understand the social reality of death, dying, and bereavement has, until fairly recently, tended to reflect parochial medical trends. For Walter, the evolution of ideas in sociological analysis needs to be grounded in social structure and to engage more directly with the work of other cognate disciplines because "death is, or can be, one of the basic motors of society: death practices and beliefs profoundly affect society" ("Sociology" 330).

It is also clear that, while death is an abstract concept, it nonetheless involves "real"—that is, material—bodies. Death is "not simply a general term", Bronfen and Goodwin contend, but "a very particular one, represented in and through the dead" (6). The understanding that bodies are shaped by the world they live in—culturally conditioned, situated, and historicised in a multiplicity of ways which makes them inarguably, and inescapably, political—is therefore crucial to any consideration of death and representation. Critical approaches to embodiment stress the importance of sex, gender, and sexuality to the study of the body. Grosz argues, for example, that "[o]ur conceptions of reality, knowledge, truth, politics, ethics, and aesthetics" are all effects of sexually specific bodies (*Volatile* ix). There are several ways in which bodies can be conceived of as sexualised: in a biological sense (that is, with respects to their anatomical difference); in terms of their gendered behaviour; and in terms of their sexual practices (Stephen 29). As this chapter suggests, the latter two have particular significance for this inquiry, concerned as it is with notions of subjectivity, agency, identity, and power. In Aaron's view, it is the body's "perilous pleasures"—the "stormy relationship between pleasure and danger"—that underlies much of the engagement with culture in contemporary Western society. Such culturally mediated perils, she argues, work to "confront the 'safe' boundaries between life and death, pain and pleasure, sexuality and gender" ("Introduction" 4–5, 10). It is over representations of the dead *feminine* body, however, that this relationship between mortality and sexuality is especially pronounced. Indeed, for centuries, death and Woman have been wedded together so firmly in art and literature that, it is claimed, Woman has become "a symptom of death's presence" (Bronfen, *Over* 215).

Over the course of this book, I will repeatedly return to this fascination with the conjunction of death and Woman because, as Bronfen argues, representations of the dead feminine body also stand for something else: They are "clearly marked as being other" (*Over* xi). According to Bronfen and Goodwin, that which aligns itself with death in any given representation is Other: "dangerous, enigmatic, magnetic". To study representations of death is therefore to examine "how not only individuals but also groups have defined themselves against what they are not but wish to control" (20). Kearl offers a similar argument when he suggests that "attitudes toward death are socially generated and serve social functions, especially as a means of social control" (*Endings* 4). For Bronfen and Goodwin, both individual executions and the collective violence of war serve as examples of those images of "alterity and sacrifice" that are necessary for a culture to define its boundaries (15–16), while for Kearl, it is not death in itself, but rather the threat of death that can operate to establish the conformity of the populace (*Endings* 87). Perhaps nowhere is it more apparent that death can be utilised as a means to ensure social order, however, than in those places in the aesthetic arena where the corpse works to delineate the boundary between acceptability and deviance— between normal and abnormal. Halberstam links monstrosity to fears of the foreign and the perverse, for example, arguing that the monster is a cultural object whose role is to articulate the presence of impurities—those aspects of the community that need to be expelled in order to support and sustain economic, social, and sexual hierarchies. Along the same lines, Aaron points to the tendency of contemporary cinema to link queer sexuality with deadliness, to align homoeroticism with potential death ("Death"). Such claims unerringly echo Foucault's contention that part of the "work" of official knowledge and discourses is to act as instruments of normalisation—to channel people and populations into "correct" and "functional" forms of thinking or acting (McHoul and Grace 17).

Despite the vacillation that exists between death's many meanings—and despite the multifaceted approaches to its study—it is evident, then, that the relationship between death and representation is one that is marked by a set of themes and ideas largely relating to body politics and power. This is, of course, a gross simplification, but in tracing the common threads that run through this chapter, I am struck by how frequently the practice of representing the dead body is negotiated over these terms. Indeed, it is these thematical and rhetorical points that form a continuous line of investigation throughout this book: death is both threat to and instrument of power; death is gendered; death is inextricably tied to sex/uality; death is the constructed Other; and death is physical. The ways in which these arguments relate specifically to the discourse of narrative fiction produced for adolescents is explored at length in the following chapters; however, by way of concluding—and by way of neatly summing up my motivation for undertaking this research—I want to close with Stuart Hall's pertinent words concerning representation:

> The great advantage of the concepts and classifications of the culture which we carry around with us in our heads is that they enable us to *think* about things, whether they are there, present, or not; indeed, whether they existed or not. There are concepts for our fantasies, desires and imaginings as well as for so-called "real" objects in the material world. And the advantage of language is that our thoughts about the world need not remain exclusive to us, and silent. We can translate them into language, make them "speak", through the use of signs which stand for them—and thus talk, write, communicate about them to others. ("Work" 62, emphasis original)

Chapter Two
Matilda's Last Dance:
Death and Historical Fiction

[E]verything about the past is only available to us in textualised form: it is "thrice-processed", first through the ideology, or outlook, or discursive practices of its own time, then through those of ours, and finally through the distorting web of language itself.

(Barry 175)

The community's idea of itself in history cannot be disentangled from the ways it represents death.

(Bronfen and Goodwin 15)

Since Philippe Ariès's *Western Attitudes to Death*, the cultural meanings derived from responses to death are inclined to be situated within the broader frame of the Western world rather than at a nation-specific site. As a result—and because death is universal—academic discussion of the topic is often over-generalised (Charmaz, Howarth, and Kellehear). The concern of this chapter is therefore with more localised (that is, national) experiences of, and ideas about, mortality. Using Australia as my model, I am going to focus specifically on some of the historical fictions produced for adolescents in this country. I am working from the notion that cultural myths have, over time, developed around particular experiences of death, and that these myths serve to "explain, eulogize, and promote admiration and acceptance of [the nation's] struggle with life and death" (Fitzpatrick 27).

History and Historiography

As a discipline, history has had a longstanding relationship with empiricist and positivist epistemologies. This means that, until fairly recently, it has been viewed as an unbiased, objective series of progressive accounts and verifiable truths which assist in both explaining the world and understanding the present. The approaches to history and historical fiction that inform this chapter, however, are based on the premise that records of the past are ideologically inspired and retrospectively constructed accounts "not of what actually happened, but of what historians tell us happened after they have organised the data according to their own version of social reality" (Munslow 127). Drawing upon ideas developed by theorists such as Karl Marx, Michel Foucault, and Hayden White, these analyses clearly illustrate history's connection with narrative, discourse, ideology, power, and language. Marx's theory of historical materialism points to the illusory nature and political interests served by older models of "disinterested" history, arguing that cultural production, including the writing of history, is inherently ideological (Spargo 6). Foucault and White insist that meaning is essentially created *by* historians, and *through* language, when the events of the past are organised into a story. Like the Marxists before them, they see this process as intrinsically ideological, given that meaning is culturally constructed in language, and that "ways of conceptualising the relations between past, present and future are themselves historically and culturally contingent" (Spargo 11). White's thesis also illustrates that history and fiction have many similarities. As Robert Berkhofer argues, both share "conventions of reference and representation and modes of narrativity" (69). Both also derive their power from verisimilitude rather than objective truth, are linguistic constructs, and appear to be equally intertextual, "deploying the texts of the past within their own complex textuality" (Hutcheon 474).

Historical Fiction for Children

These ways of looking at history emphasise the interpretative nature of any reading of the past, yet it is traditional humanist approaches which continue to influence writers and critics of children's historical fiction who largely appear to value history as a source of truth, instruction, and meaning. In "Versions of the Past: The Historical Novel in Children's Literature", Margery Hourihan argues, for example, that the best historical novels are those which espouse historical accuracy, evocative language, and convincing characterisation, invite reader-identification, and are "rich with meaning" for readers in the present ("Versions" 168). While this position has been challenged in recent critical readings which display an awareness of the textuality of history, many of even the most current fictive texts express the attributes of humanism which John Stephens (*Language*) identifies as characteristic of the genre.[1]

Historical fiction for children, he argues, tends to have a strong moral and even didactic purpose. Its lessons are usually socially conservative, and are constructed to give the impression that "a reader's present time, place and subjectivity constitute a normative position against which alterities are to be measured" (205). This area of writing also often urges readers to believe that there exists a set of universal human values that are transhistorical, and that human needs and desires are reasonably constant, irrespective of time, place, and other states of being.

The strategies by which historical fiction for children socialises its readers are, therefore, of critical importance. One of the ways these texts function ideologically is by encouraging reader identification with principal focalisers. Another is through the fusion of narratives about large-scale events with more personal stories, particularly those involving relationships. These texts additionally draw analogies between the development of the child and the formation of a culture or nation, and thus between personal and national identities (McCallum; Pearce, "Messages"; Stephens, *Language*). Historical fiction is essentially a realist genre, also inclined to avoid disclosing its own narrative strategies, and apt to conceal the mechanics of the story-making process. As both White and Foucault's approaches to history suggest, however, the means to understanding history—and, by implication, historical fiction—is to draw attention to its rhetorical form, and to emphasise the process of construction complicit in its making. History is not about the past, they argue, but more about the ways of inventing meanings from "the scattered, and profoundly meaning*less* debris we find around us [. . .] There is no story *there* to be gotten straight; any story must arise from the act of contemplation" (Kellner 137).

The Australian Context

History can have vastly different meanings depending on the sources of its "facts", what elements are left in or out, the points of view that are articulated, and the perspective from which the story is told. One of the most widely publicised events in recent Australian history illustrates this point. The disappearance of Azaria Chamberlain from Uluru (then Ayers Rock) has been narrativised in many forms since its occurrence in 1980. Azaria's death and the events surrounding it have been the subject of several books, countless official documents, a movie, and an autobiography, each of which tells a different story, although they are all based on the same set of circumstances (that is, Azaria went missing at a particular time, from a particular place). "Lindy" Chamberlain's account in *Through My Eyes* is undoubtedly vastly different to that of the proceedings from the second coronial inquiry which led to "Alice Lynne" Chamberlain's conviction and imprisonment for the murder of her daughter, even though both are presented as factual.[2] The title of the Chamberlain text is also a pertinent example of this argument: "through my eyes" makes reference to the constructedness of story and the subjective nature of telling it. In contrast, the language associated with the inquiry implies that "non-fiction" (particularly that belonging to the legal system) should be equated with truth. Both these titles—and the differing formats of Azaria's mother's name—also point to the ways in which a culture can legitimise particular versions of history.[3]

Regardless of the inquiry that finally pardoned Lindy/Alice Lynne Chamberlain, there is no doubt that many Australians continue to hold an opinion about her innocence or guilt. As an event that captured the interest of the Australian public and inspired such passionate debate for so long, the Chamberlain case was a cultural phenomenon that quickly took its place in the national narrative tradition alongside those other "great" stories that have shaped the country's past. What is interesting about the case is therefore not the "truth" of the matter, but the insights the event provided into the organisation and production of meaning in the Australian culture, especially in association with its historical discourse. Kay Schaffer suggests, for instance, that the disappearance of the baby at Uluru "allowed Australians to pour a century of fear and frustration, evidenced by representations of the bush as cruel mother, on to a woman who became the archetypally evil mother". Thus, it "is not the 'reality' or the 'facts' which deserve closer scrutiny", she contends, "but the modes of representation which enabled the population to read the events according to pre-existing systems of meaning" (65).

As the novels discussed in this chapter demonstrate, these systems of meaning continue to inform narratives written about Australian history, surfacing even in contemporary representations. They are by no means definitive, but their dominance does suggest something about the culture in which they were produced, and the ways in which the people in Australian society have come to know their past. Kate Darian-Smith and Paula Hamilton argue that popular understandings of history express the past through a set of simplified and selective myths that make historical events emotionally comprehensible and memorable. These mythic narratives do not offer a totalising and integrated history, they contend, but are rather a series of anecdotes, progressing selectively through historical time, and rendered significant by certain images and symbolic moments of revelation and action (2). For Graeme Turner, all national fictions draw on the available myths and discourses of national character and identity in their articulation of "the nation" (107). Maureen Nimon and John Foster share similar views, arguing that although Australian adolescent literature does not differ markedly at a general level from the forms of fiction aimed at adolescents in other Western nations, what sets it apart are "the special features of the Australian experience" as mythologised in the country's history (20).

Australian cultural studies such as Turner's also suggest that common or dominant forms and meanings in Australian narrative are drawn almost exclusively from the past when the concept of mateship, the legend of the egalitarian, anti-authoritarian (male) battler character, and the landscape-dominated ethos of the country were first mythologised. Thus, even as newer myths and narratives are articulated by the culture, this narrow range of meanings continues to have currency. As Turner points out, contemporary versions of "the Australian" and the Australian "way of life" owe much to the bush legend of the 1890s, and even Australia II's victory in the America's Cup provoked references to Gallipoli and World War I (107). Other studies have shown an almost seamless development between bushman and soldier and have also noted how, over time, the radical nationalist version of mateship has crossed a broad political and ideological spectrum to become the defining element of the quintessentially Australian character (Murrie, "Australian"). Former Prime Minister Paul Keating's speech to commemorate the entombment of the Unknown Soldier at the Australian War Memorial in 1993 illustrates these ideas:

> [T]he Australian legend which emerged from the war [...] is a legend not of sweeping military victories so much as triumphs against the odds, of courage and ingenuity in adversity. It is a legend of free and independent spirits whose discipline derived less from military formalities and customs than from the bonds of mateship and the demands of necessity. ("ANZAC Day")

The Australian Way of Death

If, as Australia's national fictions suggest, there is a particularly Australian way of life, are there also typically Australian styles of dying? In "Death in the Country of Matilda", Allan Kellehear and Ian Anderson argue that there *is* an Australian way of death and that it exists as an "officially endorsed set of cultural images" all of which are patriarchal, gentrified, and medicalised (1). Citing the Bushman, the Soldier, and *Homo suburbia* (the suburban dweller) as key characters in the myth-making process, Kellehear and Anderson demonstrate how experiences of death in Australia are expressed through celebrated images of national identity, at the same time noting how these dominating images—the deaths which figure in a political and historical schema as important—act to marginalise or silence other representations of death which do not conform to these systems of meaning: "dominating images of death reflect dominating influences in life itself. For national history and identity, the politics of death reflect the politics of everyday life" (12). For the Bushman or the Soldier, death was mythologised as exterior, working-class, white, public, and thus, to some extent, communal. It was attributed to the harsh Australian landscape, infectious diseases, war, and the fight against colonial authority or the Aborigine. These were the representations of death, Kellehear and Anderson argue, that were essential to the nation-building exercise. In turn, the "gentrification" of Australia's population and the emergence of *Homo suburbia* contributed to this set of images, constructing death as interior, private, middle-class, and medicalised. The focus of *Homo suburbia's* anxieties, they suggest, are those deaths which come from within the home, or threaten the home and the bourgeois dream of "privacy, comfort, control, predictability, safety and financial and marital security": suicide, road accidents, AIDS, SIDS, and the top two killers of the Western world, cardiovascular disease and cancer (7).

In Kellehear and Anderson's view, the tradition of death that is constructed by these images dominates the Australian imagination, functioning ideologically to hide from popular view broader experiences and meanings of death (such as those belonging to women, non-Anglo migrants, Indigenous people, or other non-whites). This creates an assumption, they argue, that "same *causes* of death means same *experiences* of death for everyone [...] differences included" (9, emphases original). A particular consequence of fashioning the past in these monological terms is exemplified by the absence of female images and experiences of death in Australia's death iconography. To be sure, the recording, defining and interpreting of historical events has traditionally been a male occupation, and history has often been conceived of as a progressive and linear set of stories about "great men" and their heroic deeds. Feminist theories suggest as much: "history" is a gendered term—*his* story, not hers. However, as Lesley Fitzpatrick argues in a study of the relationship between death and art, the discourse on mortality in Australia is overwhelmingly masculine; gender roles, even in recent works, are polarised to such an extent that "men die and women grieve for them" (22–23). The tradition works as well to elide other brutal or "distasteful" representations of mortality in national history and everyday life. Although death has been a central aspect of Aboriginal experience in Australia since colonisation, for example, Aboriginal deaths both in past and present times have tended to be hidden away from popular view. The myth of *Homo suburbia* demonstrates that death is a mark of disadvantage for Aboriginal peoples because it highlights the fact that the diseases and deaths which haunt Aboriginal communities (such as diabetes, chronic lung disease, car accidents, suicide, and kidney and liver disease) are those that appear to be "under control in the Caucasian community" (Dusevic and Carruthers 3). The heroic myth of the Bushman works in a similar way because it obscures much of the violence of colonisation by trivialising the devastation and death that marked so many cross-cultural encounters during this period. It does this firstly by portraying Aboriginal people as victims, "sometimes violent, sometimes passive to the onslaught of a 'superior' civilization", and secondly by suggesting that the Aboriginal presence in the myths "is submerged under the rubric of 'nature'": it was "the 'wilderness' that was conquered by these rugged pioneers"; little is said about "the impact of white diseases and delinquency in contact situations, 'peaceful' or otherwise" (Kellehear and Anderson 10).

These claims support Foucault's thesis that history itself produces continuity, coherence, and unity—a "collective mentality"—by glossing over differences and disruptions (*Archaeology*). And yet, it must be stressed at this point that Kellehear and Anderson's own discussion of "Australian" notions of death is problematic in that it refers to an "Australia" which not only assumes itself to be the normative version of the nation, but which subsumes Aboriginal perspectives. My own analyses of death are similarly influenced.[4] Aboriginal understandings of death are radically different from those of white Australia, however. Deborah Bird Rose argues, for example, that many Aboriginal people believe that dead bodies continue to live in their own country and they call out to their dead relatives when they go out hunting, fishing, collecting, or visiting the country: "Variously known as spirits, dead bodies, the old people, or the ancestors, the people who belonged to country in life continue to belong to it in death" (*Dingo* 73; *Nourishing* 71). In a study of the Yarralin people's stories and culture, Rose also points out that the community's notions of death do not constitute a cohesive set of beliefs; there is no dogma among the people on those "portions of a human being which exist before the person is conceived and which separate at death" (*Dingo* 58). Furthermore, although dead bodies are buried following European customs, and some people have accommodated Christian teachings within a general framework of ideas about spirits, beliefs about death are largely derived from Dreaming Law. The people also believe that bones endure forever, that the relationship between life and death is not imagined as a battle as it is in Western culture, and that the dead person's name cannot be spoken because, "as long as the memories are fresh and raw the dead person is there" (*Dingo* 69–73; *Reports* 26).

"There's a Black Boy Dead and a Migloo Holding a Gun": Un/covering the Murderous Past

Like Kellehear and Anderson, Rose nonetheless contends that national histories that commemorate some deaths, but are silent about others, rework monological narratives of nationhood (*Reports* 29).[5] Kellehear and Anderson argue, for example, that the image of the Bushman living and dying on the land, and doing battle with the wild forces (the weather, the harsh terrain) of an untamed country functions as a symbol of "the historical amnesia that took hold in white Australia" because "its images deflect the fact that the foundation of the Australian nation rests on the violent pacification and subjugation of Aboriginal countries" (12). It is not surprising, then, that representations of Indigenous people in past versions of Australian history were either conspicuously absent, or inclined to construct Aboriginality in terms of savagery. Similarly, colonisation was often depicted as a passive process devoid of violence or death. As Clare Bradford's study in *Reading Race: Aboriginality in Australian Children's Literature* demonstrates, the colonial discourse that informed children's school texts in the early to mid-1900s served to cover over the sorry facts of the displacement and death of Indigenous people, to ensure that Aborigines were "all but invisible" and certainly never heroes (19, 21, 26). According to Leela Gandhi, the desire to erase the bloody and painful memories associated with colonisation, to engage in a kind of "historical self-invention", is characteristic of settler societies (4). Around the early 1990s, however, a methodological shift in historical scholarship occurred in Australia. Reflecting larger social and cultural changes that were emerging at the same time, this new approach to the discipline sought to highlight the negative aspects of European settlement, and to correct the silences and misrepresentations that were such a feature of Australian historiography up until this point.

Produced in a social and political climate in which cross-cultural relations were a conspicuous issue, a number of Australian adolescent fictions written at this time therefore thematise Aboriginality and Aboriginal-white relations. Many of these texts foreground ideas about reconciliation between Indigenous and non-Indigenous Australians, while simultaneously engaging in what Bradford calls "revisionary history" (*Reading* 191). This is highlighted in Melissa Lucashenko's *Killing Darcy*, through an exchange between Darcy Mango and Cameron Menzies about Aboriginal massacres:

'Massacres?' [Cam] asked. 'That stuff happened around here?'

'Of course,' Darcy replied impatiently. 'What did ya think happened? Think a spaceship come down and kidnapped all the blackfellas round here?'

Cameron, shamed, was silent. He'd never thought too much about that side of the past. To him, history was goldfields, and 'explorers'. Sometimes he gave some passing thought to Aboriginal languages or Central Australian tribes. And of course he knew that the continent was taken by force, but, well, it was never stated that way, was it? Not to your face. Not about your own home. And not by an Aborigine. (123)

Scenes in which violence, murder, and genocide are uncovered are common to these types of narratives. In addition to *Killing Darcy*, Gary Crew's *No Such Country* and *Strange Objects*, Victor Kelleher's *Baily's Bones*, James Moloney's *Gracey* and *The House on the River Terrace*, Jim Schembri's *The Jay Beans Guild*, and Lucy Sussex's *Black Ice*, all feature protagonists in contemporary settings who find evidence from the colonial period of such events.[6] On the whole, the concern of these novels is not with the past; rather these representations of death operate largely through their relevance to— and impact upon—contemporary culture. Yet they do demonstrate some of the ways in which the past continues to inform and shape meaning in the present. A familiar theme in these texts is thus the redressing of past wrongs; upon discovering the cruelty displayed towards Aborigines in the past, adolescents (usually of Anglo descent) attempt to rectify the situation in the present while also learning to understand and value Aboriginal culture. Sometimes this involves the retelling of a historical narrative to more accurately represent the "facts", or to give it another perspective—such as *The Jay Beans Guild*—while at others, it encompasses a rejection by the white protagonist of their whole way of life. In *No Such Country* (which I will discuss shortly), for instance, one of the characters symbolically and physically leaves her past self behind when she discovers that her family was involved in the murder of a local clan.

For the most part, representations of cross-cultural relations in these fictions (particularly as they relate to death) are oversimplified, oppositional, and framed through white perspectives. Some texts, which self-consciously set out to address the issue of "white guilt" and to question whether there is an obligation to uncover the "truth" about past events, also conclude by glossing over these same issues. When the remains of an Aboriginal clan are exhumed in *The Jay Beans Guild*, for example, the narrator proclaims that "as far as he [can] tell, all skeletons look the same" (192). In other instances, stories thematising relations between races become subsumed within larger narratives dealing with an adolescent romance. In *No Such Country*, the conflation of one strand of the story involving the discovery of a mass Aboriginal grave with another chronicling the relationship between a non-Indigenous girl and an Aboriginal boy depoliticises relations between black and white by depicting these exchanges in romanticised and polarised terms. By contrast, *Killing Darcy*'s treatment of death and Aboriginal-Western histories is complex since it is constructed to engage with "a number of discourses and meanings, each provisional and incomplete" (Bradford, *Reading* 188). While this story also involves a potential relationship between an Aboriginal boy and a white girl, the relationship does not develop at a romantic level largely because of the novel's resistance to stereotyped models of gendered race relations. Its insistence on multiple perspectives and ways of being also assists in evading some of the cultural norms associated with sexuality and desire as the following encounter between Darcy, a young homosexual Aboriginal male, and his boss, Jon Menzies, demonstrates:

> Jon suddenly grabbed Darcy's slim arms from behind, marched him a few yards, then turned him to face the caravan disintegrating slowly behind the fuel shed. 'Renovator's delight? Ideal first home?'
> Enjoying the contact, Darcy began to grin. He could really go for Jon. Sometimes he felt himself on the verge of saying something stupid, something he'd really regret as soon as it was outta his dumb black gob. (89)

Killing Darcy, focalised through both Indigenous and non-Indigenous perspectives, tells of the mystery surrounding the death of a young Aboriginal boy in the early twentieth century. When Filomena Menzies, who is visiting her father Jon's horse property in the summer holidays, discovers an old camera that retains images of this event, she and her brother Cameron speculate that inside the camera is "a murderer's victim looking for revenge" (100). One of these photos shows their great-great grandfather, Hew Costello, standing over the body of the dead boy with a rifle in his hand and, horrified, the siblings assume from this image that Hew is the killer. In an attempt to find out more, Fil and Cam involve Darcy who, with the help of an Aboriginal elder, Granny Lil, performs a ritual that transports him back to the place and time of the death. The attitudes of each of these characters towards the death are very different, however. Fil's initial solution is to sell the camera: "'It was a million years ago. Who cares? I don't want to know about it, [. . .]'" she says to Cam (84). Yet Cam's response discloses the sense of responsibility he feels for the murder: "'You gutless cow!'" he replies, thinking, "We have to find out what's going on, we can't just ignore it" (84–85). For Darcy, the decision to act is not a matter of choice as it is dictated by Aboriginal Law that he must go back, even though he is terrified because "where he [comes] from, deaths [mean] payback" (124). As he tells Cam and Fil:

> '[I've got to go] . . . to find out who got murdered, and who did it and why, and how *we're* involved in it [. . .].
> [. . .] The camera wouldn't have turned up unless someone's supposed to do something. Youse can't. I ain't got no choice, see. If I run, it'll catch me. Same as you can't sell it—it's come to ya'. (182–83, emphasis original)

The point at which the mystery is solved is obviously an important one; it occurs when Cam and Fil watch their father destroy a dangerous horse and they are overcome by the similarities between the scene they are viewing and the photo. Here, past and present merge as the image of Hew, the sun behind him, "the rifle, held by the butt" and "[his] hat lying on the ground like a rock" is duplicated by Jon who, "[s]ilhouetted by the rising disc of the sun [. . .] could have been Hew Costello" (212). Framed through ideas about responsibility, authority, and knowledge, several aspects of this scene (and its outcomes) draw attention to the complexities in the novel's representation of race relations. The first discloses the kind of tensions and contradictions surrounding issues of white responsibility for the colonial past. For Cam, beginning to appreciate the scale of the mistreatment of Aborigines throughout Australian history, and the disadvantages of being Aboriginal, the boy's death has an enormous impact. Irrespective of when it occurred, he feels some sense of responsibility for this event, especially because of his kinship with Hew. This is evident in his slippage between past and present tense when he exclaims joyously "'[Hew] isn't, wasn't, a murderer! [. . .] It's OK [. . .] It's solved everything'" (213). However, because the figure of Hew is a metonym for "white Australia" (just as the novel's setting of Federation and its surroundings is a metonym for "Australia"), Cam's response can also be seen to bear traces of absolution. The dead horse (suggestive of a "dead horse matter") also seems to work against the issue of accountability somewhat, as do Jon's open, pleading palms and his apology to Cam over the horse: "'I didn't want anyone else's life on my hands'" (213). The second aspect, dealing with authority and knowledge, a prominent theme in the novel, is an example of how the text has been constructed to resist the polarisation of Aboriginal and Western cultures. Cam "[cannot] breathe, he [is] so certain" about the conclusions he has drawn from this scene (213), and there is a general consensus among all those involved that he is correct. While it is not Cam's feeling of certainty that establishes the truth about the boy's death, but Granny's knowledge of the event (available to her through the orally transmitted stories of the Aboriginal community), authority is, however, shared between both Cam and Gran. Both are wrong in some ways about the death at the same time that they are also right. Furthermore, no one method of seeking answers is privileged over another since knowledge of the event is pieced together from library records, photos, family lore, instinct, sacred ritual, and oral tradition.

As with other novels which are informed by discourses of reconciliation, *Killing Darcy*'s lessons about history and race relations are often heavy-handed (Bradford, *Reading*). However, readers of this text are also positioned to view Indigenous and non-Indigenous cultures in Australia in terms of their "long and tangled history" as Jon Menzies puts it (43). In this instance, the themes of Aboriginality and death highlight the complexities and contradictions marking such cultural exchanges. Darcy, Granny Lil, Cam, and Fil all have something to contribute to solving the mystery of the boy's death: Darcy by determining that the dead boy was Hew's son, Edward; Granny Lil by revealing that Darcy and the Menzies family are related through the union between Edward's Aboriginal mother and Hew; and Cam and Fil by deducing that Hew had not shot Edward, but the pony which had just thrown and killed the boy. Each of them also comes to appreciate and empathise with other cultural perspectives and traditions during this process, part of which involves a questioning of their assumptions about the past. Granny Lil's mistake about Edward's death, for example, illustrates how her own cultural bias has (mis) informed her interpretation of this event, and also demonstrates how the past is influenced by, and filtered through, meaning and experience in the present. "'I don't see no accident,'" she says, adding a little later:

> 'Darcy, use ya head. There's a black boy dead and a migloo holding a gun. Oh, I know [. . .] I know ya don't wanta think ya friends are descended from a murderer. But think about it, boy. They all got blood on their hands somewheres, somehows'. (196, 197)

Bradford argues that, all too often, Aboriginal culture is homogenised, and race relations in Australian children's texts "represented as fixed within a scheme of stark oppositions oblivious to historical and cultural change" (*Reading* 208).[7] From the representation of death in *Killing Darcy*, however, it is possible to see that, by situating the narrative through a variety of perspectives, readers can be positioned to view both Aboriginality and black-white relations in terms of their complexity. Crew's project in *No Such Country* appears similar because it involves several protagonists, both black and white, yet it produces a neat closure which is not only quite different to that of *Killing Darcy*, it also "fails to address the trauma of the colonised in its focus on the coloniser's perspective" (Bradford, "Memory"). Crew's fascination with history is apparent from a number of his novels; in particular, he is appalled by stories involving the mistreatment of Aborigines and has acknowledged that he seeks to address the silence surrounding these crimes by awakening modern (and, by implication, white) Australian adolescents to this facet of history (McKenna and Pearce 118, 119). Although authorial intent has little bearing on my discussion of these texts, it is interesting that even with such a clear articulation of these objectives, *No Such Country* is nonetheless pervaded with the kind of meanings that support the stereotypical or totalising representations of Aboriginality and cross-cultural exchange that I discussed earlier.[8]

The novel is, in many respects, a small-scale, compressed history of Australia since colonisation, focusing specifically on Aboriginal-white relations. Set in the fictional isolated fishing village of New Canaan, the plot revolves around the secret of the town's murderous past. Two local girls—Rachel Burgess and Sarah Goodwin—and Sam Shadows, a university student working on an Aboriginal shell midden near the village, uncover the bodies of an Indigenous clan who were murdered by the men of New Canaan a generation ago. Until this time, the collective community silence about the event and the despotic rule of the priest known as Grey Eye, or the Father (an unsubtle symbol of the Church, the Empire, patriarchy, and white power), has ensured the mass grave remains buried beneath the lantana. Besides his anthropological work on the midden, Sam is also in the village to uncover some family history. As an orphan, the only information he has about his parentage is that his teenage Aboriginal mother, Hannah, left New Canaan and sought refuge in a government "retreat" in preparation for his birth. As the secrets of the village are revealed towards the conclusion, Sam discovers that Hannah—the sole survivor of the massacre—was the last of the Indigenous clan in the area, that she was raped by the Father, and that the priest is actually *his* father.

Brendan McKenna and Sharyn Pearce argue that the Father "represents the patriarchal corruption that has affected Christianity in the past because it permits men to oppress, to lie, to exploit" (121). Thus, besides the predominant theme of cross-cultural relations, *No Such Country* addresses the issue of the Church, patriarchy, and women's oppression. One of the defining features of adolescent novels is the struggle for power between adolescent protagonists and the various social institutions in their lives (Trites, *Disturbing* 8). For Rachel and Sarah this is represented—as it is for all of the females in the text—by their relationship with New Canaan's domineering males and, most importantly, with the Father. To overcome the entrenched systems of power operating in New Canaan, the girls must therefore defeat the Father and uncover the secrets of the past. Secrets and silence function symbolically to represent the oppression of females in the text, and to reflect the silence about Aboriginality common to colonial discourses. New Canaan seems to be slowly collapsing under the weight of the secret as the atmosphere of doom conveys. Its symbolic death can be seen in the disasters and deaths which plague the village, and in its derelict atmosphere. The houses are sullen and brooding, and encrusted with salt (19), the boat sheds' splintered timbers are pale and fading (30), and the church is constructed entirely of pine packing cases (48). Of the female characters featured who know about the massacre, Hannah is dead, Eva (Rachel's mother) dies in the opening chapter, and only Miriam Goodwin still lives, although she has withdrawn into silence after Eva's death (16). The colonial figure of the silent, suffering Aboriginal feminine is also present in the text. Hannah's story is only shown in the Father's book, and divulged in a letter written by the Matron of the Retreat. Her narrative silence is echoed by her refusal to speak; when she does appear in the narrative, she will not "engage in conversation sufficient even to name her own child" (81). Furthermore, almost everything the reader knows about Hannah is constructed through white frames of reference. Even Sam only relates the little he knows of his mother's history to Rachel and Sarah as a preface to the Matron's letter which becomes the "real" story. As Robyn McCallum argues, "the subjectivity of a historical other can only be inferred from the texts and discourses within which s/he is constructed and made present as a subject" (230). Readers who align themselves with the kind and beneficent Matron, Elizabeth Hibbert, are positioned to view Hannah in a way which divulges the many colonial ideologies that inform the novel: she is frail and powerless, with a "simple and childlike manner" containing "no artifice", is "utterly naïve and ignorant of all but the most elementary forms of social intercourse", and she takes to her work as a general domestic at the institution "as though she had performed such menial duties all her life" (81–82).

Hannah's story illustrates how pervasive Aboriginalist discourses and attitudes can be, even in texts like *No Such Country* which are so patently designed to resist such ideas.[9] By essentialising Aboriginality and universalising Aboriginal spirituality, the narrative constructs Sam's search for his family history and identity in ways which draw upon stereotypes of Aboriginal culture, even though at one point the text is attempting to interrogate such assumptions. On the bank of the lagoon, Rachel asks Sam: "'[A]re you so smart that you can tell the sex of birds?'", and he replies: "'Naturally [...] Can't all us Abos?'". But this apparently parodic allusion to white imaginings is countered once he adds: "'When I swam in here the other day, it was like I'd done it all my life. Every day of my life [...] I felt at home. Like I belonged'" (154–55). Significantly, "home" for Sam is the site of the massacre, and his Aboriginality is dependent on "intuition", on being "at home [...] near the lagoon and that mountain" (155) where he can feel "the heart of the earth" (95).[10] Such statements create a homogeneous or singular version of Aboriginality that "falls back onto colonial views of the undifferentiated Other" (Bradford, *Reading* 11) and, by tapping into this romanticised, timeless version of Aboriginality, negates the particularity of the past. In itself this is problematic as such representations construct Aboriginality in ahistorical terms and, in this instance, also negate the seriousness of the massacre.

The conflation of Aboriginality with traditional discourses of femininity in this exchange (highlighted by the association between words like "intuition", "naturally", "heart", "home") is of more concern, however. Representations of Aboriginality, femininity, and death often occur together in *No Such Country*. This is due to the close alignment of the two major themes—women's oppression and cross-cultural relations—but also a function of the plot since it is implied that atonement for the murderous crimes of the past, and the erasure of the old patriarchal order (through the death of the Father) is achievable only when the characters of Sam, Rachel, and Sarah work together. These outcomes are also tied to female sexuality, evident when Sarah and Rachel unravel the town secret and prepare to take on the Father, proclaiming "'[w]e're women now'" (154); when the massacre is revealed to Sam in the Father's book only after he bleeds onto it (192); and when Miriam leads the girls to the burial site. Here they find her kneeling, "naked, the shocking white of her skin smeared with blood [. . .] shoving her fingers between the black rocks that [lie] partially exposed at her knees" (128). The sexual overtones that are a feature of this episode are also evident in the description of the massacre, illustrated by the helpless clan's "shrieking and crying" as the men of New Canaan "have their way [. . .] dragging the black bodies, moaning and whimpering" into the sea (193).

Hannah's death, too, is constructed in terms of sexuality, as her demise at the "Retreat for Wayward Women" suggests. As the only Aboriginal woman in the novel, Hannah functions metonymically, revealing the tensions surrounding both miscegenation and white constructions of Aboriginal female sexuality. According to Bradford, although interracial sexual relationships are rarely addressed in fictions for Australian adolescents, the few that do explore the theme are inclined to represent these relationships in tragic terms, sending a clear message that they will not work (*Reading* 106). Such tensions are often manifested as episodes of violence, destruction, and death, exemplified by *The House on the River Terrace*, in which an Aboriginal girl commits suicide after she is rejected by a white boy, and Julia Lawrinson's *Bye, Beautiful*, where it is implied that an Indigenous boy's death is directly attributable to his sexual relationship with the white town-policeman's daughter. Where *No Such Country* is concerned, death is used as a form of "punishment" for the sexually transgressive female. The "sex-leading-to-death" motif is common in literary history (Bassein 60), but for Hannah, this is emphasised by her Aboriginality because she alone escapes the fate of the rest of her clan, only to die after falling pregnant and giving birth. Although the Father dies too—he is engulfed in lava and flames when a nearby volcano erupts—he is dehumanised to some extent by the Armageddon-like climax, giving his death an abstract quality and disassociating it from his sexual relationship with Hannah. Furthermore, the traditionally masculinist image of the devouring Mother Earth in this scene (a symbolic representation of feminine retribution) merely serves to reveal the anxieties regarding female power that are such a characteristic of the text.

These ambiguities undermine the more positive aspects of *No Such Country*, as does the volcanic eruption at the novel's conclusion. Alice Mills sees the town freed of its guilty past by this event ("Writing" 29), but because much of the story revolves around Sam, Rachel, and Sarah's unearthing of the past, when the volcano covers up the evidence of the massacre and the midden, their efforts are rendered futile—particularly after Sam has told Rachel that "'burial sites and rubbish dumps provide more information about cultures than anywhere else'" (157). Like the town graveyard, the atrocity of the crime is buried once again, and New Canaan is then, in fact, "new"—and "no such country", where a large scale massacre of the Indigenous population can occur *and* be covered up, really does exist. The text is a lesson in history as its omniscient mode of narration and hieratic register signify.[11] However, it does not seem to support any meaningful dialogue between past and present, nor interrogate any of the issues it raises. Crew's novels are often constructed to resist ideas about "historical truths" and unmediated views of the past. As McKenna and Pearce argue, white Australia has "a national moral amnesia" about the aspects of history that *No Such Country* confronts, and texts like this can assist in righting this wrong, hopefully by inspiring readers to seek out "the historical truth" like Sam, Rachel, and Sarah (126). Yet by erasing the village's history altogether, the novel ultimately works against the themes it purports to address.

Given its obvious attempt to critique traditional or ethnocentric versions of the past, the approaches to history that characterise *No Such Country* are therefore unsettling. Attempts to locate the massacre at a particular time and place are destabilised, for instance, by a sense that past and present exist simultaneously, or are constructed in causal terms. This is represented by the singular temporal setting, the Father's book—in which New Canaan's Indigenous history is illustrated quickly and superficially (192–93)—and by the Father himself who, albeit old, has existed from "the beginning" and lives throughout the novel. The implied analogy between evolution and colonisation, evident in the following passage, also encapsulates these ideas:

> There were those who believed the Father had existed from the beginning, that in some dark and primal time he had come up from the sea, flying like a white bird, or a vessel, some said, a white-sailed vessel, and that he had first appeared out of the surf at the entrance to the lagoon. (Prologue)

In turn, the strategy of framing the reconstruction of the clan's death through a traditional narrative model of adolescent sexual development reduces the gravity of the massacre, as does the shift from "realism to adventure romance" at the novel's conclusion (Mills, "Writing" 29). Most important, however, is the novel's closed ending which positions readers to view the events of the past as "an old, sad story best forgotten" (Bradford, "Memory"). Sam and Rachel leave the town together with no plans to return except to visit Sarah; the unrepentant Father dies; and though it is possible that Sam and Rachel will tell the story of the massacre to others, the reader is left in New Canaan with Sarah whose liberation rests with the inheritance of books salvaged from the wool clipper, Liberty, an instrument of imperial power.

The Agency that Heals the Wound: History, Mortality, and the Feminine Subject

In "Preying on the Past: Contexts of Some Recent Neo-Historical Fiction", Peter Pierce argues that, over the last five or so decades, Australian historical fiction has turned away from "unconstrained and idealistic affirmations about Australia's future" to empathise instead with those figures in the historical landscape who were previously marginalised: "victims of imperialism, patriarchy, racism, capitalism" (307). According to Stephens, this trend is particularly applicable to historical literature for younger readers which now often tries to renegotiate history by providing a counterpoint to the meta-narratives of the past ("Always"). Regardless of how "successful" they are in dismantling entrenched concepts of national history—or, to use Bradford's words, "representational and narrative habits and patterns privileging Western over Indigenous perspectives" (*Unsettling* 119)—*Killing Darcy* and *No Such Country* are a case in point. My focus in this section, however, is upon texts which "reinstate" other such marginalised figures—specifically women, whom Schaffer argues are hardly mentioned at all as historical subjects in the dominant texts about Australian nationalism (76).

Earlier, I alluded to the masculinist bias that characterises the discourse on mortality in the national fictions, so it is not surprising that there are few YA historical novels which support a meaningful dialogue with female experiences of death. Indeed, it is rare in such texts to find a female character who is not merely cast as a shadowy presence, relegated to the periphery of the story, or given a symbolic role. I am reminded here of the character of Cecelia Hainsworth in David Metzenthen's *Boys of Blood and Bone*, whose primary function in the narrative is to act as a dead soldier's memory keeper, waiting for the appropriate moment when his diary can be passed on to a (male) recipient of a following generation who is deemed worthy of comprehending the sacrifices and hardships involved in fighting a war. Like other women in the imagined community of the nation, Cecelia is positioned largely as a mourner: watching, waiting, coping, and then grieving. Although she builds a life for herself after the soldier's death, she never leaves the small town where they met and where the local teens sometimes avoid her, knowing of her tendency to bring the subject around to the injustices of a war that was "terrible beyond understanding" (157).

In the texts I am concerned with—Garry Disher's *The Divine Wind*, Anthony Eaton's *Fireshadow*, and Mark Svendsen's *Poison Under Their Lips*—female characters are central to the story, but even then they do not possess a narrative voice. In *The Divine Wind*, for example, which documents an interracial relationship between Mitsy, a Japanese-Australian girl, and Hart, an Anglo boy, readers are positioned to identify with Hart because the romance is viewed entirely from his (white, male) perspective. Through Hart's eyes, Mitsy is constructed as an exotic Other, and thus, as Sharyn Pearce argues, she becomes the archetypal narrative object "to whom Hart, as a representative of the dominant group, extends understanding" ("Messages" 244). Another feature of these texts is that they are inclined to be set in liminal spaces; that is, domains "in-between" cultures, languages, and subjectivities, where individual and group identities are shaped, where differences are played out, and which are marked by "relations of power and by histories of cross-cultural exchange" (Bradford, *Unsettling* 158–59, 168). In *The Divine Wind* and *Poison Under Their Lips*, this in-between space is representative of the frontier landscape, in that it "overtly expresses both an extension of the subjectivity of those who choose to inhabit it, and a primary object which must be opposed or come to terms with" (Stephens, *Language* 210). This notion is encapsulated by Hart in *The Divine Wind* when he muses that he has "a duty to grow up quickly in a country where the frontier snatches your loved ones away from you" (45). In *Fireshadow*, the protagonists inhabit both normative and liminal spaces, but even in environments where they are most at home as members of the majority culture, they are nevertheless positioned as Others.

In this sense, what binds all of these texts together is the theme of alterity. The motif of otherness is not troubling in itself because such settings often function as borderlands, allowing for the destabilisation of order, or of contact with alien ways of being and knowing, and thus they cannot help but evoke an association with death, however figurative. As these texts are apt to annex death to (sexual) secrets and scandals, however, this theme can become problematic, since the ideological effect of rhetorically yoking death, femininity, and otherness together in this way is to suggest, as Elisabeth Bronfen argues, that the Other is "semantically encoded as the site on to which anxieties about loss of control and boundary dissolution are projected" (*Over* 190). In *The Divine Wind*, this pattern is played out against the backdrop of World War II, when the White Australia policy was in full force and the Japanese were advancing into the South West Pacific. Set in Broome, a north-western town renowned for its multi-racial history, the novel is, to use Pearce's phrase, "rather brave" in its exploration of European-Australian tensions (a subject that has hitherto been underrepresented in Australian children's literature), yet it has a "discernible tentativeness" about it too that hints at white anxieties about difference ("Messages" 243). A number of stereotypes cluster around the character of Mitsy and the romantic relationship between Hart and Mitsy, for example. The relationship begins after Mitsy's father, Zeke, a pearl diver, is killed rescuing Hart when their lugger is caught in a cyclone; however, it does not become sexual until the height of the war in the Pacific. At this time, the whites of Broome are shocked by the "extent and vigour" of the Japanese attacks, and the Japanese occupants are seen as "aliens in [their] midst" (104, 113). Mitsy and Hart's trysts, which represent a retreat from a "world going insane" (117), are therefore conducted in secret. In the tradition of Orientalism, Mitsy then comes to symbolise the mysterious Other because she "inhabit[s] the dark hours"; in the light of the day she retreats to become "a dream in [Hart's] head", but in the filtered moonlight she takes command, helping him to achieve "slow pleasures" (116, 118). She is also described as sly and not classically beautiful (that is, by European standards), although Hart still sees her in romanticised terms. The novel additionally tends to represent the Orient as a feminised, sexualised, and domestic space: Each day the pair scrub sheets stained by the evidence of their lovemaking, washing shirts and underwear with the sheets to convey their "innocent intentions" (117); Hart learns to brew Japanese tea and cook traditional dishes; and the two rarely leave the house together, except to deliver food to the Japanese locals who are interned in the jail. Mitsy also functions to stabilise the identity of the Anglo male subject, firstly because Hart becomes her protector when the family offer her sanctuary, and secondly because she represents his redemption. This is made very clear at the beginning of the narrative when, looking back on this period of his life, Hart muses that "Mitsy saved me from myself" (9).

Non-whites are often constructed as less sexually repressed than whites, as "naturally" sexual (Robert 72), and this is another problematic aspect of the narrative. When the pair first begin to experiment, Hart declares: "I knew nothing about making love. Mitsy taught me how. Neither of us was experienced, but Mitsy had an instinct for it [. . .]" (116). Hart's redemption is also tied up with his sexual relationship with Mitsy; he sees Mitsy as the source of his salvation, evident when they are exploring each other's bodies, and she takes the "knobbiness, [the] carven ridges and dead tissue" of Hart's damaged leg—the symbol of his emasculation since his injury prevents him from joining the war effort—and returns it to "normal" (116). Here, the text points to the regenerative power of Woman, a theme that is common in the discourse of Orientalism, but is also familiar to male-authored/narrated fictions which tend to portray women by their relation to men, or in terms of their sexual and reproductive functions.

In *Fireshadow*, similar ways of seeing and constructing the female subject suggest that this is an enduring pattern in Western fictions. Like *The Divine Wind*, the narrative of *Fireshadow* is also set during the Second World War, locating its German protagonist, Erich, in an environment marked by unsettling politics and relations of power. At seventeen, Erich runs away from his family in Germany to join the army. Captured in Libya and brought to

Marinup, a prisoner of war camp in Western Australia, a patriotic and fiercely proud Erich finds himself at odds with Marinup's other complacent prisoners who are only looking to resume a peaceful life once the war is over. He finds solace in a tentative friendship with Doctor Alexander, the camp physician, learning to slowly let go of the fear, bitterness, and grief that are a feature of both his journey as a soldier and his difficult relationship with his father, an officer in the German Army. Although Erich's story is intertwined with that of Vinnie's in the present, the multi-stranded narrative is largely concerned with the romance between Erich and the doctor's granddaughter, Alice. The camp acts as a backdrop against which exchanges between the two can be played out, because it mixes people of different rank, class, nationality, and loyalties. In this way, their relationship functions to explore ideas about nationalism and group identity, and about differences and similarities between cultures. Such differences inevitably act as obstacles to their union. Erich is not "the sort to bow to pressure in the face of the [perceived] enemy" (29), for example, and so for his relationship to develop with Alice, he must first relinquish the desire to place duty to his country above his personal feelings. For Alice, this is "the only way to be human" (184), but the pair do not come together until Erich learns that his father and other members of the *Wehrmacht* have been executed on Hitler's orders. Feeling betrayed, that his father's death "make[s] it all a lie" (197), he turns instead to Alice for something "to believe in [...] to hold on to" (197, 198). Symbolically, this occurs just moments before the two hear that the war is over.

As Stephens explains, the ideological effect of displacing the large-scale events and politics of war into a personal romantic relationship is that "historical particularities [are transformed] into universals of human experience" (*Language* 238). This is reflected in the moral message inscribed within the text (which also applies to the present-day strand of the narrative): that the ability to develop meaningful relationships is crucial for the adolescent's development into a well-adjusted adult, and, more importantly, that differences and prejudices can be overcome by love and understanding. The message is somewhat complicated, however, by Alice's pregnancy, which she discovers not long after Erich has been shipped back to Germany. Alice clearly occupies a position of privilege at the camp, but in the mistrustful and xenophobic community she returns to after Erich's departure, she is doubly inscribed as Other: first, because she is unwed and carrying Erich's child, and, second, because she maintains a close, public association with Gunter and Francesca, one a former POW and the other an Italian immigrant. Alice's ostracism is brought into sharp relief when the three take a trip to Cottesloe beach. The beach is a site where the Australian ideals of classlessness, egalitarianism, and community are perceived to combine, but it works here to demonstrate how alienated she has become:

> [She] is aware of people's eyes on her as she drops her [...] towel and walks to the water's edge. She can feel the judgement in their gazes. She

can feel the other mothers sitting under their umbrellas and radiating disapproval at her. She knows she doesn't look respectable, swimming at a family beach in her condition. Especially with Germans. (243)

Ideas about loyalty and national identity are further disrupted during an encounter at the local grocer's. Here, the shop assistant tells Alice and Francesca to "piss off", that Francesca should not have been allowed to enter the country because she is "the reason [his] old man got shot in the leg" (251). Some of the customers agree, but others, like the grocer, are horrified by such bigotry. Through these exchanges and events, readers who sympathise with Alice's predicament are positioned to view the values associated with nationalism as parochial and divisive.

A telling moment therefore occurs when, after hearing Alice's story, her friend, Anne, a war widow with two small children, says: "'One day our kids are going to play together [. . .] and if I've got anything to do with it, then none of them, not yours or mine, or anyone else's for that matter, is going to give a bugger about where their fathers came from'" (231). Anne's desire to see her own children at play with Alice's child never comes to pass, however, because Alice dies immediately after the birth of her daughter. The child is called Matilda, a name that has special significance in Australia, but is also an Anglicised version of the German Mathilde (Erich's sister). She therefore acts metonymically to signify the union of enemies and to suggest a future Australia in which diversity and pluralism will be embraced. Yet, in what is typical of more recent Australian children's fictions, this future is not represented as certain or free of problems. Indeed, Alice's parents withdraw Erich's access to his daughter and make it clear that he is not welcome to return to Australia to become a part of Matilda's life. As the narrative is largely concerned with Erich, and as Alice's parents are mostly represented as harsh and intolerant (Alice is slapped by her mother when her parents find out about her pregnancy, and the words "shame" and "disgrace" are used), it is likely that the audience will align themselves with the two lovers.

There are obstacles to reading *Fireshadow* as a counterdiscourse of cultural homogeneity, however, the principal one being Alice's death. Much of Alice's story is focused on her struggle to overcome the prejudices connected with her pregnancy and with her choice of partner, so when this section of the narrative ends on such a tragic and unexpected note, it is difficult not to associate her ostracism with the "tearing [and] searing" pain and the pooling blood that she experiences not long before she dies (272–73). As I argued earlier, the scene at the beach is a pivotal one in this respect because it situates Alice at the centre of a domain that is of particular significance in the national culture; taken together, the two events therefore suggest that Alice is paying for her transgression, both as a woman and as an Anglo-Australian. This blunt reading of Alice's death is ameliorated somewhat by the events that occur in the years to come (especially in the present-day strand of the narrative), because

Erich is reconciled with Alice's parents and eventually returns to Australia. Nonetheless, the appearance of the woman/death trope remains a troubling aspect of the novel because it reinforces the age-old idea that death is the price that women will pay for sex outside marriage. The discrepancy between story and significance (or the explicit and implicit ideology) that is apparent in the closure of Alice's story also suggests that the positive messages about cultural difference that are promoted elsewhere in the novel are fragile and unsound.

The final novel I wish to consider in this section is *Poison Under Their Lips*. The narrative of the text (one of very few texts to explore Aboriginality and death purely from a setting in the past) follows the events surrounding the murder of an Aboriginal man and the rape of an Aboriginal woman by members of the Queensland Mounted Native Police. While largely the fictional journal of eighteen-year-old cadet Arthur Bootle Wilbraham, the novel is also interspersed with documents such as letters, depositions from actual court hearings, and newspaper articles and editorials that have been sourced by the author from archival libraries. As the juxtaposition between the personal and the official suggests, the novel works to interrogate authorised versions of Australian history; it juggles differing perspectives and uses strategies that position readers to be confused or unclear about the narrative's status as "truth". Much of the text is concerned with the discrepancy between official government policy and the ways in which the Native Police put such policy into practice. A good example is the conversation between Judge Lutwyche and Arthur, where the word "disperse" takes on two very different meanings. The judge begins with a rhetorical question to Arthur: "'So, young Wilbraham, you've come to scourge the blacks for us?'". Arthur's naïve answer—"'Well, to disperse them if troublesome, Sir'"—causes much hilarity between the judge and the violent, racist Lieutenant Wheeler, the troop's commanding officer. "'Disperse? Quite so, lad, quite so!'", the judge responds, adding in an aside to the lieutenant: "'I think you've backed a winner with this one, Wheeler'" (53). For the judge and, as the reader comes to learn, for Wheeler, the Aboriginals are depraved animals, who in "social function and intelligence are more closely related to the apes than [the] average Britisher", a view which justifies whatever means they choose to "breed the last vestiges of the savage out of the [British] race" (53–54).

The ideologies of *Poison Under Their Lips* are quite clear so that exchanges like this one, in addition to the entries in Arthur's journal, only serve to further emphasise the text's sympathy for the predicament of the Indigenous people during colonisation. Nonetheless, the seemingly straightforward story is muddied by two factors. The first is the position of the Native Police themselves, an armed force made up of (often unwilling) Indigenous troopers under the command of white officers. The complicated power relations (between different Indigenous clans and between Aboriginals and Europeans) that such a grouping produced and/or exploited is self-evident. The role of the Police, ostensibly to keep the peace between Aboriginals and pastoralists in frontier districts, in practice worked to open up the land for settlement. The Queensland Force had a reputation for violent confrontations during which traditional land-owners were either dispossessed or killed; the ways in which they frequently dispensed "justice" were also questionable. The second is Arthur's participation in one such event. After a wild night of drinking at the camp barracks, Arthur awakes to the sound of women screaming and men swearing. Two Aboriginal women and a young Aboriginal man (who is unknown to Arthur, but is called Jemmy by the Troop) have been restrained. One of the women, the object of Arthur's infatuation whom he has named Eurydice, is bloodied and dishevelled. The blame is laid on Jemmy by Lieutenant Wheeler, who handcuffs him, beats him, and then commands one of the black troopers to whip him. Arthur tries to walk away, but is ordered instead to start his "proper training" and to show the "filthy nigger what to expect from the Queensland Native Police" (31). Seeing what he thinks is devastation on Eurydice's face, Arthur proceeds to kick Jemmy, cracking several of his ribs. Jemmy later dies from his injuries. As Arthur blocks much of the night from his memory, and as the time sequence of his story is jumbled and incomplete, the text's audience is unlikely to garner a clear sense of his role in the incident. Readers are therefore positioned to view Arthur with ambivalence, and this is further confused when his version of events is contradicted by the text's extraliterary discourse. His struggle between the two dominant models of masculinity that the narrative offers—the bawdy, and sometimes cruel and immoral model that characterises the Native Police and the chaste, humane, and devout version that he has been raised by—also creates a tension.

Another contradiction that works against a reading of the narrative in the colonial tradition is the alleged assault of Eurydice and "her black sister" (30). Accounts of the rape and sexual exploitation of Aboriginal women by Aboriginal men are familiar to the colonial texts from which *Poison Under their Lips* draws its narrative style and subject matter. According to Bradford, such incidents function to imply that white men would never treat women, white or black, in this way (*Reading* 82). Thus, when Arthur acts to "defend [Eurydice's] honour" (163), the text appears to reinstate the stereotype of the white man as saviour and protector of Aboriginal women, and to sustain colonial European judgements of Aboriginal culture, namely that Aboriginal women were "degraded and oppressed within their own societies" (Robert 73). However, Arthur (and, thus, the reader) belatedly learns that Jemmy is Eurydice's husband, and that the two women were gang-raped by the Troop's white officers after Arthur's apparent disappearance from the scene. Symbolically, the camp where these incidents occur is called Mistake Creek, and Arthur is too traumatised to remember whether he is also guilty of sexually assaulting the women. In this way, the narrative fulfils a requirement of the postcolonial project in that it not only returns to the colonial scene to revisit, remember, and interrogate the "forgotten archive of the colonial encounter", but it tells a story in which the coloniser "concede[s] its part or complicity in the terrors—

and errors—of the past" (Gandhi 4–5, 10). This is neatly encapsulated in a conversation towards the conclusion. Here, the Troop's Sergeant Thomas is attempting to make Arthur see that Wheeler was once an honourable man. "'But we live in the present and not the past'", Arthur counters. "'True'", the Sergeant agrees, adding "'but it is the past and nothing else that leads us to where we stand now'" (185).

In conjunction with the particular features and events of the narrative that I have discussed so far, this textual moment functions to give a sense of the complexity that characterises the origins of settler societies and which marked episodes of conflict during the colonial era, since it suggests that history is not objectively knowable, not a matter of one "side" being right and the other wrong. At one level, then, the text works to destabilise notions of imperial power and thus to critique monolithic versions of the history of white settlement. This is not to say that it is free of colonial meanings, however. Indeed, although readers are unlikely to support the (often vicious) colonising practices referred to in the journal and the peritextual material, the text's principal claim—that whiteness should not be viewed in superior terms—tends to falter when the narrative's treatment of Eurydice is subjected to examination. Eurydice is central to the narrative because she plays a part in Wheeler's downfall, she appears in almost every entry of Arthur's journal, and she is the reason for his willingness to commit an uncharacteristic act of brutality—she is the "love that [drives his] actions" (163). Yet she is denied a narrative voice and she is often mute, and thus she works to signify the silence and absence that is such a familiar aspect of Aboriginal experience in the colonial tradition. In addition, Arthur does not know the woman's name, so he chooses a name he feels is appropriate. Not only does naming constitute power within colonial discourse (Bradford, *Reading* 39), but in drawing on the tale of Orpheus and Eurydice to explain the connections between the pair, the narrative replicates the male-centred plot of a myth which is essentially concerned with the quest for a dead woman. Although, in the end, it is not Eurydice who dies, but Arthur, as with the mythic Eurydice the Aboriginal woman's downfall is represented here in phallic terms. The myth tells of Eurydice's death after she steps on a poisonous snake while fleeing from the unwanted advances of Aristaeus; in *Poison*, Eurydice must live in exile after her husband is murdered and she is sexually assaulted. "'She bin havem piccaninny'", one of the Aboriginal boys at the camp tells a sergeant who is trying to piece together the events of the night: "'That snake bin bit her good'" (164). In a move which evokes other stereotypes of "helpless Aboriginal women and predatory white men" (Bradford, *Reading* 107), Eurydice is therefore firmly positioned as a victim of imperial and patriarchal power.

The colonial intersection of gender and power, in which the Aboriginal woman is the object of the white male gaze is also present in the text (Bradford, *Reading* 107). Indeed, an obvious, but familiar, ambivalence haunts Arthur's descriptions of Eurydice because they are stereotypical fantasies of the racialised Other (particularly as there is little in the text to suggest that the pair interact much at all). Arthur sees Eurydice as his "beloved dusky virgin of the bush" (27), as "chaste as the driven snow [. . .] as noble as she [is] savage" (86). "Hers is a proud bearing", he writes, "almost aloof [. . .] Eyes so brown as to be almost black, intense and mischievous [. . .] yet, at the same time, pliable and alluring" (75–76). Such accounts bring to mind Freud's trope of the "dark continent" (a phrase borrowed from colonialist images of Africa) in which the feminine represents unexplored, and thus mysterious, territory. The dark continent trope, Mary Ann Doane argues, "indicates the existence of an intricate historical articulation of the categories of racial difference and sexual difference". It welds the erotic and the exotic together in such a way, she contends, as to lay blame with black women for "the victimization inflicted upon them by white males" (212–13). Eurydice is also represented as the means to the male subject's absolution—the way to freedom from sin or error—because, irrespective of who fathered her unborn baby, Arthur vows to find her and to parent her child, to beg her forgiveness and to be redeemed. Thus, he "carr[ies] her as [his] wound" (194), but at the same time, she is his "only path to redemption" (141). Like other women in the Western tradition, Eurydice therefore occupies a double position; she is "the agency that heals the wound of death's presence in life" since as a desired sexual object, she "undoes the work of death by promising wholeness", but, at the same time, by virtue of her alterity, she is also seen as its source (Bronfen, *Over* 69).

The Australian Warrior: Death, Masculinity, and Heroism

In contrast to the novels I have considered so far, the texts that I wish to discuss in the remainder of this chapter are those featuring what may be deemed "lauded" aspects of Australian history—either iconic figures and images, or key moments in time that pay tribute to what it means, in popular terms, to be "Australian". The experiences of mortality represented in these fictions are what Kellehear and Anderson call the dominating cultural images of death in Australia—those politically and historically celebrated images of national identity that "act as cultural pointers for which deaths count as important" (1). The first is the soldier, because, as Keating's earlier speech suggests, the particular qualities of mateship, fortitude, courage, and physicality that define the "Australian legend" come together in an especially potent way in this figure. Indeed, the myth of the Australian warrior is a powerful and recurrent one in Australian death iconography because it belongs to a narrative tradition that is characterised by its tendency to construct manhood as a heroic state of being—to celebrate the kind of male characters whose legendary status is associated with honour, bravery, and altruism; forged through violence, conflict, and death; and linked with important events in Australian history. In this way, the meaning of an individual death has often been transformed into the type of heroic act that promotes nationalistic sentiments and ideals. A shootout between police and outlaws, the battleground at the Eureka diggings, the bloody fight at Gallipoli; each of these images draws together ideas about masculinity, national identity, and heroism.

There are few events in Australian history that have had such an impact on constructions of masculinity and national identity as those of World War I, however. As many social commentators have noted, then and since, this period is often referred to as Australia's "coming of age", and ANZAC Cove as the place where the birth of the nation occurred. A federal commonwealth for only just over a decade, the new national government was keen to prove itself and establish a reputation in the international arena. In an era when the notion of sacrificial death (or "blood sacrifice") was seen as a necessary rite of passage or an initiation ceremony, it was felt that the difficult task of storming the Gallipoli peninsula would assist with this goal ("The ANZAC Day Tradition"). Patriotism was so highly valued during the period when Australia became involved that thousands of men rushed to enlist and, even after the failure of the campaign in April 1915 (over 8,000 Australian soldiers were killed), enlistment numbers rose significantly; the highest number of enlistments of any month during the war was recorded in July of this year. Perhaps this was because of Australia's long tradition of making heroes out of noble failures: the defeated Eureka rebels, Ned Kelly, the suicidal Jolly Swagman in "Waltzing Matilda"; as Frank Bongiorno contends, Gallipoli certainly seemed to fit this pattern. Bongiorno also notes, however, that the physical superiority of the "bold and ferocious" Australian soldier (at the time, a prominent theme in much of the writing about the War) confirmed some popular Australian self-images about masculinity and nationhood (qtd. in "ANZAC Day"). Indeed, the figure of the Australian and New Zealand Army Corps (ANZAC) soldier, Deborah Edwards argues, "valorized a nation prepared to sacrifice its best—its young men—to what was perceived as an appalling but noble cause" (478).

The sacrifice of male life in war has often been configured in terms of glory and Australia was no exception. What distinguished Australia's preoccupation with warrior manhood, however, was its persistence after the war (Garton 88). Since this time, both popular and "high" culture in Australia has embraced the legend of the soldier hero and the macho male image he represents: the ANZAC has been immortalised by artists in paintings, drawings, sculptures, and poetry; embodied on national monuments; and celebrated (particularly in death) for his youth, beauty, physical prowess, endurance, and courage. Today the ANZAC soldier is often remembered in terms of his "ultimate sacrifice", and celebrated for his part in the nation-building exercise. The ANZAC "gave new definition to what it means to be an Australian", Andrew Fraser, Member of Parliament, enthuses: "These brave souls risked their lives and died so today we can enjoy the freedom and democracy upon which this nation was built" (*The Spirit of ANZAC*).

The valorisation of the "Australian legend", even in contemporary histori-cal fictions produced for Australian youth audiences, suggests that the myth is an especially enduring one.[12] At least in part, this trend is due to the tendency of the genre to invoke past systems of meaning, and to use the hero as a peda-gogic device for teaching children about history. Unlike the exemplary models which influenced Anglophone children's literature throughout the nineteenth century and well into the twentieth century—texts featuring great men and women, legendary acts, and stories of nobleness (Jones and Watkins, "Intro-duction" 4–5), accounts of heroism today are, however, marked by tensions and contradictions. As Kerry Mallan contends, portrayals of the traditional warrior hero in adolescent literature continue to celebrate conventional forms of heroic masculine subjectivity at the same time that they unsettle the norms of traditional gender representations ("Challenging"). These kind of ten-sions are evident in Metzenthen's *Gilbert's Ghost Train* and *Boys of Blood and Bone*. Both texts advocate a version of masculinity that is firmly linked to the kind of rough-and-ready, practical, brave, and honest ideals embodied in the authentically "Australian" character, but both also problematise traditional constructions of heroism which glorify masculinity and death by foreground-ing the fragility of the male body. The novels are influenced by discourses of nationalism, pairing manhood with death by framing masculinity through the myth of the ANZAC hero; however, by suggesting that boys *are* made of blood and bone and that death *is* absolute, they also question the sustainabil-ity of such conventional constructions.

In *Gilbert's Ghost Train*, thirteen-year-old Dallas Dean has terminal leu-kaemia. The narrative is set in Dally's home during the last stages of this ill-ness. Metzenthen utilises the largely masculine and working-class worlds of the railway worker and the soldier as a background for the novel, so that as Dally and his brother, Martin, are learning about death and dying, they are simultaneously being inducted into a version of masculinity which constructs death in terms of heroism and courage. It is Gilbert, of the novel's title, who is instrumental in assisting the brothers through this period: A train enthu-siast and ex-railway worker who appears at the old railway line on the Dean's property, Gilbert was also once an ANZAC. Every few days, he sits with Dally and Marty and tells them a story from his past, each of which contains a subtle message about death and dying. For Dally, these stories help to prepare him for his own death, largely by suggesting to him that being brave is important. Signalling the novel's concerns with heroism, at one point the boys discuss what is happening to Dally as his illness progresses, and whether he is fright-ened about "where he is heading". Marty tells Dally: "'I know you're not scared kid [. . .] Because you're a hero, Frog, that's why. You bloody are'" (133). The poignant and lengthy scenes detailing Dally's death provide a counterpoint to such episodes, however; not only do they highlight how weak and insubstan-tial Dally has become, they also unsettle traditional notions of bravery, not only by emphasising Marty's vulnerability but also by suggesting that there is a similarity between the two boys' positions: "Man, this is hard", Marty thinks. "If I let myself, I could crumble like dry clay into dust and blow away. I haven't got much strength left. My hands are sweaty and my stomach swills around" (154–55).

Boys of Blood and Bone, in particular, foregrounds the corporeality of death because, here, the reality and violence of war become, to appropriate Mallan's phrase, "unpalatable truths which destroy the appeal of the heroic myth" ("Challenging" 153).[13] This is vividly described in a scene in which Australian soldier Andrew Lansell witnesses another soldier's death—"boys were dotted with blood and small pieces of flesh like the rind of some sort of strange fruit" (138)—and also when he waits in a trench for backup:

> Andy crouched, the trench to his right blown wide apart, a dead Australian half-buried as if he had been caught in a mudslide, the sky above the body yawning dangerously wide, steel-grey, flogged by wind and rain.
>
> [. . .] He waited, fear swelling like a sickness, as vulnerable-feeling as if he was a bubble [. . .].
>
> [. . .] There was nothing [he] could do but crouch and shake. He felt as if he was continually screaming, his bones seemed bent with tension, a feeling like a dam of blood at the back of his throat was about to spew out, the sound and concussions dashing more and more thoughts from his head until he relinquished the idea of fighting anybody or anything, tried to wrap himself up in his own arms, and breathed in the animal heat of his own moaning, the dugout shaking, lumps of dirt knocking him sideways. (180–81)

The heroic myth is further undermined by Andy's failure to return from the War; he dies in a field hospital in France of injuries sustained almost a year after the above event, viewing his time as a soldier in the moments before his death as a duty constituting no more than "a second of his life" (277). It is at this point that the phallic fantasy of the strong, impenetrable male body is destroyed.[14] After the explosion that smashes into his chest, Andy's mate Darcy begs him to hold on, but Andy doubts that anybody could take the insurmountable force of the shell that has thrown him onto his back, the pain tearing screams out of him: "whatever had hit him had hit him too hard" (276–78).

The anxieties that have surrounded the ANZAC legend since its inception show that warrior masculinity in Australian culture is both diverse and uncertain. World War I demonstrated, for instance, that "the primitive energies of the male body (virility, physical strength and aggression) were no match for modern technological warfare" (Carden-Coyne 139). While the warrior ethos and the heroic virtues of ANZAC manhood were embraced by Australians after the war, at the same time, confidence in this masculine ideal was weakened by the vast losses of life and the fact that so many soldiers had arrived back physically and psychologically damaged (Murrie, "Australian"). Later conflicts in which soldiers returned as emaciated victims of prisoner of war camps, or to vocal anti-war protests (such as after the Vietnam War) also compromised the manly ANZAC ideal. Thus, one of the few ways Australians could make sense of the enormous loss of life in the twentieth century wars, Stephen Garton argues, "was to see these sacrifices as part of a rich tapestry of 'history', where societies flourished and grew because of the actions of their soldiers". In this way, the legend, which may once have reflected an older bushman ideal, was "translated into something national and hence more readily available for a broad, popular and cross-class audience" (91, 94).

This idea is clearly expressed by Fraser when he writes that it is the "determination, courage and strength" of the ANZACs "which has helped Australia grow into the strong nation it is today". By confronting the "impossible challenges" set in front of them, Fraser contends, these men inspire young Australians today to "stand tall and to succeed" (*The Spirit of ANZAC*). Fraser's statements also illustrate some of the ways that the myths of the past can be mobilised so that they have meaning in—and for—the present. In *Boys of Blood and Bone* this idea is especially pronounced because the novel links Andy's war experiences with a contemporary story about Henry Lyon, another eighteen-year-old boy, fusing them together in such a way that, in the end, the story of Andy's life and death entirely alters Henry's subjectivity. A telling example of this strategy occurs in the narrative's epilogue when Henry revisits the Avenue of Honour in Andy's home town of Strattford. Not only does the road of memorial trees represent a special place where he can "actually see where the past, the present, and perhaps [the] future" meet, but it also defines in some way what he plans to do with his life from then on: "[. . .] plenty, he hoped. Plenty" (292). As John Fiske, Bob Hodge, and Graeme Turner argue, monuments such as war memorials signify death speaking to life, functioning to give lessons from the past to the present. They "occupy a central place in the version of history offered by official culture"—a version of history that both acts as "a foundation myth" and "serves to legitimate the present order" (137).

The refrain "Lest We Forget" has become a familiar one in recent times. In the last decade or so, attendances at all forms of ANZAC commemorations have increased, and this trend is reflected in the number of children's books dealing with war (particularly World War I) that have appeared since the early 1990s (Meiklejohn). In Metzenthen's words, war is "a carnage that no one can really understand" (qtd. in Hamer). And yet, in *Boys of Blood and Bone*, the focus on "remembering", the suggestion that "it would be a mistake to think that the things people have done before us have nothing to do with us now" (196), and the tendency to parallel the lives of the two boys so that Henry's engagement with the past is linked to what he learns about death and war, constitute an attempt to achieve just that. The boys' paths cross when Henry (who is driving up to the south coast of New South Wales from Melbourne on a windsurfing holiday) breaks down in the small country town of Strattford. Stuck for a few days until his car can be fixed, he befriends young local couple, Trot and Janine, and, acting on their advice, finds himself staying in the pub where Andy downed his last beer before leaving for the War. Here he meets Andy's fiancée, Cecelia. After noting Henry's physical resemblance to Andy, Cecelia shows him a photograph of Andy and his mates. In the photo, Henry thinks, the boys smile as if they know things that he could know too:

> Just believe in us, cobber, they seemed to be saying, and eighty-five years'll go up in smoke because it's only a bit of bloody time standing between you and us, and time's nothin' if you truly believe, if you truly want to be one of us. (32)

For a moment, Henry does, but it all seems so difficult: "It was like looking at the rusted cogs of machinery long-abandoned; any explanation of history was too long seized in time [. . .] he was looking at them through the years, them in their lives, him in his, and that was that" (25, 32). Nevertheless, Henry's vague interest is truly piqued once he begins to read Andy's diary. He wonders where and how Andy died, tries to imagine what war would be like, and starts to ruminate on life and death, at one point asking himself how it would feel to pick up someone who was dead: "[M]aybe take an arm, a still-warm wrist, and help carry the person to a rough hole and lower them in. They'd be heavy. There would be blood and wounds. You'd shovel the dirt in carefully. At the start. He could imagine. And then they'd be gone" (38).

The narrative alternates between Henry's story in the present and Andy's in the past. Extracts from Andy's diary provide brief accounts of his life; however, as the front cover illustration signals, the experiences and thoughts of both boys are treated equally. Divided roughly in half, the cover depicts a sepia-toned soldier at the top and a brightly coloured beach scene featuring a windsurfer at the bottom. Faint handwriting, which overlays both pictures, provides a visual link to the diary entries inside the novel at the same time it demonstrates how central the diary is to the story, and the impact it will have on Henry's life. This is also clear from the different visual weighting given to the figures of the two boys: The figure of the soldier, symbolically cut off at the neck and floating amongst the clouds, is much larger and looms over the smaller figure of the windsurfer beneath it. The suggestion that the boy on the lower half of the cover is embarking on a journey is apparent from the long line of footprints behind him as he trudges along a thin path of sand towards the distant horizon. There is a sense that he is also travelling *to* the soldier who is standing above him, and the soldier's static pose reinforces this concept.

As the major concern of the novel is the meaning that Andy's life and death have for Henry, this reading seems apt. The manner in which Henry's masculinity is worked out in reference to Andy's also highlights the journey motif. The characters of Henry and Andy represent very different ways of being male and their pairing weighs one model of manhood against another, each of which is influenced by socio-economic ideologies and stereotypes in its depiction. In this way, for example, country is juxtaposed with city, blue-collar with white, physical with intellectual, and acting with thinking. The construction of Andy's character is grounded in a romanticised notion of the past and draws on nationalist rhetoric and ideas about the "national type": an inscription on his gravestone reads "A son of Australia" (288); he is described as "fit and capable" his face "even and strong", and as looking "so *Australian* [with] those clear eyes that [can] look forever" (102, emphasis original). By comparison, the picture of Henry that builds up is of a somewhat aimless youth, troubled in his relationship with girlfriend Marcelle, and largely dependent on his wealthy parents for many aspects of his life. Andy at eighteen, the text implies, is already a man, while Henry, at the same age, is still a boy. The masculine type associated with Andy is thus valorised and the trajectory of maturation that the novel offers for Henry involves modelling his own subjectivity on this type.

The character of Trot (Andy's present-day double who befriends Henry) also functions to reinforce this idea as his initial meeting with Henry illustrates. Using the masculine image of the car, the differences between them are not only immediately apparent, but presented in a way that emasculates Henry who, in this scene, is depicted walking away from his mother's overheated Volvo, the P-plate "stuck crookedly onto the glass". Stranded, his mobile phone "unwilling to provide him with a carrier", he is rescued by Trot in a "spitting" V8 Holden Commodore, "gold mag wheels like stars", and P-plate tossed carelessly on the dash under a pack of cigarettes. Henry's embarrassment over his mechanical ignorance, and his awkwardness, is contrasted with Trot's ease as he sits in the Holden "as comfortably as Buddha in his temple", asking questions about the Volvo's problems as though "it was unthinkable that Henry wouldn't know the answer" (1–3). The male schema associated with Henry is also devalued by Henry's lack of "authentic" Australian credentials, particularly those associated with class, the ANZAC ideal, and with the past. "[E]ven today middle-class Australians accept a definition of their national identity represented in terms that derive from radical working-class ideals", Bob Hodge and Vijay Mishra argue (xiii). Thus, with a sailboard *and* a Volvo in rural Strattford, Henry feels "like a bit of a wanker" (16). As a city boy, more at home on the coast, he finds Strattford strange, unlike Andy and his mate, Darcy, who says as they sail away from the country: "'Funny how me last sight of Aussie is gunna be somethin' I don't even recognise. I've never been to the bloody beach in me life. Not a friggin' gumtree in sight'" (54). Henry's Canadian heritage provides him with few "authentic" links to the Australian soldier, and he is somewhat ignorant of this aspect of history as well. To him, the First World War is like "something from the Middle Ages" (2). This is emphasised by the admission that his great-grandfather "didn't get killed. He got gassed or something, and they sent him home" (20).

The shift in Henry's outlook is first signalled when he revisits the Avenue of Honour, looking for Andy's plaque. Spying a stand of cypress trees in a paddock across the road, he imagines they belong to "the time of the war, their darkness hinting at death, secrets, and the unspoken" (26). After this, the mood of the place stays with him and the past does not seem so far away, and he muses that if he had been around when Andy was, he may have seen first-hand "what the darkness of the trees could only suggest [. . .] whatever it was the old war footage never showed" (25–26). At this stage, Henry's knowledge of death is vicarious, but when Trot dies after losing control of his car, the word "dead" begins to "take on some form, as if it was solidifying" and he understands that, until that point, "[he'd] never had to deal with the word or the world like this before. Trot was *dead*. He was gone. *Now*. Gone" (174, emphases original).

Trot's accident points to the fragility of the male body (particularly as it occurs not when he is driving dangerously, but when he is trying to avoid a hay bale left on the corner of the road). It also highlights some of the ways that contemporary notions of gender have influenced and modified traditional masculine norms. The eulogy at Trot's funeral, given by his girlfriend Janine, shows him to have something of the Sensitive New Age Guy (SNAG) about him. Janine alludes to rural society's role in shaping Trot's masculinity at the same time she stresses that he broke the mould. She makes reference to his emotional strength and depicts him as "one of the most thoughtful people" she has ever met—a gentle, kind and generous man whose desire to help others defined much of his life (193). Nevertheless, as a physically strong man of action, a hard worker, and a doer not a talker, Trot also shows how "persistent [the] tug of conventional images of masculinity" can be in Australian narrative (Lucas 146). His death demonstrates how notions of masculinity can be informed by macho images of living hard and dying young as, even after the finality of the burial, Henry continues to feel like "a bit of a wuss driving along in a Volvo when he [thinks] about Trot's car which was definitely a hard-goer" (255). Like Andy in the past, Trot is an exemplary model of "Australianness"— the national "everyman" for whom the ANZAC was such a potent symbol in 1920s Australia (Edwards 478). Accordingly, his death is defined in terms of heroism and courageousness by both Janine and Cecelia. Janine wishes that when he had died "it could've been doing something heroic rather than an awful accident, because that was the sort of person [he] was [. . .] bigger than what happened to him [. . .] Much bigger" (192), while Cecelia believes that, although she "would not have wished that war on anyone", Trot "would've done better eighty-five years ago with something heroic to do" (195).

The tendency to "refract contemporary images of Australian masculinity through the template of past images and mythologies" (Lucas 138) is reinforced by the comparison between Trot's death and that of the soldiers. Furthermore, by framing Trot's death through references to the warrior figure and the past, heroic notions of death are valorised and contemporary models of boy/manhood devalued. This is emphasised when Henry and Janine travel to France to visit the small war cemetery where Andy is buried. The journey, which involves Henry leaving "[h]ome—*Australia*—twenty thousand k" behind him echoes

Andy's own journey, but as "the biggest adventure in [Henry's] life", it also illustrates the extreme difference between each generation's experiences of life and death (274–75). Thus, although Henry comes to appreciate the immensity of war, to "more than admire" Andy for his bravery and his sacrifice, and to shape aspects of his own subjectivity in Andy's image, at the novel's conclusion, death becomes a marker of masculinity that separates the two. In thinking about Andy's death as an individual rather than as "a part of the collective death of all soldiers", Henry concludes that while Andy wasn't necessarily "a mythical ANZAC", his death had certainly made him one (247–48). This is illustrated in the final chapters as Andy lies wounded in the field hospital. Organised around images that fuse death with the national and the masculine, Andy's final moments encapsulate the familiar legend in every way. Unable to order his thoughts, he finds snapshots of his life running through his mind, seeing himself with the people he loves, drinking in the pub, playing football, at the railway station, sniping at Germans. And then, in his thoughts, he begins heading for home and the hills around Strattford where his horses graze under the gums, the trees are "mere puffs of colour, more blue than green, the sky [is] silver" and his house shines "like a white beacon at the end of the track" (277, 286). "'[. . .] by Jesus I'm proud to be yer mate'", says Darcy in farewell. "'And don't worry, I'll tell everyone what ya done'" (290).

Heroic myths, of course, gain their power from the telling and retelling. As Darian-Smith and Hamilton see it, mythic narratives like the ANZAC legend are "the wellspring of nationalism and they are constantly mobilised to serve differing ideological purposes" (2). Bruce Scates notes, for instance, how "the meanings of that great conflict [World War I] have changed with each succeeding generation". Scates also argues, however, that many young pilgrims to the Gallipoli cemeteries today see the suffering and the loss of human lives from this war as pointless, and some are "appalled that so many epitaphs [speak] of glory" (21). The idea that war deaths are pointless is indeed a prominent one in *Boys of Blood and Bone*, in part because the novel debunks the attraction of warrior manhood that is suggested by images of the virile young soldier, frozen at a point in time when the male body is in peak physical condition (Buchbinder 19). And yet, although the loss of Andy's life is depicted as a waste (and Trot's death can be seen in this way too), the myth is obviously an enduring one since it is clear that the narrative draws not only on popular understandings of this aspect of Australia's history, but from the same set of meanings and images that the myth was founded upon.

Convicts, Crime, and Punishment: Ways of Being Male in Jail

I want to turn now to another myth which has proved to be influential in constructing particular versions of "Australia", and of Australian history—that of convictism. The text I will use to frame this discussion is Gary Crew and

Philip Neilsen's *Edward Britton*. Although a collaborative project between the two, the novel incorporates a number of the themes and preoccupations that are familiar to Crew's work. Both an account of life in a Tasmanian prison and a story about two teenage convicts, Edward Britton and Izod Wolfe, the novel explores notions of power, authority, death, morality, and justice in a similar manner to—and with many of the Gothic overtones of—several of Crew's other texts. In this instance, however, the aim is not to self-consciously interrogate a particular version of history, nor to explore the links between history, narrative, and representation (as with other Crew fictions), but rather to call attention to some aspects of Australian history—namely, the special boys' prison established at Port Arthur in 1834—that "few people know about" (back cover). Crew's tendency to blend fact with fiction is thus evident in his referencing of historical works in the acknowledgments section, and in the prominently featured single-line summary on the rear of the book which describes the text as a "haunting novel based on cold, hard facts".

It is fact that white Australia began its life as a penal colony when convicts were transported to New South Wales in 1788. Without doubt, the system that incarcerated them had punishment as its primary aim. Yet it has been suggested that fewer than ten percent of the prisoners transported to Australia ever saw the inside of a penal settlement and, according to A. W. Baker, the average convict experience was not, objectively speaking, horrific (3, 53). Nevertheless, as studies in Australian convict fiction invariably note, there is a marked discrepancy between what historians would consider factual accounts of this period and the literature that has become, for many Australians, the principal source of knowledge about convictism. Popular conceptions of convict life portrayed in works such as Marcus Clarke's *For the Term of His Natural Life* which construct convicts as victims of sadistic punishments, enduring brutal living conditions in jails, "more sinned against than sinning", have been extraordinarily influential, for instance (Hergenhan 2).[15] Hodge and Mishra see representations of crime and punishment from the foundation of the colony to the present as ambiguous and complex, serving the different interests and portraying the different experiences of various groups (121). This is evident in the complexity that has marked the relationship between convictism and nationalist ideology throughout Australian history. Official attitudes towards convictism have fluctuated, reflecting the changing times, needs, and politics of the nation; at times the convict past has been suppressed, while at others it is seen more positively. Laurie Hergenhan cites its political usefulness to various nationalistic programmes, its function in German propaganda against Australians in World War II, and its social appeal in the contemporary period (3). Prior to the late 1800s, the stigma attached to the country's criminal origins meant that convictism was viewed in shameful terms, and convicts themselves as immoral, ignorant, and uncivilised beings. Once the Australian nationalist movement had begun the campaign to promote a distinct non-British identity, however, convict narratives began to construct the convict as a victim of poverty, industrialisation, or the brutal British Empire. *For the Term of His Natural Life* is often cited as a key text in this process which saw transportation and incarceration represented as an injustice, and Australian convicts as exiles both from society and their native land.

Regardless of its departures from the historical facts about the average convict experience, Clarke's work "succeeded in articulating an acceptable understanding of the convict era" which, even now, typically informs contemporary narratives about convictism (Baker 136). It is therefore unsurprising that *Edward Britton*'s representation of Australian convictism calls on a number of schematic stereotypes that originated in this period, and that it provides a synthesis of the common themes that are expressed in this definitive version of the myth (such as freedom, exile, rebellion, reformation, self-sacrifice, oppression, brutality, and heroism). Its setting at Australia's "Junior Port Arthur" is also pertinent since Port Arthur has acquired a depth of meaning like few other places in Australia.[16] As a kind of public memorial to the past (both recent and centuries-old), Port Arthur occupies a place in the Australian memory that is both a symbol of convictism in its entirety, and of human suffering and tragedy at a collective level. As Maria Tumarkin argues, it is a place "materially and discursively bound by traumatic repetitions" (199).

While Point Puer, the juvenile prison that features in *Edward Britton*, was not located at the site of the Port Arthur settlement, but approximately three kilometres across Opossum Bay, the two settings are nevertheless semiotically linked by these meanings. Thus, while the novel is centred around adolescent rather than adult convicts, it follows familiar conventions in its narration of the convict experience. Both Edward and Izod are portrayed as victims of a powerful regime: Edward, an English actor, is wrongly accused of stealing costumes from a theatre, and Izod is one of the many dispossessed Irish, arrested in England for vagrancy and illegal immigration. The harshness of their sentence outweighs the triviality of their crimes, and each of them is singled out for especially cruel treatment at the hands of their hated jailers. For these two boys, the Point Puer prison is a place of horror, suffering, and death. Like those earlier constructions which place the virtuous convict in opposition to an unjust society, *Edward Britton*'s treatment of convict life is, therefore, a form of protest. Yet it simultaneously possesses the kind of meanings which work against this idea, and this is most clearly articulated through the novel's representations of masculinity, sexuality, and death.

According to Clive Moore's study, there were several models of manhood extant in colonial Australia (35–36). Convicts as a group formed a distinct under-class in society at large, yet within the convict system itself, there was no singular version of masculinity but rather "a range of competing masculinities, often in dramatic interaction with each other" (Evans and Thorpe 22). This is evident in the characters of Edward and Izod: Although both boys are convicts, they represent very different masculine types, each associated with a particular social class. Once a travelling entertainer in England, at the time of his arrest Edward belongs to a Shakespearean theatre company, a profession which is linked in the novel with respectability, beauty, and culture (16–18). An intelligent, well-spoken, "tall and fair" boy, he reads, writes, and speaks better than most of the officers. The narrative explains that, unlike most of the other "common criminals" in the jail, Edward is not guilty and, thus, "a cut above the rest" (12). He is likeable, and many of the other boys look up to him. By contrast, Izod is described as small, thin, and colourless. His Irish nationality, his work (both in the prison pigsty and assisting the surgeon with undertaking duties) places him in a class that is, in many ways, lower than any other in the prison. Like other protagonists of the convict or prison narrative, Edward and Izod are constructed as solitary figures.[17] Edward's aloneness relates to his difference from the others, and references to his height—"almost a head taller than the rest"—operate as a symbolic reminder of this. Izod's isolation from the community is self-imposed (he is not "one for socialising"), and while he too is already marked as "other" by the very same features that contribute to his social position, it is largely his familiarity with death that sets him apart: "It was death that separated Izod Wolfe from those about him. Death that had shaped his life" (12).

The negotiation of Edward and Izod's masculinity is played out, therefore, through a comparison between differing masculine schemata, a common textual strategy in adolescent literature (McCallum and Stephens, 344–45). As the novel is concerned with the penal system, their maturation is also framed through ideas about reformation. Foucault's study of prison regimes in *Discipline and Punish* shows that during the period in which *Edward Britton* is set, the penitentiary (of which Point Puer is an example) had become a common form of incarceration. Its object was to reform or rehabilitate the prisoner through such practices as hard physical work, training in practical trades, or religious and scholastic education. Raymond Evans and Bill Thorpe argue, for instance, that sentence to transportation "was ideologically regarded as a means towards transforming working-class male criminals into reformed masculine types—men who conformed to the ruling, early nineteenth century bourgeois ideals of earnestness, respectability and manly integrity" (30). For Edward, this process is both simple and almost unnecessary. Soon to be released when he turns eighteen, already the kind of educated, principled, and heroic figure championed in the text, he lacks only love—the "princess imprisoned by her tyrannical father" whom he can rescue (8). This occurs with the arrival of Susan Buckridge, complete with the sadistic and cruel parent (the new lieutenant-governor of the prison) at Point Puer. For Izod, the path is more complex. A small-framed boy, who is sexually under-developed, bony, and slight (38), his subjectivity is clearly represented in terms of growth and "becoming".

In the almost exclusively male domain of the prison, Izod is offered various potential role models. He rejects the type of masculinity associated with the other boys in the prison, and although he comes to find a friend amongst the boys, he never counts himself as one of them. This is evident in the way he shuns contact with them, rarely washing because he refuses to stand naked next to the other boys: "Their playful splashing and teasing at the water troughs sickened him and their tugs and slaps and flicks intimidated him [. . .] and he hated the louts who flaunted their genitals" (37–38). With their camaraderie and physical presence, these boys embody the legend of Australian mateship, a version of masculinity that is, in fact, said to trace its antecedents back to the convict era (Moore 46).[18] Izod is repelled by the cruel but cowardly Sergeant Hecht, who corners and then rapes the boys when he has the chance. The authoritarian version of masculinity associated with Commandant Buckridge is also pejoratively constructed. Closely resembling the "gentry masculinity" described by Evans and Thorpe in "Commanding Men: Masculinities and the Convict System", Buckridge's way of being male is represented as violent, racist, and sexist. Thus, while Izod sees the surgeon Patterson (the only man in power who befriends the boys) in a positive way, it is Edward who comes to fascinate him.

It would seem, then, that Izod's coming-of-age is constructed in terms of a (hierarchical) conversion from one masculine type to another because, as the descriptions of the boys' physical appearance and social position suggest, it is Edward's version of masculinity that is consistently advocated. At various points in the narrative, Izod's desire to be like Edward is glaringly evident, particularly after Izod watches him act in a play staged by the boys of the prison for the local community. Izod is "entranced" and in awe of Edward, seeing him as employing "some kind of trick or magic" in the performance. "Here at last is someone to trust and believe in [he thinks]. Someone who [rises] above fear and filth and bullying" (196–200). This magic Izod attributes to knowing how to read and write, and he sets about acquiring the skill himself. When this is accomplished and Izod reads aloud in class from a bible with such fluency, expression, and character that his teacher and classmates listen in amazement, the transformation appears possible.

The two boys also exhibit many similarities. Most notable is a dislike of overt displays of sexuality (hence their friendship with the somewhat asexual Patterson). In Edward's case, this is usually expressed as a preference for romantic and chaste love, but for Izod, any form of sex or sexuality is repellent: "The random coupling, the writhing and grunting, confirmed his suspicion that humans were two-legged pigs" (219). Indeed, it is Izod's intense and often contradictory association with carnality and death that eventually complicates the (re)modelling of his masculinity. His extreme aversion to carnality is at odds with the "primal excitement [that flutters] through him" when he attends an amputation and performs his first burial (117), and his desire to kill the lieutenant-governor encompasses almost every aspect of his life. Soon after Commandant Buckridge arrives at Point Puer, Izod recognises the man responsible for evicting his family from their home in Ireland, and he prays to become a "weapon of revenge" so that he might get rid of the man he holds responsible for their death (37).

When the relationship between Edward and Susan is exposed by Buckridge—who claims Edward is a "filthy disciple of the Devil", a "beast in human form" who has "violated" his daughter—Izod is provided with this opportunity: He seizes Hecht's gun and shoots Buckridge dead.

These dramatic events resemble scenes from the play, especially as they occur on the same stage. Then, Edward's captivating lead role in the performance saw him fighting against injustice and killing to defeat evil. As the focus of this newer drama, Izod symbolically takes Edward's place. However, it is at this point that it is made clear that Izod can never truly be like Edward: In the upheaval, Edward has escaped, yet for the murder of Buckridge, Izod is sentenced to hang. The ideological implications of granting Edward freedom while Izod is executed are expressly tied to the kind of class-biased masculine schema valued in the text. Thus, Izod's masculinity (and identity) is represented as innate and unchangeable for it seems that no matter how many times he "performs" a particular version of masculinity, not only will he be impeded by his socio-economic circumstances, but his death constructs him as ultimately defeated by the systems and institutions which determine what these circumstances will be. Turner argues that convict characters are often constructed in terms of their powerlessness, and death or conclusive defeat are typical modes of resolution in Australian narratives dealing with imprisonment (71). Izod's death is, therefore, almost an inevitability, particularly as it is clear from the beginning of the novel that death has already marked him as "other" and set him apart. This is emphasised in a number of ways: Firstly, towards the end of the novel, when Izod describes Edward as dazzling, graceful, beautiful, and accomplished (he even likens him to an angel) but, in comparison, sees himself as disgusting, ignorant, and less than human (201); secondly, when Izod states that he has killed Buckridge for Edward and Susan—"To set the beautiful free" (249); and lastly, when Edward thinks: "It was as if Izod was saying, I take [Buckridge's] life and I give you yours. Go. I can endure anything" (242). Thus, by the conclusion of the narrative, it is not Izod who is represented in terms of becoming but Edward. For Edward, possessed with the "knack of changing himself into someone else" (197) and on a ship leaving Tasmania with Susan, life has numerous possibilities. In contrast, the only choices left to Izod are those concerning his death.

Kim Wilson speculates that death is invoked in YA fiction "to illustrate the complete failure of the subject to assert their agency and thus fulfil the desire to create an identity" (30). This notion is not only clearly expressed by Izod, but is also familiar to the convict narrative tradition in general; here, convention dictates that oppositions between self and society will emphasise the futility of individual action. Turner sees such negation of individual power as having a distinctly colonial meaning (59), an argument which supports the kind of civilised, bourgeois masculinity valorised in the text. The murder of Buckridge, which at least partially turns Izod from basic criminal to man of honour, can be seen in this way as the motive behind the killing is transformed from the singular desire for revenge into something far more altruistic: in championing the idea of romantic love, bravely speaking out to clear Edward's name, providing the diversion which allows Edward to escape with Susan, and killing the hated Commandant, Izod's name comes to signify "honour" rather than "bog-Irish scum" (233). Yet Izod's death also illustrates how various contradictions and ambiguities in meaning and value have informed the convict myth (and, more generally, the historical representation of Western outlaws) over time. As Hodge and Mishra argue, convicts were constructed by the ruling order (and those in favour of the existing penal regime) as romantic figures, celebrated for their "noble and convenient suffering and demise" (120). The melodramatic description of Izod's final moments and the transformation of his death into a legend can be viewed in similar terms, particularly as the glory of his death ultimately overshadows the brutality of his life. Significantly, however, in also becoming the kind of principled outlaw figure celebrated in protest texts when he dies unafraid and resisting authority, "launching himself from the scaffold into the void" before the hangman can release the trapdoor (254), his death is also constructed in heroic terms. As one of his convict peers relates years later in a Sydney pub:

'I seen the making of the legend, I did. And happy he was, you know . . . Even more than happy . . . *Complete* [. . .] Died for all of us boys he did. Died for all of us . . . A martyr he was, if ever there was one. A martyr . . .'. (249, emphasis original)

In this way, Izod is not only mythologised as a brave hero who perished for the good of the greater community, but as in traditional tales of convictism, the story of his execution also becomes a form of resistance that performs a community-sustaining role by contributing to the identity, cohesion, and morale of a whole group (Hodge and Mishra 121).

Whistle Man: Death and the Bushranger Myth

Edward Britton demonstrates that contradictory representations of criminals are a prominent feature of narratives dealing with crime and punishment in the Australian context because they were originally influenced by two very different system of values. Like the convict narrative, the bushranger myth also exists in two polarised forms, both of which continue to find meaning today. As Ina Bertrand points out, "the myth comes in two, mutually exclusive, versions". One strand constructs bushrangers such as Ned Kelly as "vicious [. . .] murderers of policemen who are just doing their duty in protecting the citizenry against [the outlaw's] depredations" ("New Histories"). More typical representations, however, depict bushrangers as national heroes; here they are celebrated as noble champions of the underprivileged and as symbols of resistance against Britain, the convict system, and the colonial authorities. In this familiar and popular version of the legend that Turner traces in part to the iconic paintings of Sidney Nolan—which, he argues, thoroughly encode the 1890s definition of nationalism (111)—the past is romanticised and politicised by positioning the honourable and brave individual in opposition to an unjust society. Undoubtedly, Ned Kelly is the most recognisable embodiment of this particular representation of the outlaw figure: As a potent icon in Australian popular history he is the subject of innumerable biographies, theatre and film productions, exhibitions, documentaries, and memorabilia. In fact, according to some accounts, Kelly and his gang have had "more books, songs and websites written about [them] than any other group of Australian historical figures" ("Ned Kelly").

The exploits of the Kelly Gang have become one of Australia's most enduring myths; Ned, Joe, Dan, and Steve continue to live on after their death in both the Australian imagination and commodity culture, and Ned has even been absorbed into Aboriginal legends of group survival as an ally against white oppression (Innes). The majority of contributions to the making of the myth—including those of Gang members themselves—celebrate Kelly and his men as heroes, but, inevitably, questions remain about "what really happened" during this period of Australian history. Was Ned just another thieving, murdering bushranger or a bona fide victim of the system? Recent Kelly fictions, such as Peter Carey's *True History of the Kelly Gang*, examine this question, deconstructing the legend through a heavily-researched narrative containing some of the "facts" relating to the man behind the myth—or the "human being behind the iron armour" as Andreas Gaile puts it (37). In *True History*, Gaile argues, Carey's emphasis on laying open "the irregularities and flaws, and ultimately, the lies and the myths of officially authorized versions of Ned's history" acts to cast doubt on the validity of established and objective views of this aspect of Australia's past.

With its insistence that "one man's tale is but half a tale" (121), and its exploration of the role of "truth" in history, Brian Ridden's *Whistle Man* follows a similar path. From the brief synopsis supplied on the back cover, the words "injustice", "charismatic", "hero", "avenge" and "Irish poor" operate as a schema to suggest that the novel follows a familiar set of narrative conventions. In this version of the myth, Ned is constructed as a rebel hero, fighting on behalf of the Irish Catholics who are oppressed by the wealthy, a corrupt justice system, squatters, the police, and the redcoats. As in *True History*, Ridden's Kelly Country is a place where "the old oppositions between 'convict' and 'jailer' have only been replaced by new—and no less harsh—ones" (Gaile 37). The novel chronicles the escapades of the Kelly gang from when Ned is first released from jail for horse theft, to the infamous siege at Glenrowan, and to his execution soon after. It is focalised through Garrett Clancy, friend to Ned and a Kelly Gang sympathiser. Fathered by a man who fought at the Eureka Stockade and later died of the wounds he received in this battle, named after an Irish hero, and with links to Banjo Patterson's famous drover, Garrett appears defined by the authentically Australian male characters associated with his heritage. When Ned crosses his path, however, Garrett is a teenage orphan whose uneasy relationship with old family friend Magnus, the only father-figure in his life, finds him looking for other masculine role models: "I was fifteen then, and finished with school—wishing I could grow taller and heavier overnight and sprout an instant beard. Ned was four years older, and already the tough bushman I wanted to be" (7). Garrett's hard manual work with Ned signals his development into adult masculinity; soon he becomes "more man than boy" (45), and by joining the Kelly Gang sympathisers— running messages, acting as a decoy, and even helping to collect the steel for the famous armour—it seems likely, as his mother assures him early in his life, that he will grow from a boy into an important man (28).

The idea that males were destined to enlarge the nation and its history is deeply embedded in both popular and "high" culture in Australia (Walker 124). By earning the respect of Ned (who praises him for his bravery), and contributing to Australian history just "like [his] father did" (209), Garrett's masculinity is therefore constructed according to well-established patterns. Both Ned and Garrett's stories in *Whistle Man* imply a connection between heroic masculinities and nationalist agendas. There are frequent references to the Eureka rebellion (often quoted as a key event in the development of Australian democracy), and the Gang's final stand at Glenrowan is linked to the death of Ned's republican vision. A witness to the siege, Garrett reports that: "The police would not rest now. For them, it had to end with all the out-laws captured or killed. The boys would not surrender [. . .] they were part of Ned's dream for a republic [and] I could not see our dream whimper off like a beaten dog" (202). The green and gold cummerbund that Ned clutches as he lies "riddled with bullet holes" in the station master's room is thus also significant since it was awarded to him for an act of bravery in his youth.

In Australian bushranger legends, heroes often outwit the police, but their capture or death is always inevitable. While some Kelly stories have Dan and Steve escaping from the Glenrowan Inn, most accounts conclude with the death of all members of the Gang. As Magnus warns Garrett: "'[T]wo of Captain Moonlite's bushranger gang [. . .] died in a battle with New South Wales police. Four others [have] been sentenced to death'" (147). Thus, in this case, the myth is also offered as a warning pertaining to the dangers of rebelling against the authorities. Under these terms, the events of history are depicted as repeatable and are valued, as is common in historical fiction for children, for their ability to provide instruc-tion and meaning. In Magnus's words, "'[Ned's] story is not new, and there are lessons to be learnt from the past'" (89). This ideology is reiterated later in the narrative when he adds: "'The Irish never beat the English. Rebellion in Ireland, crushed. Rebellion in New South Wales, crushed. Rebellion at Eureka, crushed'" (148). He then tells Garret to lead his own life, not his father's, because "'[t]oo many men die young'" (148). From Magnus's speeches, it is clear that one of these lessons is concerned with the role that choice and self-government—rather than fate—have in shaping male subjectivities, evident when he says: "'If [the Kellys] want to live, they should sail for America'" (147). This is reinforced by Garrett's feeling that the Gang's recklessness can only lead to their arrest as, from quite early in the novel, he is afraid of what it will cost to be one of them (71). In this way, the Gang are represented more as masters of their own destiny and not so much as victims of the various systems that oppress them—and, therefore, their ultimate deaths are rendered somewhat foolish rather than heroic.

In the end, it is not the death of the outlaws that separates Garrett from the Gang, but the discovery of the deadly ambush that is planned for the police and, most importantly, the killing (at Ned's request) of alleged whistleblower Aaron Sherritt. For Garrett, the significance of this event lies less with the breaching of the code of mateship than with the slaughter of one mate by another: "[Aaron's] cold-blooded murder in front of his wife could never be justified [...] How wrong I had been about Ned. Exile had changed him" (173, 227). From this episode it is possible to see how the legend has been informed by a number of binary meanings; these are the kind of brutal acts that Hodge and Mishra claim "tarnish the romantic image" (131). Garrett's decision to turn from a life at the margins of lawlessness to a settled existence on a farm close to his intended bride, Moira, would seem to support this idea, particularly as he begins to look to Magnus for guidance on many aspects of his future. His choice signals a rejection of the manhood embodied in the Gang and a move from one model of masculinity to another (albeit one still tied to the bushman ethos). And yet, by the conclusion, Ned is nevertheless represented as a hero once more. As Magnus argues, "'[m]en like [Ned] are dangerous, but they manure the tree of liberty'" (215). Thus, although Moira insists that Garrett "let the ghosts [of the past] go" and become "her hero", he still feels bound by the heroic stories of his father and of Ned who "always seemed so much bigger than he was" (240). When, just prior to Ned's execution, Garrett has a final meeting with him (which significantly occurs during the Melbourne Cup celebration, an event of national importance) this is clearly evident. In tones reminiscent of other freedom-fighters Ned declares that "'[t]hey will bury my body within the walls, but they have no power to keep my soul'" (232). His defiance shows that the "establishment" is incapable of truly defeating him, and depicts his death in the celebratory and familiar anti-authoritarian terms of the legend.[19] Fittingly, Garrett stands under the arch of bluestone block that marks the entrance to the jail and plays "Londonderry Air" on his tin whistle, a tune which operates in *Whistle Man* as a symbol of Irish resistance, but which also becomes a lament for Ned's death.

Conclusion

David Price says that "history consists of a larger vision beyond the level of the individual, a vision that attempts to make sense of the collective experience of nations, groups, and entire races" (92). The majority of novels that I have discussed here would seem to endorse such a view because they express a familiar understanding of historical experiences of death in the Australian context. In fact, this was the idea behind the title of this chapter: "Matilda's Last Dance". By referring to "Waltzing Matilda", the unofficial national anthem—and a song which is celebrated for its ability to embody the attributes of the national Australian character—I wanted to suggest that there *is* an Australian way of death that can be traced throughout my readings. At the same time, however, I am aware that in so doing, I am working from a precarious position. Not only am I mindful that as a white Anglo-Australian many of my ideas about "the nation" are normative, I am also conscious that a project which uses an umbrella term like "the nation" in the organisation of its arguments can serve to override and silence the less powerful voices in the culture (G. Turner xiv). The anthem itself can be seen to operate in similar ways because its origins in white colonial Australia imply that the version of "Australia" it conjures up is a masculinist and nationalist one, and because "the lyrics privilege a man's story about death, asking who will dance with Matilda when he is gone. Matilda is behind the song, not in it" (Kellehear and Anderson 13).

Given that I have focused predominantly on novels which pay tribute to the "foundational" events and figures that the national fictions are based upon, it could also be argued that my sample supports the very same narrow interpretation of Australia's past, and therefore gives acceptance to its status as "truth".[20] To be sure, there is an absence of females in hegemonic definitions of Australianness, and a scarcity of YA texts which provide a counterpoint to the dominant masculinist myths. As Foucault has trenchantly argued, however, exclusions and silences speak volumes about the distribution and operation of power within discourses and societies. A telling example of this thesis is the ways in which the ex-centric subject is represented in *The Divine Wind* and *Poison Under Their Lips*. While each novel seeks to empathise with the victims of the imperialist, patriarchal, and racist regimes that dominated past eras of Australia's history, there are nonetheless problems in the ways these issues are addressed. This primarily occurs because the racial Other is a female who is not only denied a narrative voice, but is also subject to the desirous gaze of the white Anglo male protagonist from whose perspective the story is told.

It is for this reason I would argue that *Fireshadow*'s multi-stranded narrative is more effective in positioning its audience to come to an understanding of perspectives belonging to those who are located outside the boundaries, or at the borders of, hegemonic representations of Australian history. Even so, *Fireshadow*'s treatment of sexuality and otherness suggests that there are limited ways in which the female presence in Australia's past can be understood. In part, this occurs because, by subsuming the female experience under the male's, the narrative reinforces the idea that history "belongs" to men. The death of the novel's female protagonist also acts to re-establish boundaries and control, and to imply that there are codes which govern ways of being and acting, not only as a woman but also as an Australian. As Stephens contends, then, there is no guarantee that the reinstatement of marginalised figures in the historical landscape will correspondingly lead to "representations of people in their otherness" ("Always" xiii). This is made very clear, for example, in *No Such Country*. Unlike earlier accounts of Australian history, the novel unquestionably equates colonisation with the decline of the Indigenous population. At the same time, however, its capacity to contribute to a truly revisionary history of Australia's racial wars is arguable because it is inclined to construct the kind of neat endings and outcomes which effectively "re-bury" the past, and thus to foreclose on the ethical issues raised by such violent events. In contrast, *Killing Darcy*'s depiction of relations between black and white (especially as it concerns death) is marked by complexities, tensions, and incomplete meanings, and its use of multiple perspectives serves to politicise and historicise the effects of colonisation upon Aboriginal people both in the past and the present.

It may be that *No Such Country* (and other novels in the genre that were produced around this time) reflects the spirit of social progressivism that marked early-1990s Australia because it suggests that "to expose old wrongs is enough to correct them" (Bradford, "Memory"). Yet, as Bradford argues, merely to acknowledge the genocidal practices carried out in the colonial period is not enough; these "terrible stories [...] must be heard [and] incorporated into national consciousness" ("Memory"). Although postcolonial theory has assisted in highlighting various attitudes towards race that have informed Australian children's texts over time, it is therefore reasonable to argue that the colonial past is still powerfully present in many of the attitudes and ideologies that feature in contemporary texts thematising Aboriginality and cross-cultural relations (Bradford, "Centre"; *Reading*). The same may be said for those historical texts which feature the deaths of iconic figures like the convict, the bushranger, and the ANZAC soldier, because they too call extensively on a narrative tradition which is apt to privilege imperialist regimes, and European culture and practices. The myth of the heroic bushman figure (from which the warrior and the bushranger draw their appeal) is one which elides the violence and disruption of colonisation, for example, because it focuses instead upon the growth, progress, and development of the (white) Australian nation. As Kellehear and Anderson point out, it is only by ignoring the earlier interracial wars that the myths associated with the "heroic courage of a virgin (white) nation", and with such figures as the unsullied soldier, were able to be articulated (11).

Without doubt, the appeal of the hero figure has waned over time. Amongst the number of alternative masculinities on offer in both literature and film for adults and children in Australia, various critics have noted the continued presence of traditional heroic models, but have also drawn attention to their increasing unpopularity (Lucas; Mallan, "Challenging"; McCallum and Stephens). Robyn McCallum and John Stephens claim, for instance, that "narrative fictions which target a contemporary Australian adolescent audience now characteristically eschew any kind of traditional male heroic image" (343–44). By treating the narratives that I have examined here as discrete texts, it can certainly be argued that each of them works in its own way to problematise traditional constructions of heroism and heroic death, and thus to unsettle the norms of traditional gender representations. The confronting representations of death in *Boys of Blood and Bone* function to undermine this idealised model of manhood because they depict war as violent and futile, and because they emphasise the vulnerability and corporeality of the male body. While the meanings that are attached to death and heroism in *Whistle Man* are similarly articulated through ideologies concerned with masculinity and nation, this novel complicates the tradition too by challenging those celebratory versions of Kelly Gang history which condone acts of violence and murder committed for the republican cause. Finally, although *Edward Britton*'s account of convictism provides a synthesis of the common themes that are expressed in the definitive 'protest' version of the myth, its employment of the anti-hero character also works at various points to create tensions and contradictions within this familiar tale of heroism. Nonetheless, generally speaking, the vision of the past that these three texts construct is a gendered, selective, and masculinist one, particularly since the dominating images of death are played out entirely within masculine domains. Despite the widespread inclination to turn from traditional concepts of heroism (which are now often acknowledged as gendered and raced) and from physically aggressive depictions of masculinity, these texts therefore offer, to use Rose Lucas's words, a "nostalgic and celebratory adherence" to conventional forms of heroic masculine subjectivity (143). Notwithstanding specific shifts in the construction of masculinities, they can be seen to continue the tradition of patriarchy that Kellehear and Anderson claim characterises the life and death images of "the country of Matilda" (9).

Chapter Three

Verisimilitude:
Representing Death "In the Real"

A fiction's claim to be re-presenting truth can be supported in two complementary ways: by the use of conventions which affirm the text's veracity; and by avoiding discoursal elements which foreground its literariness.

(Stephens, Language 251)

Realism is plausible not because it reflects the world but because it is constructed out of what is (discursively) familiar.

(Belsey, Critical 44)

The development of the YA label during the 1960s coincided with the emergence of the adolescent "problem" novel which introduced readers to a variety of personal, social, and political problems (Nimon and Foster; Saxby). Although this direct confrontation with "serious" issues previously considered to be beyond the bounds of children's fiction was considered innovative at the time, today it is said to be a defining feature of the genre (Nimon and Foster 3). Indeed, there is now virtually nothing that is off-limits in contemporary YA fiction (Owen 12). As this chapter illustrates, one of the characteristics of the genre is its willingness to engage with the traumatic and harsh aspects of life; readers can vicariously explore a plethora of topics including sexual abuse, incest, teenage pregnancy, homosexuality, violence, suicide, and terminal illness. The genre also tends to be dominated by realist discourses—to such an extent that it is often viewed as a body of work that tells "real" stories about "real" people. All of the narratives I discuss here therefore share a commitment to veracity—to representing stories about life and death accurately and "truthfully". They are also notable for their differing approaches to such subjects, however. Many depict death as a catalyst for growth. Some work to suggest that death is a punishment for transgression by subscribing to the notion of adolescence as a dangerous period of development, and by implying that there are severe consequences for teenage children (particularly girls) who operate outside socially prescribed boundaries. By framing mortality through themes of sexuality, still others can be seen to demonstrate how normative judgements work discursively to divide the "normal" from the "abnormal". As a group, these narratives also provide an interesting cross-section of experiences of death, thus building a picture of the particular patterns, tensions, and themes that can be said to represent Western death culture in the contemporary era.

Realism

The aim of the realist novel is to create an authentic or faithful reproduction of "reality", to represent "life" in such a way that is consistent with the/an external reality and human experience *outside* the text. The standard for success of any realistic work is thus dependent on its semblance to "truth" or actuality (verisimilitude), its accuracy in transferring common experience into a fictional form, and its ability to match a reader's expectations of reality. The idea that a realist novel can somehow *reflect* reality is untenable, however, because a realist text is as much a fictional construct as any other literary text. The process of representing "reality" necessarily entails discoursal choices about the selection and arrangement of a narrative's story elements, about the ways in which one strand of story is related to another, and about how the story is told—from mode, to point of view, to vocabulary, to syntax (Stephens, *Language*). A consideration of the role that language plays in representing a subject or the world also disrupts the notion that a realistic fiction can be a transparent, reliable representation of what actually "is". Narrative does not imitate reality, it only creates "an *illusion* of mimesis, since the moment an object, character, setting or event is represented in language it is subject to the assumptions, ideologies and modes of thought embedded in the language used to represent it" (Bradford, *Reading* 139, emphasis original). In their commitment to verisimilitude, realistic texts, as a rule, systematically seek to conceal their own methods of construction, and hence to disguise the relationship between fiction and reality. As Terry Eagleton argues, realist literature "tends to conceal the socially relative or constructed nature of language: it helps to confirm the prejudice that there is a form of 'ordinary' language which is somehow natural" (117).

Realistic Fiction for Children

Although the ideological implications of an audience equating representation with "truth" are a focus of critical practice concerning literature for children, the importance of verisimilitude in children's fiction is nonetheless overstated. The capacity to produce writing which contains "the essence of realism" (language that evokes the "real world", "real" characters with "real" voices) continues to be regarded as a marker of a "good" novel (Stephens, *Language* 4). Catherine Bateson's *Painted Love Letters*, a text I discuss in the latter part of this chapter, is highly recommended by reviewer Anne Hanzl, for instance, because it is "a thoughtful and moving story [that] is sad, but not depressing as [the protagonist] Chrissie realistically explores the meaning of love and relationships within the family, and of life and death itself" (38). As it is used here, the term "realistic" is a slippery one, because notions of realism are culturally and personally relative. Hanzl's evaluation demonstrates that the meanings and values that can be drawn from the novel rely not only upon a particular expectation about the nature of reality—a general agreement about what constitutes "the norm"—but also upon those "truths" and values that match the reviewer's own. John Stephens also points to the problems associated with the excessive focus on verisimilitude when he argues that it assumes "that words and things are directly equivalent" (*Language* 244). Even simple representation involves interpretation, he contends, and thus to grasp the different ways a reader may perceive phenomena (and also the different ways that power is implicated in language), it is essential to take the encoding discourse into account (*Language* 244–45).

According to Stephens, there are two complementary ways by which the discourse of realism functions to construct a coherent fictive world for readers: "by the use of conventions which affirm the text's veracity; and by avoiding discoursal elements which foreground its literariness" (*Language* 251). The most pervasive strategy for effecting the illusion of realism, he suggests, is the use of first-person narration (where narrator and principal focaliser are the same). This strategy encourages audiences to share a narrator's view, and thus to adopt a stance which is identical to the focalising character. However, in aligning themselves with this character, it is argued that readers are also likely to undergo textual subjection—that is, to be susceptible to the ideologies of the text (*Language* 68–70, 251). As realist fictions strive to create the illusion that events are represented linearly, another strategy is to "mask the inevitable fissuring of simple story linearity (and hence of verisimilitude)". It is by these means, Stephens contends, that random sequences of typical story existents are drawn into a meaningful relation and, therefore, that the significance of a story is constructed (*Language* 250–51, 288). Finally, Stephens argues that realism is apt to "efface self-conscious textuality, displacing the presence of word-play, ambiguity, figurative language, and so on, to the level of character interactions". In this way, "overtly literary features are not a prominent part of the narrator's discourse", and literariness is "instead rendered implicitly by means of the metonymic mode of realism" (*Language* 288).

Expelling the Monstrous-Feminine in *Touching Earth Lightly*

In order to explore some of these ideas further, I want to turn now to Margo Lanagan's *Touching Earth Lightly*, a text which discloses a number of tensions in the meanings that are constructed for its readers at different narrative levels (that is, between the narrative's story, and the significance it constructs in the course of representing these story elements). The novel explores notions of femininity and the female body through two very different protagonists. One girl, Chloe, is conventionally beautiful, caring, and interested in romantic love, possessing qualities typically associated with orthodox models of femininity. Janey, the other, is by contrast "promiscuous", reckless, and wild. Their particularly close relationship is the focus of the narrative; however, it is a story of female friendship that is tinged with sadness since Janey dies part of the way through its telling. For Chloe, Janey's violent, sordid death means that there is "a dark wound in her where Janey [has been] cut off", a wound that "never quite closes [but] sours everything, slows everything, bleeds mystery and sadness" (169). Yet it also signals her own growth, away from the time-consuming and sometimes suffocating relationship she has with Janey.

Roberta Seelinger Trites argues that an acceptance of losing others and awareness of mortality shapes much of the discourse surrounding death in YA novels, because adolescents commonly gain their first knowledge of the pain and powerlessness involved in permanent separation when someone they love dies. The "corollary that inevitably follows", Trites contends, is the "recognition of their own mortality" (*Disturbing* 119). Demonstrating Chloe's own acceptance as Being-towards-death, Janey's death makes Chloe feel "as if she's just a cipher for her dead friend, as if she's death itself" (151), and it also gives her life some significance—"an edge of portent, a kind of unwitting courage it didn't have [prior to this] time"(168).[1] However, because in many ways, Chloe and Janey believe that "together [they] make up one gifted, gorgeous person" (139), Janey's death is also an extremely important aspect of the narrative's ideological framework. When the two girls greet each other, for instance, "it's as if the remaining part of [their] self has appeared" (163). And yet, at the same time that descriptions of them focus on their extreme closeness, they also emphasise—in unequal terms—their difference, contrasting physical appearance, class, and, in particular, attitudes towards sex and sexuality. As Clare Bradford points out, for a number of reasons, the construction of the girls' relationship through a scheme of binary oppositions is problematic: It consistently undermines Janey's search for agency by depicting her as "abnormal" next to the uncomplicated and under-control Chloe; it associates class difference with sexual pathologies; and it creates a kind of determinism for Janey ("Embodied" 114–16). Readers are thus cued not only to expect Janey's exit from the narrative, but to see it as a consequence of her risky behaviour, her social position, and her way of being female.

According to Robyn McCallum, the double in adolescent fiction can be represented as an aspect of the developmental process; that is, "the double represents another possible position the character might occupy" (77). In a sense, Janey operates as Chloe's double: she is "an other", but most importantly, "another" aspect of the self—an internalised other (McCallum 75). This is evident in the way that Janey never "speaks" her self in the text but is rather focalised always through Chloe (Bradford, "Embodied" 114). Chloe perceives herself to be "[c]olourless, boring [and] directionless", while she sees Janey as marvellous, with "all the talent, all the sex appeal [and] all the initiative" (130). Yet because of the pejorative construction of Janey's sexuality, at a psychological and figurative level she becomes a manifestation of the most threatening or dangerous aspects of Chloe's self. In Freudian terms, Janey represents Chloe's id, her instinctual, biological drives and desires. In the face of the socially controlled dictates of the super-ego, however, she is forced to operate as a monster of excess. Like the nineteenth-century literary figure of the madwoman in the attic—that repressed aspect of the (female) self that is confined by the dictates of patriarchy (Gilbert and Gubar)—Janey functions as an asocial and uninhibited surrogate for the conventional, nicely brought-up, often docile Chloe. In ways similar to other representations of psychological doubles, the two are juxtaposed to reflect this: Janey is dark where Chloe is fair, and Janey is "oversexed" and passionate in contrast to Chloe who is "happy-ish" and not particularly interested in sexual activity (39). Symbolically, then, when Janey dies, Chloe's body hurts, "actually *hurts!*" (131, emphasis original), and her period arrives early to "make the bleeding literal" (120). As the reference to menstrual blood (a signifier of Woman) indicates, here it is as if Janey—and therefore the monstrous aspect of Chloe's sexuality—is being expelled, for in Julia Kristeva's view, menstrual blood "stands for the danger issuing from within identity (social or sexual)" (71). As Elizabeth Grosz explains, "proper" sociality and subjectivity are based on the expulsion of the improper, the unclean, and the disorderly elements of the body's corporeal existence from its "clean and proper" self, and thus "the subject must disavow part of itself in order to gain a stable self" ("Body" 86).

Kim Wilson's more literal reading of Janey's death argues that it is "a function of the plot to illustrate the effect of abjection on subjective development" (27).[2] For Janey *is* abject: She can see that her "whole life disgusts people" because it is "a big dirty *hole* that [she is] always having to be dragged out of" (82, emphasis original). Janey is also an example of what Barbara Creed calls "the monstrous-feminine". According to Creed, representations of the monstrous-feminine are, in psychoanalytic terms, manifestations of male castration anxiety, and thus their presence in a text typically operates to reinforce the phallocentric notion that female sexuality is abject (*Monstrous* 151). This is signalled by the way her character is constructed as a "devourer" and as a threat to the males she engages with. When Chloe suggests that Janey needs a "nice, steady, tolerant man" such as her brother, Nick, he protests: "'She's dangerous, that girl'", adding "'God, she'd take over [and] I don't think there's enough of me [...] I've got a life to live'" (128). Her monstrosity is starkly evident, too, in another episode very early in the novel where she is likened to a deadly spider: "The moonlight fell through the car window onto Janey's tight black-widow clothes, on her bag, split open on the floor, spilling foil-wrapped condoms like treasure" (15).

Trites points out that "death and sex are cultural and biological concepts that are linked inviolably" (*Disturbing* 122). In these scenes, however, notions of sex and death are also closely intertwined with femininity, making it difficult not to connect Janey's death with her way of being female. According to Bradford, Janey dies of "an excess of femaleness" because she is driven purely by her sexuality; she is constructed as "subject to corporeality, ruled by the phases of the moon and of her menstrual cycle" ("Embodied" 114, 116). From a patriarchal perspective, then, the figure of Janey is, to use Kerry Mallan's term, a "disruptive feminine presence" that must be "silenced and annulled" ("Fatal" 180) and she is, therefore, killed off. Significantly, this occurs at the very place where she often goes to have sex: She is raped and beaten, and when Chloe finds her, her dead body is displayed in a manner which "incites a sexualising gaze" (Mallan, "Just" 43) since she is naked and positioned lying on her back. Almost in a grotesque parody of orgasm (or, symbolically, in preparation to submit to the phallic order), her mouth and eyes are open and she is draped across the back of a car, an object often associated with the male (103). Janey can transgress the hetero-normative construct of female sexuality, the text appears to say, but she will pay for her sexual aggression. This is emphasised by Chloe's mother, Joy, when she informs Chloe "that most people don't do sex like that" (120). Consequently, Janey's death is violent, evident in the look of "glazed surprise" fixed to her (dead) face, her body "marked up and down with bruises", a cape of blood flowing "down around her from the back of her head and off over the edge of the boot" (104). Here, death has not caused a "destruction of the gendered body", but has rather ensured the "objectification of the woman's body-as-image" (Mallan, "Just" 44), because, as Chloe notes after placing a coat over Janey, covered and with her eyes closed she looks only like an accident victim rather than a victim of a violent sex crime (105).[3]

Nevertheless, there are moments when Janey's sexuality is privileged by the text. Wilson points to one episode where, unable to wait until evening, Janey chooses to have sex during a lunch break at school (27). In contrast to the descriptions of the disgusted, bitchy, and cold girls who whisper about her afterwards in the classroom, Janey is represented in positive terms: Her "lips are very red and her eyes and skin are as bright as dew with sunlight on it" (123). In another, the double standards characterising phallocentric notions of female sexuality are highlighted when a boy Janey has just "done over" suggests that Chloe is either frigid or a lesbian because of her lack of interest in having sex herself, while in the same conversation informing her that boys don't go for girls like her and Janey. "'You're just angry because she calls the shots,'" Chloe replies, adding: "'You'd go for her, no worries. She wouldn't *want* you to stick around, though—that's why you don't like her" (12–13, emphasis original). Janey's clear enjoyment of her sexuality and her body, and the subversive use of her father's pornographic magazines to create a decoupage egg in craft class, covered with "strange pink leaves and buds [. . .] little vagina-mouths, surrounded by petals of thigh and breast and bottom" (118) also provide evidence of feminist agendas and strategies (Bradford, "Embodied" 114).

However, as Wilson also suggests, the text constructs Janey's death as a *fait accompli* (29), making these incidents, as a whole, little more than a surface ideology which ultimately fails to disturb the more pervasive message underscoring the novel (that is, that female sexuality is abject). In fact, Janey's deathly fate is evident almost from the outset. She conducts her "trysts" at an auto-wrecking lot—a graveyard of rusted car bodies and parts, infested with rats, from which at one point she emerges "like some kind of mysterious extrusion from [their] corpses" (14). Another scene links her with decay when she is described as "all black-legginged legs, with a tiny snarled black jumper, like a wisp of some kind of mould around her shoulders and arms" (30). Thus, although after the court case, Chloe thinks how arbitrary the accident was "a matter of timing and slips in someone's concentration [. . .] and the wrong constellation of people and fluids" (164), she also feels that she has "been drawing this one event towards her all her life" (122), has known without admitting it the danger surrounding Janey:

> Police, morgues, injuries—she's gone along in all innocence, never dreaming these words might be used of Janey, but now that she looks back, of course they were coming—she should have seen them flapping like vultures over Janey all along, from way back in the schoolyard, and in a tall column spiralling up on the thermals of evil grotty heat from Janey's house. (113)

Chloe and her mother accept some responsibility for Janey's death— Chloe for her choice to leave Janey in a distressed state after she has been raped by her brother, Nathan, and Joy for her own passivity—for not doing more to avert the looming tragedy. Joanna Harris argues that the episode when this occurs provides evidence of Chloe's maturation into adulthood. It is also presented in a way which suggests that an adult view of the situation is a complex one: a "realistically" unresolved and unresolvable way of seeing (44), because although Chloe feels culpable she also firmly reassures her mother that they cannot be guilty: "'[I]n the end we're not the ones on trial. We're not the ones who did it" (182). This statement is echoed by Chloe's father, Dane, when he says it was "just bad *luck* as much as anything" (182, emphasis original). However, as Harris also argues, it is at moments like these that the novel's impression of realism becomes a powerful ideological tool since they assist in promoting a "misleadingly simple perspective to explain the circumstances of Janey's murder". Rather than "extending an understanding of the social forces which shaped Janey's existence", she argues, this scene merely reinforces the idea that Janey was destined to die (44). By the novel's conclusion, this has become abundantly clear: Janey has been replaced by Isaac, Chloe's new boyfriend, creating a romantic and conventional closure that is only possible in narrative terms because of Janey's death (Bradford, "Embodied" 116).

In Wilson's words, "those who transgress and who are subsequently abjected are an example to all to conform to the regulations imposed" (28). As I have argued, this is made especially clear in *Touching Earth Lightly* by the association between Janey's non-conformity and her violent murder. Several episodes, in particular, highlight this idea, not least those detailing Janey's "promiscuity", but also those that make reference to her unplanned pregnancy, and the sexual relationship she has with her father and brother. Like other adolescent novels featuring teenage pregnancies, this one operates as a cautionary tale relating to the dangers of teenage sexual activity. According to Trites, authors who depict young adults experiencing "extreme sexual pleasure" tend to minimise the repressive use of ideology, in part by allowing characters to feel empowered by their sexuality (*Disturbing* 96). In this instance, however, rather than gaining a sense of empowerment from her obvious enjoyment of sex, Janey is punished. Not only does she suffer depression and moments where she "hates herself" as a result of relinquishing her child after the pregnancy, she is disempowered by the knowledge that this occurred in spite of the responsibility she took for contraception: "'I guess, you know, statistically. The number [of condoms] I use, I'd have to get a dud some time'", she explains to Chloe (157). Here, the anxieties surrounding adult views of adolescent sexuality are clear. Disturbingly, they intersect with another set of ideologies concerning maternity, sexual abuse, and class, for it is suggested that the quality of Janey's mothering skills has been predetermined, and that the potential to harm her child is a given. It is as if, the text implies, she has inherited a gene that will ensure she is "hopeless", and always doubting her ability to "stop the tradition". In a vulnerable moment, she says: "'You hear, you know, how 'abused' people abuse their kids and I . . . just wonder, is that something you could control?'" (159). Spoken from within the "generalised niceness" of Chloe's house, where everything is organised and clean, and parents are helpful and caring, this statement only adds to the sense that Janey's freedom of choice is entirely limited by her social situation.

Where the brutality of Janey's existence manifests itself in episodes of sexual abuse, the connections between class difference, sexual pathology, and Janey's death are particularly evident, for it is these incidents that point to the extent to which she has disturbed the social order, and thus also to her abjection. In the adolescent novel, Trites argues, "nothing demonstrates the power relationships between adults and adolescents as effectively as the abuse of sexual power" (*Disturbing* 96). As a function of the narrative plot, Janey's sordid home life provides the reason for her escape to, and refuge within, the Hunter household. In fact, the novel opens with Janey declaring "'I've got to get out of that house'" (7), followed by juxtaposing representations of the depressing search for new accommodation and her "dirty old man" with Chloe's liberal, friendly home and her "civilised brothers" (Harris 42). Both Janey's father and brother have been sexually abusing her for some time, and her fear of them is demonstrated by the lengths she will go to in order to conceal from them any details pertaining to her new life, even when this involves drastically changing her appearance. Under these circumstances, the power the men have over Janey is explicit. At a discursive level, however, readers are positioned to view Janey's abuse, including the later rape by Nathan, as a consequence of her subversive sexuality. Drawing on the familiar (patriarchal) image of the woman with the short skirt who is "just begging" to be raped, the text suggests that Janey's casual and often aggressive approach to sex means that she has foregone her right to refusal in *any* sexual encounter. This is illustrated firstly by Chloe's question about how Janey feels in regard to the abuse, to which she replies: "'[W]ho am I to complain?'" (38), and secondly by Janey's mother who is constructed as ineffectual and blank, but also—with her pretence that nothing untoward is happening—complicit in the crime. The significance of these small, but meaningful, snippets of information is then imposed retrospectively when they are drawn together at a point later in the narrative (importantly, after the scene involving Janey's death) when Chloe asks Dane: "'Is it child sexual abuse if the child doesn't really *mind* the sex?'" (136, emphasis original).

Lying Down with Dogs: Death, Defilement, and Sexual Taboos

Another text featuring an "unknowing" and ineffectual (yet culpable) mother living within a family where physical and sexual abuse are common practice is Sonya Hartnett's *Sleeping Dogs*. This heavily symbolic and disturbing tale is, in Heather Scutter's view, about "reversing, even perversing, common assumptions about love, marriage, childrearing and family" (261). For at Bonaparte Farm where the Willows reside, there is an incestuous relationship between brother Jordan and sister Michelle, and a history of paternal physical abuse. Griffin, the domineering alcoholic father of this dysfunctional group, is inebriated each time a child is conceived, and his wife, Grace, has become silent and withdrawn, rarely leaving her chair in the dim lounge-room. Death and decay lie like a shroud over the farm and the dilapidated caravan park which is attached to it. The house is huge and ancient, no wall is straight, it lacks paint, and its corrugated roof has holes. Inside, "hammocked drapes of cobwebs" hang from the ceiling, mirrors sport clouds of mould, and the hallway is "a tunnel of a catacomb, fallen inward like lungs expelling air" (50, 52). As the synopsis on the jacket cover suggests, the Willows occupy a dog-eat-dog world where the only currency is power: from "this house, this land, that father, that mother", there is "no pity", "no mercy", and "probably no escape" it warns.

The narrative of *Sleeping Dogs*, which begins with a number of seemingly disconnected passages of dialogue and events, follows a short period in the family's life. During this time, Bow Fox, a park tenant who is intrigued by the insular family (and who will not let the metaphorical sleeping dogs lie), uncovers their secrets and sets into motion a series of incidents that culminate in the shocking murder of Jordan. Like *Touching Earth Lightly*, the narrative positions readers to view Jordan as both victim and criminal since, in using similar strategies to the Lanagan novel, it suggests that although it is Jordan who is abused and exploited, it is also he who will be punished because of the family's transgressions. The text cues readers to expect Jordan's death, for example—to see it as a given—as, from the outset, he is depicted as an Other. When contrasted with the dark, cruel, and ruthless pack comprising his siblings and father, there is little doubt that this yellow-haired and fragile twenty-year-old represents the runt of the litter. This is emphasised by the portentous association of his character with the figure of the crow, "a timid [and] easily harried" bird (43–44), but also a symbol of ill omen or death. Besides the sense of fatalism surrounding Jordan's character in the opening chapter, there are also few instances where he is the focaliser; rather, the point-of-view is, for the most part, shared progressively between every member of the Willow family bar Jordan. Scutter argues that, as a function of the narrative, this signals that "Jordan is bright enough only to perceive himself in others' terms" (261); however, it also works textually as a means of setting him apart.

It is significant, then, that when Jordan's perspective is first introduced in detail, it occurs directly after a beating from his father. During this episode, Jordan's position as an outsider is stressed even further when the reader learns that it is only he who bears the brunt of his father's anger, and when Griffin shouts: "'I look at you and wonder from where the hell you sprung'" (16). Not as obvious—at least at the beginning of the narrative—is the association between Jordan's death and his relationship with Michelle. Although readers are directly confronted with incidents of violence, there is no explicit description of sexuality; such "realistic" information is withheld so that awareness is by inference only (Scutter 254). Nevertheless, there are several episodes which occur early in the text that assist in creating a connection between the two. In both, the notion of (sexual) crime and punishment, a theme central to the novel, is explicit. The first occurs immediately after the abovementioned beating when Jordan is administering to his injuries:

> Sometimes, when his father hits him it strikes him as ludicrous, twenty years old and still being hit. So once he'd hit back, had, to his embarrassed astonishment, knocked his father off his feet. He was eighteen then. Michelle had been angry for days. She said to him, 'That was the most disgusting thing I've ever seen, Jordan.' And then she'd sat beside him and said that, in a way, they deserved to be hit, both of them. They knew what they did wasn't *right*: you read about it in books and it was never right in them. If Griffin hit Jordan, wasn't that a sort of punishment for them? And if they were being punished, didn't that give them freedom to go on doing what they did? 'Do you see what I mean, Jordan?' she'd asked. 'Sometimes, two wrongs *can* make a right. Can *give you* a right.' (18, emphases original)

In the second episode, the story of a violent thrashing Jordan receives from Griffin is juxtaposed with another concerning the beginnings of the siblings' inferred sexual relationship, twining them together with Michelle's statement that "[. . .] there was no denying it: Jordan had done something to make their father mad, so it must have been Jordan's fault. He had brought this harm upon himself" (58).

The link between the incest and the death becomes abundantly clear when Oliver (Michelle and Jordan's younger brother) spills their secret to Bow. Shaking and ill, Oliver feels "he's done something fatal, something terribly treasonable, something he should die for" (74). Pleading with Bow, he says: "'Don't tell Dad' [. . .] 'Please don't tell Dad'" (74). As the reader is likely to learn from this incident, under the Law of the father that operates at the farm, two wrongs most definitely do not make a right. Thus, by the conclusion when Griffin *has* been made aware of the relationship and is hunting Jordan down with his rifle, Jordan's future in the narrative has already been assured: He is "doing nothing but accepting his fate" (124). Here, the ideological implication is that, in breaking the laws governing licit and illicit forms of sex and sexuality, Jordan is susceptible to punishment. Or, to use the words of warning contained in Michel Foucault's study of the discursive regulation of sexuality, "strange pleasures" will "eventually result in nothing short of death" (*History* 54). That Griffin literally gets away with murder reinforces this idea too, because the sin of sexual perversion is given greater weight than the sin of filicide. As Joanne McPherson argues,

> [whilst] murder and incest are equally abject in the eyes of both secular and religious institutions it is the defiance of the word, the Father, the symbolic and patriarchal, through the performance of incest, which is punished in *Sleeping Dogs*, and not the murder of the son. (15)

In this way, Jordan's sin is not merely a sin against God or a transgression of the incest taboo, it is "an insult to Griffin's authority", and he dies, therefore, in order to reaffirm patriarchal power and control (21). This idea is encapsulated in the text when Michelle chastises Jordan for the one occasion where he strikes out at Griffin in retaliation: "Never, *ever*, hit him back [. . .] He's our *father*, remember'" (18, emphases original).

The power differential that is evident in this exchange is a characteristic feature of the siblings' affair, for Michelle controls each encounter as much as Griffin tyrannises the family (McPherson 20). Due to her status as her father's favourite, Michelle already wields a certain amount of power; indeed, Griffin is as drawn to Michelle as he is repulsed by Jordan. McPherson explains the dynamics at work in the Willow household in psychoanalytic terms, arguing that the relationship between Michelle, Jordan, Griffin, and Grace, is conducted within the context of the Oedipal myth (15). In this instance, however, the love of the mother is substituted for that of the daughter/sister, and it is the son instead of the father who is murdered. Michelle embodies that particular stage of the process when the female child has turned from her mother and has begun the project of seducing her father because, of all the Willow children, it is she who is most alienated from her mother but most adored by her father. By contrast, it is Jordan who is violently estranged from his father but has yet to detach from his mother; unlike any of his siblings, Jordan is devoted to Grace and this devotion both emphasises his difference and implies an "ongoing connection to their pre-Objectal relationship" (McPherson 19). In McPherson's view, Griffin's adoration of Michelle is purely platonic, yet it creates the underlying motivation for his abuse of Jordan because, in focusing upon Jordan, Griffin has identified his competitor for Michelle's love. Moreover, McPherson contends, in accepting the abuse as "his due punishment for Michelle's sexual attention", Jordan simply reinforces the Oedipal drama that will result in his death (18).

At the conclusion to *Sleeping Dogs*, the remaining Willows simply pack up and move on. Bow, who remains ignorant of Jordan's death, imagines that their sense of liberation as they cruise away, "running and free" is great; he "actually smiles to remember [them]", and "he is gracious enough to wish them luck" (130). In terms of story closure, the suggestion here is that the Willow family will not be held responsible for their transgressions; rather, their behaviour is sanctioned since it is implied that they will merely set up somewhere else to begin the cycle of abusive behaviour anew—albeit minus Jordan and Michelle's incestuous relationship. Robert Cormier claims that the text pushes "the boundaries of YA literature to their outer edges and perhaps beyond", so that even while readers "shudder at the terrible truths of [Hartnett's] vision", their notion of socially and morally acceptable behaviour is challenged.[4] Jordan's death is the most problematic obstacle to viewing this text as truly subversive, however. Situated within the theme of punishment dominating the narrative, his murder works against the perception that the forms of subjectivity embodied by the Willows are either transgressive or resistant. Readers are, furthermore, encouraged to view the maternal in the context of orthodox patriarchal ideologies: Grace, who sits as "still as the dead", in a dress which is "perfectly without colour at all" (52–53) is constructed as powerless, a figure who represents a "constant, inadequate opposition to the paternal, rule-governing symbolic order" (McPherson 21), while Jordan, the child who has the closest connection with the maternal body, is eradicated.

For several reasons, Francesca Lia Block's *Wasteland*, which also deals with incest, provides an interesting contrast to *Sleeping Dogs*: One, the relationship between siblings Lex and Marina is represented as loving and affectionate instead of abusive; and, two, the narrative's predominantly lush and saccharine imagery—flowers, rainbows, lemonade, baby powder, bugglegum, perfume, warm breezes—has none of the Gothic overtones of the Hartnett text. Thus, whereas in *Sleeping Dogs* the abject nature of the sexual union between Michelle and Jordan is reflected in the decaying farm (which has unquestionably gone to the dogs), in *Wasteland*, the fanciful and sensuous—if, at times, barren—vision of Los Angeles that is the backdrop for the story signifies an entirely different association between character/s and setting. At one level, then, the text would seem to condone, if not celebrate, the siblings' deep connection. Besides the narrative's dreamlike register and the soft, pinkish hues of the front cover—each of which works to create an impression of romance—there are many instances, for example, when the pair's extreme closeness is highlighted and their relationship is almost defined in terms of mutualism (that is, where mutual dependence is necessary to social well-being). A case in point occurs when Marina thinks: "[E]verything I did, everything that happened to me [. . .] I asked myself—what does this mean for us" (18), while on another occasion, Lex remembers a moment when he first became aware of their special bond:

> When you were a baby I sat very still to hold you. I could see the veins through your skin like a map to inside you [. . .] I stopped breathing so you wouldn't [. . .]
>
> Then you reached out and curled your fingers around mine, so tight. I knew you recognized me. That was the first time I knew I had a heart in my body. (1–2)

Each also addresses the other with the same term of endearment—the pronoun "you": "You, that's me. You called me you and I called you you" (19).

The narrative has clear associations with Romantic portrayals of sibling incest which, according to Alan Richardson, are presented "not as a perversion or accidental inversion of the normal sibling relation, but as an extension and intensification of it" ("Rethinking" 554). The emphasis in Romantic incest is on a shared childhood rather than blood ties, he contends, and on the notion of perfect sympathy in love (or total sympathetic fusion) ("Dangers" 741);

thus, it promotes "virtual identity in spite of sexual difference", nurture over nature, and experience over birth ("Rethinking" 556). And yet, Richardson says, unions between co-socialised pairs nonetheless tend to end in disaster: Romantic erotic relations between cross-gender siblings are repeatedly disrupted by "a conflicting but conscious acknowledgment that such relations just do not work", and therefore they typically follow a trajectory from "childhood association, through adolescent romance, to separation and death". In this way, they construct a paradoxical view of sibling incest that is both ideal and aversive ("Rethinking" 564, 565, 569).

The kind of narrative ambivalence that arises from such conflict clearly marks *Wasteland*, because while the indisputably loving connection between Lex and Marina creates a justification for their relationship, on several occasions the text's handling of meaning and ideology appears to suggest, to the contrary, that their union constitutes a violation of the primary social law. The most obvious example which supports this reading of the text is the novel's determinate closure. The narrative is largely concerned with Marina's quest to understand her brother's death (which occurs soon after an erotic and, it is implied, sexual, incident between the siblings) and, in the latter part of the novel, with the search for her absent father. She is accompanied on the journey by her friend, West, who is with her when she tracks her father down and discovers that Lex is adopted. Satisfied that she has all the answers to the puzzles, Marina then begins a romantic relationship with West (who loves her despite—and because of—his knowledge about her relationship with Lex). The message that is contained in the conclusion, therefore, is that healthy sexual development for Marina is dependent upon finding an appropriate (that is, culturally approved) substitute for Lex. This is reinforced by the strategy of positioning readers to view West as a suitable partner for Marina from very early in the novel (significantly, his perspective is first introduced immediately after Lex's death), and by Marina's response to West after he asks her whether it is "harder now", now that she knows that Lex is not her biological sibling and thus could have remained her lover: "'He was my brother anyway. When someone is something to you, it's always like that'" (149–50). Rather than rendering the pair's love as "star-crossed" (Brabander 741), like Romantic treatments of erotic relationships between siblings, the novel's dénouement therefore serves to suggest that all unions between co-socialised pairs are implicitly incestuous.

The narrative's opening sequence functions similarly. It begins with one of the book's tag lines. Located on the first page of the front matter, it reads: "Your whole life you can be told something is wrong and so you believe it". While clearly a hint to the secret concerning Lex's adoption, it is also a reference to the prohibition of incest, and so it works to yoke the book's main theme (that of secrets) to the notion of illicit behaviour. The section then ends with a short passage about Lex's death. As with *Sleeping Dogs*, the ideological effect of such ordering is to imply that there is a cohesive and consequential link between "crime" and "punishment"—that there are penalties for crossing socially prescribed boundaries. That these limits are concerned with sexual practices and ways of being is then firmly established by the juxtaposition of this passage with another detailing Marina's memory of her first menstrual period. Here, she has become unhappily conscious of her own sexual difference: "I was old all of a sudden. I wanted to be a little girl. A little boy" (18). In Marina's view, menarche has the potential to bring the siblings "closer than [they have] ever been", to grant them the ability to "disappear into each other", but she also recognises that from this time on she will be "further away" from Lex too (18). This episode marks the point at which sexual tensions and desires are set into play between the two and the romance enters a new stage. It is not until Marina is sixteen, however, that the pair's love for each other becomes physical, but once this occurs, Lex's suicide—his need to "sever [him]self" from Marina—quickly follows (124–25). In the tradition of Romantic sibling incest, then, the point at which the romance is allowed to fully develop, "paradoxically comes both to represent the ultimate fulfilment of sibling love and to demand its disruption" through the death of one or both partners ("Rethinking" 557).

There are several other ways that the text functions to suggest that Lex and Marina's behaviour should, in the long run, be regarded as taboo. The first concerns the theme of secrets, which is played out not just through the events of the story, but also at the discursive level. I have demonstrated how this works in the opening sequence, but it is apparent, too, in the way that the narrative operates like a mystery. The reader is positioned to gradually piece the events of the story together through hints and indirect references rather than explicitly detailed episodes, a process which is further complicated by the fractured temporal sequencing and structure of the narrative, and by the slippage between perceptual points of view that occurs when one of the pair addresses the other as "you" (this latter strategy makes it difficult to discern which of the protagonists is focalising or speaking). In my opinion, the enigmatic mood or tone that is created by conveying the story elements in this manner serves to give theme a status equal to that of story, thus embedding the notion of "secrets" more firmly into the narrative. The use of symbols, allusions, and intertextuality also acts to construct a similar significance for the novel. The narrative directly draws on two of T. S. Eliot's poems: "The Waste Land" and "Marina". In "The Waste Land", the themes of moral decay, sin, and sterility jostle with others that are concerned with spiritual salvation and the quest for moral regeneration. The poem traces a trajectory from despair to hope that is paralleled in *Wasteland* by Marina's journey. At the opening to the novel she knows there is a world beyond the "vast barren waste" that she sees herself mired in— "canyons full of coyote and monarch butterflies [. . .] purple and yellow wildflowers [. . .] parks and palms and palisades" (11), but it is not until she has spent hours immersed in Santa Monica Bay, until she and West have become "new, together" that the ghost of Lex is gone (150). From the perspective of the close, it is not difficult to associate Marina's rebirth with her new relationship, to view one union as "wrong" and the other as "right", particularly as Lex's death is, in narrative terms, the event that makes this romantic ending possible.

The wasteland motif that is central to Eliot's work has its origins in a myth which connects sin with impotence or infertility—a tale in which sacrificial death (often a ritual death by water) is necessary for life to continue (Davidson 125). These aspects of the poem are also alluded to in *Wasteland*. On several occasions, it is implied that Lex dies by drowning himself in the ocean, while on another it is clear that he sees suicide as a necessary step in order for Marina "to be free [to] have some kind of life" herself (124–25). Again, the suggestion is that erotic attachment between co-socialised pairs is unhealthy, that it cannot be fruitful. The strategic placement of the poem "Marina" in the final section of the narrative adds emphasis to this message. The poem evokes the Romantic belief in the innocence of childhood, and it reflects the dreamlike, introspective, and nostalgic tone of the rest of the novel; however, at the same time, it too relates loss to rebirth, sin to death, pathos to becoming. The second part of the poem is particularly important in this respect because it can be interpreted as "a commination or denouncing of anger and judgements" against those who have committed a cardinal sin (Moody 154). This is apparent in the verse which begins and ends, respectively, with the following: "Those who sharpen the tooth of the dog, meaning Death [. . .] Those who suffer the ecstasy of the animals, meaning Death" (126). Taken on its own it would be difficult to read too much into this section of the work, but the references to dogs and animals have a retrospective significance because each symbolically appears in an earlier stretch of narrative dealing either with the incest or with death.

Finally, the novel's overarching ideology is amplified by the suggestion that the blame lies with Marina for breaching the law. This is evident in the way that the siblings' (suspecting) mother directs her antipathy towards Marina and not Lex; in Marina's association with the mermaid, a creature both beguiling and destructive; and in the textual focus on Marina's, rather than Lex's, coming-of-age. Marina is also persistently constructed as an object of desire, as sexualised, and it is she who takes responsibility for what happens between the two of them when she says: "I called you. I wanted a refill on my wine. I wanted to give you the jasmine and the wind chime stars. I'm sorry" (65). Her concession is then reinforced by Lex when his later recall of the incident is couched in the same terms: "[Y]our eyes were still watching me that way, the time I came to you in your crib. Almost as if you had been calling me (100).

Skeletons in the Closet: Homosexuality, Same-Sex Desire, and Death

Perhaps it is fair to say, as Trites claims, that "in Block's novels, ultimately, nothing all that radical really happens" (*Disturbing* 150) because while *Wasteland* has the potential to interrogate orthodox sexual practices and behaviours, on the whole, it merely demonstrates the power of discourse to communicate notions of "normality". Like *Sleeping Dogs* and *Touching Earth Lightly*, it suggests that alternative forms of sexuality are perverse and, thus, to borrow Foucault's words, it constructs a distinct "division between licit and illicit" (*History* 37). Indeed, it is implied by each of these three texts that, regardless of their (sometimes graphic) representations of transgression, the death of the protagonist occurs as the result of a violation of the rules governing sexual experience. A fourth text which positions its audience to make this connection is Charlotte Calder's *Settling Storms*. In this novel, the suicide of Steve Overton, an adolescent male attempting to come to terms with his homosexuality, is presented as senseless—"[j]ust a dumb waste of a life. A sheer, fuckin' waste" (152). However, the secrecy which surrounds his death simultaneously suggests that the event and the circumstances which precipitated it are shameful. For example, neither the reader nor Mel Childs, the girl at the centre of the story who comes to occupy Steve's house after his death, discover the reasons behind his suicide for some time, and it is not until a year after his death that this information is revealed to Phoebe Benbow, one of Steve's closest friends.

The narrative is organised around several strands of events and themes. One of these relates to death, another to sexuality, and a third to family. The motifs of alienation and dislocation are common to all three. Mel, a recent arrival to the tropical town in which the story is set, is positioned as an outsider amongst her new peers and also within her family where the fragile relationship she has with her often absent, "hysterical TV-star" mother, Davina, is slowly disintegrating. Phoebe's need to work through her grief over Steve is hampered by her overbearing mother, Ruth, who would rather she put the past behind her, and also by her inability to recognise that there are other ways of being that do not conform to heterosexual standards. And Steve's alienation is attributed almost solely to his father, a demanding and hyper-macho man who not only sees homosexuals as "filthy poofters", but at the time of Steve's death, was trying to pressure his son into joining the notoriously homophobic armed forces. Trites argues that contemporary adolescent literature is defined by such interactions because YA novels "rely on adolescent protagonists who strive to understand their own power by struggling with the various institutions in their lives"—sexuality, death, school, religion, gender, family (*Disturbing* 8, 20). The outcome of these struggles, of course, has implications for the ideological messages contained within a text. Wilson points out, for example, that constructions of the self in adolescent fiction tend to be based on humanist models that advocate "a belief in an essential self that requires the exercise of one's own agency" (25), while Trites argues that, in order to achieve maturity, characters in YA novels must come to an acceptance of their environment, and the social institutions with shape both it and them (*Disturbing*).

For Steve, attempting to negotiate his way through a minefield of institutionalised sanctions relating to sex and sexuality, the quest for agency ends with his death. His story, although told retrospectively, nevertheless acts as a frame through which Mel and Phoebe's own growth is charted. Phoebe's progress towards understanding the circumstances leading to Steve's suicide is represented as an awakening which occurs because of her friendship with the less parochial Mel. In one episode, where Mel tells her that Seth Jones, the "wickedly babish" star of the television soap opera *Endless Beach*, is gay, she is both incredulous and horrified: "Judging by Pheobe's expression [Mel thinks] I might just as well have said he's a serial axe murderer". "'What a waste . . .'" Phoebe says, to which Mel replies: "'It's only a waste for the girls, Phoebes! Only for the girls!'" (161, 165).[5] By the conclusion, however, Phoebe has been sufficiently schooled by Mel to appreciate that the worth of people is not determined by whether they are "[b]lack or white, tall or short, straight or gay", so that when she becomes aware of Steve's homosexuality her embarrassment and fury at "being about the only one who didn't twig" to Steve's sexual orientation is quickly replaced by sympathy for his predicament (189–90). For Mel, an accident involving her beloved cat, Teapot, is enough to spur her into repairing the fractured relationship she has with Davina. The links between this incident and Steve's death are clear, because it is here that the themes of death and alienation coalesce: Teapot's near-fatal experience forces Mel to recognise that there is no joy in fighting with her mother and that "life is precious" (a prominent ideology in the text). Mel then apologises to Davina for her attitude, and her mother, who is away filming a mini-series, catches the next plane home.

The narrative's insistence upon a closure that brings all of the story elements together in this way discloses its limitations for a number of reasons. For instance, in aligning Steve's isolation and suicide with the Childs's problems, his crisis becomes trivialised. This is made apparent by the uneasy juxtaposition of the episode where Phoebe comes to an understanding of the traumatic events precipitating Steve's death with other episodes involving Teapot's broken leg and the melodramatic reconciliation between Mel and Davina. The effect of Steve's suicide and the discovery of his body—an event which is replayed in the final pages of the text—is also reduced by the resolutions to the girls' stories because both conclusions act to subtly reaffirm parental authority and privilege heterosexual forms of subjectivity. Mel's story is predicated upon a normative heterosexual resolution, demonstrated by her growing romance with Alfie, a friend's brother. Given the novel's concerns with issues of homosexuality and patriarchal power, this is problematic, as is the fact that closure for Mel entails restoring harmony to the (heterosexual) family unit, an institution that was the source of Steve's disempowerment. Phoebe's journey towards alternative ways of seeing and thinking is negated, in the end, by several incidents which suggest that her mother's advice is sound and that it is best to move on and forget the past. The first occurs when Steve's friends decide to hold an informal memorial for him at the reserve where he died. This involves the group "claiming the reserve back again" for themselves and encouraging Phoebe, like Ruth, to "let go of all that" (187). In the second, the girls watch a catamaran capsize. Two figures struggle to right the boat in the fierce wind, but soon after, with "their gazes forward", they are heading out to sea (190–92). An overt nod to the girls' own experiences during the period in which the novel is set (and a link to Steve who loved sailing), it too implies that there is no sense in looking back.

As novels such as *Settling Storms* demonstrate, contemporary adolescent texts which feature same-sex relationships are apt to associate these "alternative" forms of sexuality with pathology or with a crisis in identity. Ray Misson has also pointed out that, more often than not, it is usual for such literature to treat homosexuality as a source of angst (229). In texts where non-heterosexuality is associated with death, the tensions surrounding such representations are particularly clear. The connection between Steve's homosexuality and his suicide is explicit in *Settling Storms*, for instance, while in *Touching Earth Lightly*, Morris Gleitzman's *Two Weeks With the Queen*, Sue Hines's *Out of the Shadows*, and Doug MacLeod's *Tumble Turn*, where the lovers of gay/lesbian characters have died or are dying, it is implied that being homosexual is fraught with danger.[6] Like *Settling Storms*, both *Tumble Turn* and *Out of the Shadows* have a very obvious agenda—to question notions of the normative—yet both nevertheless link being gay/lesbian with secrecy, and construct homosexuality in terms of grief. In the humorous *Tumble Turn* (which is aimed at an audience younger than that of other texts in this chapter) orthodox ideas about sexuality (such as the hetero/homo dichotomy) are questioned in a way that discloses the arbitrariness of (gender) labels and categories.[7] However, Dominic, the text's protagonist, does not learn that his Uncle Peri is gay until he also discovers that Peri's partner, Lex, was killed in a car accident (which occurred while Peri was driving); both the accident and Peri's sexual orientation are presented as a family secret that Dominic pieces together via a series of email communications with his uncle.

Like *Tumble Turn*, which makes a point of how fearful mainstream society is of the "gay label", in *Out of the Shadows* there is also a conscious attempt to dispel entrenched ideas about homosexuality. The text is focalised through Rowanna and Jodie, switching from one to the other so that the narrative is structured as a dialogue between different ideological positions. Rowanna lives with her dead mother's partner, Deb, in a small country town. Both women have moved from the city to escape the bad memories associated with Sara's death, for which Rowanna blames herself. Jodie, the newest arrival in the town, is attempting to start afresh in a place where nobody is aware of her sexual orientation; after being "outed" and then socially isolated at her previous school, she is terrified at the thought of anyone uncovering her secret. The point of reference for the two girls (which they realise much later) is this prejudice. Rowanna's heterosexuality is established immediately; however, so is the torment she suffers as a child when other children draw attention to Sara's relationship with Deb: "'Your mother's dirty. Sick. A sick, dirty lezzo'" (40). Much is made of the discrimination the girls, and other homosexuals, face—from anti-gay sentiments, to stereotyping, to hostility, to outright ostracism. The text attends to an exploration of relationships in which sexual orientation is deemed irrelevant by representing love as "a sort of meeting of the selves and an unquestioning acceptance of those selves" (186). In drawing attention to the fact that lesbian is "just a word, like *curtain* or *automobile*" (47, emphases original), the narrative also exposes the instability of the relationship between sign and thing, and thus perhaps encourages audiences to question the fixedness of apparently elemental categories such as heterosexual and homosexual (Barry).

Nevertheless, there are a number of tensions which mark the representation of lesbian experiences in this novel, and which therefore work against the text's purported aim to deconstruct the hetero/homo hierarchy. As with *Wasteland*, some of these are played out through the theme of secrets. It is clear from the outset that this is a chief concern of the narrative; on the back cover, the synopsis reads: "RO thinks her family is totally unlike anyone else's; JODIE is afraid of herself. So they spend a long time stepping carefully around the TRUTH, hiding SECRETS that they know are too terrible to reveal" (emphases original). These secrets, once divulged, provide a real bond between the girls. However, as the association between the words "too terrible" and "secrets" suggests, the novel's emphasis on keeping "the truth" hidden constructs a negative rhetoric about being gay by representing it as scandalous. The consequences of bringing the skeletons out of the closet are also played out frequently, pointing to the narrative's characteristic twinning of homosexuality with punishment. This is most apparent when readers learn the story behind Rowanna's continuing distress over Sara's death. After her classmates inform Ro about Sara and Deb's sexual relationship (to which she had previously been unaware), Rowanna mounts a campaign against Deb that culminates in an accusation of sexual abuse. This is construed as a betrayal by Sara, and, horrified that her mother would side with her lover and not her child, Rowanna leaves home, only to end up living on the streets. It is illness that forces her back, but when the women reunite, Rowanna apologises for her "disgraceful behaviour" (188). The joyous homecoming is cut short, however, because Sara is killed soon after by a drunk driver when she is out on an errand for Rowanna who is still sick in bed. Thus, although Rowanna's new ways of seeing enable her to begin repairing her relationship with Deb after Sara's death, and then to speak out against homosexual discrimination, the cause and effect message behind this sequence of events is that, one way or another, Sara pays the penalty for her transgression—both as a lesbian and as a "bad" mother.

Given that the narrative deliberately and passionately claims a deep concern for gay and lesbian rights, and that it has a positive closure built around Rowanna's growth and atonement, this is a rather harsh view of Sara's death. As Rowanna declares shortly after the accident: "Stuff the people who were blind to everything outside their own narrow world, who thought love was only legitimate if it followed a certain, prescribed pattern" (195). Yet, I would argue, because this ideology is undermined in several ways by the double-edged treatment of lesbianism in the text, in the end, Sara's accident *can* be seen as a consequence of her atypical behaviour. The narrative's depiction of female sexuality is problematic for this reason. There are many textual moments, for instance, when the politicising of homosexuality is weakened by the tendency to frame the lesbian subject through both orthodox (hetero) and patriarchal forms of representation: Female-to-female relationships in the novel are based on ideas about romantic love and lifelong partnering; gendered identity is essentialised through the text's insistence on constructing subjectivity as fixed; and, for both gay and straight characters, it is suggested at all times that monogamous relationships are preferable to casual sexual encounters. Furthermore, in an overt endeavour to avoid the "dyke stereotype" (30), Jodie is described as "stunning" with "[s]un-streaked, honey-coloured hair", "[p]roper green [eyes]—not hazel", and a "long-limbed slenderness" that hints at her potential to be a "supermodel" (2). Not only a troublesome reminder of the durability of masculinist representations of women within Western discourses, the cumulative effect of depicting female subjectivity (and in particular, lesbian sexuality) in this way is that it reinforces notions of "normal" or appropriate behaviour—ironically by reinscribing the kind of entrenched norms and practices that, on the surface, the narrative seeks to contest.

In fact, the novel's pervasive emphasis on the unusualness of the girls' lives and ways of being only constructs a very definite picture for readers of what "the norm" should be. As Foucault's theories have demonstrated, when so much attention is paid to sex and sexuality, it is difficult not to focus on it, to think about what is approved and what is not (Danaher, Schirato, and Webb 144). Mallan argues that the "makeover" of the lesbian body into a conventional heterosexually attractive form is a homogenising process which represents the attempt to fix lesbian (and gay) characters in stable, recognisable sexual identities. In this way, she argues, the lesbian body is "normalised, made consumable, and by implication, less threatening" ("Feeling" 116). It is in this way, too, that the dangerous sexuality of the lesbian, and the liminal and disturbing aspects of the feminine, are contained. With this in mind—and regardless of whether the normative order is assured or critiqued by the conclusion of the text—Sara's death can be read as an extreme form of implementing closure against the disturbance the (homosexual) feminine causes by eliminating "the barred radically Other" (Bronfen, *Over* 217).

According to Elisabeth Bronfen, there are countless examples in literature and art that illustrate how the death of a woman helps to remove destructive forces from the masculine economy (*Over* 219). As texts like *Out of the Shadows* demonstrate, this argument can be equally applicable to the queer subject. Indeed, the representation of homosexuality in *Touching Earth Lightly* works in similar ways. In a text which is so overtly concerned with depicting transgressive sexualities, the function of the homosexual relationship between the Hunters' friends, Carl and Gus, is ostensibly to emphasise how liberal the family is, and also to communicate ideas about sexual diversity to readers. Carl's presence serves a dual purpose, however, as it is he who assists Chloe to come to terms with Janey's death, having recently suffered a loss himself. Carl is a regular visitor to the open-house Sunday lunches hosted by Dane and Joy, and until his death, Gus is also present at these gatherings. By implication, Gus has died of AIDS. The details of his sickness and death are never revealed, but in a moment of remembering, Chloe recalls him during one of their final outings, "shrunk to almost nothing, his smile ghastly and luminous at the same time, his eyes enormous" (148). This scene echoes an earlier one in which Chloe, struggling to understand Carl's grief, looks at him and wonders "[h]ow can the same face, the same bones and skin, look so radiant one year and so desolate the next?" (126–27). Taken together, these two brief episodes acquire a special significance, not only because they equate homosexuality with pain, but also because, in constructing an image of Carl that so closely resembles that of Gus in the period just before his death, they suggest that perhaps Carl will share the same fate.

As Trites contends, the tendency to construct gay and lesbian experiences in this manner demonstrates the limits of queer discourse at work in adolescent literature, as rather than providing the readers of this genre with transformative experiences, many novelists portray homosexuality in distinctly non-celebratory ways (*Disturbing* 104). Mallan makes a similar claim by arguing that even when narratives about gay/lesbian characters seek to challenge conventional notions of sexuality or are presented as celebratory, they are often "diluted" to secure mainstream acceptance; as a result, she argues, the aberrant often becomes incorporated within the dominant heterosexual framework ("Feeling"). A reading of *Touching Earth Lightly* which approaches Chloe and Janey's relationship in terms of same-sex desire discloses much the same ideas. With its conventional closure that is dependent upon the transferral of Chloe's passion from Janey to Isaac, the text not only illustrates the pervasiveness of the heterosexual romance model, it also suggests that "being female is to fit within social and ideological structures created and sustained by masculine desires" (Bradford, "Embodied" 115). Kate McInally argues that the novel clearly specifies that Isaac, rather than Janey, affords Chloe healthy psychosexual resolution, and that, like other texts featuring desire between young female characters, it too can be seen to represent girls' passions for each other as merely a stage in the journey towards attaining a (fixed) heterosexual identity ("Reading"). That the text's romantic outcome involves Janey's death perhaps says something about the threat that female-to-female desire poses to patriarchy as well, for in killing Janey off and representing Isaac as "the corrective to all [her] flaws", the conclusion to the narrative locates the female subject firmly within phallocentric systems of representation (Bradford, "Embodied" 115–16).

The violence and absoluteness of Janey's death, and the connection between it and her aberrant sexual behaviour, makes it difficult to construct a reading of *Touching Earth Lightly* that is not grounded in patriarchal ways of seeing and thinking. Nevertheless, as I, and others such as Bradford ("Embodied") and Wilson, have argued, there are many moments where the text does attend to resisting male universal norms by encouraging readers to resist dominant ideas about female sexuality. These disruptions and contradictions are noticeable, for instance, in passages where Janey questions the notion of romantic sex, either with her behaviour or her words, where Janey's courage and curiosity is privileged over Chloe's docility and timidity, and where the girls' relationship is shown to be of paramount importance. The latter occurs regularly in the narrative, demonstrating the power of the bonds that bind Chloe and Janey to each other: Chloe chooses Janey over her lover, Theo; the girls hug and laugh about jealous boys who feel excluded by their intimacy; and Chloe articulates her feelings for Janey in words that entirely transcend all others she uses to describe her relationships: "[I]t isn't something she thinks about any more than a magnet thinks about snapping onto the fridge—it's not a matter of discussion or agreement that keeps them together, but an unquestioning force" (148). In McInally's analysis of the text, these points of intense connection between the girls can be seen to coalesce into an image of "the positivity and possibilities of girls' desires for each other". With its refusal to align desire with dominant definitions of what constitutes a sexual relationship, and to engage with a conventional linear reading that prioritises closure, she argues, this "rhizomic" reading of the text works to resist patriarchal maturational models of subjectivity ("Reading"). Under these terms, Chloe and Janey's close and passionate relationship is a celebration of female desire, and Janey's death can be viewed not as the event that forces the girls apart, but the one that draws them permanently together. This is clearly evident when Chloe visits the crematorium garden where Janey's ashes are scattered. In this episode, readers are positioned to accept growth (even amidst death) as a positive value because there is sense of optimism pervading the scene, signalled by the emphasis on closure for Chloe, by the acknowledgment that the girls will always be bound together, and by the association between death, jonquils, and humour:

> But sitting alone here, she doesn't feel any urge to speak aloud, to whatever is left of Janey here, whatever hasn't blown away in the smoke. What's left that isn't jonquils, it seems to Chloe, is scattered through Chloe's life, and Chloe's family's, as comprehensively as a Kleenex through a load of

washing. It's just there, in their bones and brains and speech patterns, built into their sense of humour and each of their separate histories. (208)

Everything I Need to Know About Love and Death: Mortality, Gendered Subjectivity, and Growth

Of the texts available to adolescents that represent subjectivities in dialogue with the processes of death, dying, and grief, there are a number which frame mortality through themes of growth. In such narratives, what the protagonist/s learn about death often has implications for how they formulate and perceive their own sense of (gendered) self (this trend is clearly articulated in both *Settling Storms* and *Touching Earth Lightly*, for example). The narratives of such texts use death as a catalyst with which to alter protagonists' perspectives— their ways of looking at, and being in, the world, and, most importantly, their ways of conducting gendered lives. While this process may not always be a conscious operation, nor appear as an element of story, it tends to be inscribed in the narrative in two ways. In the first, where growth is represented as a "becoming" (that is, in terms of the subject's nascent sexuality), experiences of both death and adolescence are rites of passage that occur simultaneously. This pattern is present in *Painted Love Letters*, Gary Crew's *Angel's Gate*[8], Jenny Downham's *Before I Die*, Scott Gardner's *Burning Eddy*, Jane Godwin's *The Family Tree*[9], John Green's *Looking for Alaska*, Alison Stewart's *The Memory Shell*, and Sarah Walker's *Water Colours*. Secondly, growth is evoked as a "regendering" of the subject, as in Moses Aaron's *Elijah Greenface*, Alyssa Brugman's *Walking Naked*, Archimede Fusillo's *Sparring With Shadows*, Phillip Gwynne's *Deadly Unna?*, David Metzenthen's *Gilbert's Ghost Train* (which I briefly referred to in Chapter 2), and Celeste Walters's *The Glass Mountain*. Here, the experience of death induces a crisis in the subject's feminine or masculine self-concept, meaning that the trajectory of growth that the narrative offers for its protagonist involves a reconstruction of a particular way of being female or male.

The novels which follow the patterning that is characteristic of the first group of texts are inclined to feature female protagonists, although the extent to which they seek to alter adolescent girls' behaviours and practices ranges from the subtle to the overt. *The Memory Shell*, an example of the latter, represents a very obvious attempt to influence female ways of being, for instance, because it uses the concept of danger to coerce its protagonist, Hannah (and thus, potentially, its reader), into choosing a path that is quite different to the one which led to her sister's death. The narrative follows Hannah as she approaches the age of fifteen, the point at which her older sister, Sally, died in a drink-driving accident, and the point at which Hannah worries that "death [will] come for her too" (85). The novel's concerns with constructions of the feminine are focused upon Hannah and her quest for autonomy; however,

Hannah's choices as a gendered subject are limited to two polarised versions of femininity, one of which is privileged to such an extent that the very idea of "agency" takes on a hollow meaning. Stewart's strategy for advocating one way of being female over another is to construct a cause-and-effect sequence of events for the female characters which leaves them punished for their crimes. This is played out firstly by suggesting that there is a link between bad behaviour and "bad looks"; various references to physical appearance associate party girls Maz, Lily, and Ashlyn, with pimples, a "big nose", a "fat bum", and "wild hair", while good girl Lauren is "pretty", and Hannah is thin with the stereotypical blonde hair, blue eyes, and ample bust. The second way that the cause-and-effect strategy functions is by implying that there are consequences for wild behaviour; getting drunk, taking drugs, and going out without parental permission results in punishments that include a car accident, hospitalisation, and a near sexual assault. As with many adolescent fictions, growing up for Hannah is thus framed through notions of responsibility, and this largely involves a choice between the "right" and "wrong" type of friend. One of the rewards for the correct choice is a romantic relationship with a sensitive and caring boy; another is that Hannah is able to "think of her sister without crying, without imagining the violence of the accident, without seeing Sally's pale, dead face" (185). The crime and punishment theme can also be demonstrated by connecting images from two separate episodes. In the first, which occurs during the period Hannah rebels against her parents' strict regulations and rules—against "paying for Sally" (19)—she must struggle to banish from her thoughts "the Sally who lay crushed by the side of the road with her life oozed out of her" (149). The second occurs at the conclusion to the novel, once Hannah has fallen into line. Here, her "crushing terror [has] departed", and the "dark place inside [has] gone" because "light [has] come, so bright and pure, it [extends] all the way to the horizon and beyond" (178).

Like *The Memory Shell*, *The Family Tree* also defines becoming within a very narrow set of parameters. Here, the theme of death functions to signify transformation or change—in particular, the changes that adolescence brings—because one narrative strand which deals with the text's pre-adolescent protagonist, Harry, coming to terms with her father's death is closely connected to another which details her emerging sexuality. Although the death occurs when she is a small child, Harry's continuing identification with her father is represented as a source of confusion in the novel. The narrative states, for example, that Harry "look[s] like a boy" (1) and is often mistaken for one since she has her "dad's eyes, his chin and his smile and his cheekbones" (5). Unlike her sister, Annaliese, whose shiny, "long dark hair [looks] like something from a shampoo commercial" (7), Harry's "straight, brown hair [is] always cut short", and she doesn't "own one dress" (15). However, as Harry begins to reach an understanding about her father's death, and to experience other changes at school and within her family (thus beginning the developmental move from solipsism to maturing social and self awareness—

towards agency), not only does she accept that it is "not [her] responsibility to be" her father (140), she becomes "Harriet" instead. The conclusion to the narrative focuses upon a number of episodes which suggest that, through her experience of death, Harry/Harriet has been inducted into a particular way of being female. In the final chapter, the family moves into a new house, and Harry/Harriet effectively lays her father to rest, begins to grow her hair, and receives a hairbrush as a gift from her new stepfather. She also assumes her new persona by telling the neighbour: "'I'm Harriet [. . .] It's a girl's name [. . .] And it's mine'" (148).

The version of femininity that is advocated in *The Family Tree* is an orthodox and patriarchal one, perhaps because this process of gendering is played out in the context of the (step)father/daughter relationship. The narrative also implies, like that of *The Memory Shell*'s, that there are very few subject positions available to the maturing adolescent girl that are not influenced by male-derived paradigms. In *Painted Love Letters*, which also tells of a young girl's experience of her father's death, there are a number of points at which the narrative appears to resist the stereotypes associated with such psychosexual models of development, yet it too produces a similar outcome. In the author's own words, the novel is "a map charting one man's journey into death, showing the ways his closest companions took to be with him" (Bateson 13). The narrative, which traces artist Dave Grainger's final months, from his lung cancer diagnosis to his death, is focalised through his daughter, Chrissie. It is structured as a series of exchanges and interactions between Chrissie, her family, her friends, and her teachers, each of which adds to her understanding of Dave's illness and impending death. Dave's idiosyncratic approach to his death is signalled by the way he includes Chrissie in the preparations for it, asking her to record his preferences for body disposal, for the wake, and for the funeral; involves her in the decoration of his home-made coffin; and encourages her to participate in discussions about the dying process. Significantly, however, this period in Chrissie's life occurs at the same time that she is beginning to formulate a sense of herself as a sexual subject, meaning that what she learns about death is also framed through her notions of what it means to be female.

A clear example of the intersection between these two themes occurs in an episode where Chrissie has decided she needs new clothes because she has grown out of her old ones. By this point, Dave is ill enough that he spends most of his time lying on the couch, "slowly dying" (25). However, he summons up the energy to take Chrissie on a "shopping date" after they have the following conversation:

'Oh Dad, look at me! Can't you see? My overalls are too short, this top rides up all the time and I need a bra.' I stuck my chest out at him and waited for him to laugh. He looked me up and down and nodded slowly.

'Yes, you're right Chrissie. You're growing up fast. So, do you have any ideas about these new clothes?'

'Not overalls,' I said quickly [. . .] 'I want a skirt, a leather skirt. A short leather skirt. And a top with laces and big floppy sleeves. And sandals. Sandals with a little heel.' (32)

Chrissie's choices are heavily influenced by her friend, Dee, who has already been socialised into a discourse of femininity within which females are objects of sexual desire. These ideologies appear somewhat at odds with the unorthodox values that Bateson has assigned to the Grainger family, yet when Dave takes Chrissie out to buy the new clothes, the trip becomes something of a rite-of-passage during which Chrissie is inducted into way of being female that is similar to that of Dee's. Chrissie undergoes a makeover during their outing which symbolically transforms her from girl to woman as Dave styles her hair, chooses her a long, almost formal dress to wear at his forthcoming exhibition (the event which, it is suggested, is "keeping him going" and thus delaying his death), and makes her "parade in front of him as though [she is] a model" (34–35).[10] Throughout this episode, readers are encouraged to align themselves with a masculinist and normative view of the female body. Chrissie is unaware that she is being objectified and commodified by a process which signals to her that "sometime in the future [she'd] be nearly as pretty as her mother" (38), Rhetta, and there is no narrative strategy that enables an audience to recognise this. Indeed, Rhetta appears to collude with this version of the feminine when, observing Chrissie that evening doing her "catwalk strut" and modelling the new clothes, she agrees that "the dress [is] beautiful, very beautiful" and that Chrissie looks "very grown up in it" (37). When Chrissie and Dave leave the shops, the rite-of-passage motif surfaces again in an incident that, at times, becomes erotically-charged. It occurs when the pair go out to lunch and Chrissie samples oysters for the first time. "'[T]here's a time in every person's life when they have to eat oysters,'" Dave tells her. "'Long ago I promised myself I'd introduce you to your first [one] and now is the time'" (36).

The metonymic significance of these episodes is also demonstrated by a similar incident during which Chrissie's increasing fears about Dave's illness are given form. After a history lesson about a missionary priest in Hawai'i who gives aid to sufferers of leprosy, Chrissie imagines that she too is dying of the disease and begins to wear a glove to cover the "hardening skin and give-away red dot" on her hand (64). The symbolic meaning of the "white, lady-like glove" is suggested by Dave, when, after a tussle with Chrissie, he peels it off, examines her hand like it is "a small sick animal", and exclaims: "'Nice fingernails [. . .] they certainly have grown under [there]'" (66, 68–69). Fingernails function here as hair does in *The Family Tree*—that is, as a metonym for womanhood—and this moment suggests the extent to which Chrissie has grown up, particularly when juxtaposed with an earlier one in which she would rather play on a trampoline than have Dee paint her fingernails (29). I would argue that this episode is problematic for two reasons, however, both of which centre upon the notion of becoming. The first is related to Chrissie's horror at the "terrible" goings-on that are occurring under the glove because, until the point at which Dave makes her remove it, she refuses to take the glove off, imagining that she "might speed up the rotting process" that is "spreading from [her] left palm to the tips of [her] fingers (66). If, as I have argued, the removal of the glove is symbolic of Chrissie's transformation from girl into woman, then this episode can also be read to suggest that the processes involved in female sexual development are abject (especially as it is accompanied by graphic descriptions of disease and decay). The second concerns the narrative's representation of womanhood as a stable point at which to "arrive" at. This incident is just one amongst several in the novel that implies that, rather than being subject to constant transformation, there is an endpoint to the process of developing a gendered identity. Admittedly, it is suggested that Chrissie's growth continues after Dave's death; however, I think the idea that becoming can occur indefinitely is undermined, on the whole, by these small moments, and also by the narrative's closing lines which see Chrissie declaring: "I knew everything now about love and death, everything I needed to know" (93).[11]

The final text I want to consider in which growth is represented in terms of sexual development is *Before I Die*. As with *The Family Tree* and *Painted Love Letters*, the narrative of *Before I Die* is largely framed through a father/daughter relationship. The journey of its protagonist, Tessa Scott, is similar to that of Chrissie in that it traces the familiar adolescent path from innocence to experience (one that I will explore in more detail in Chapter 4). However, at the same time, it differs dramatically because Tessa is one of only a few characters I have discovered in the course of my reading who acts as a focaliser but also dies.[12] The narrative therefore acquires a particular poignancy and meaningfulness that, needless to say, is far more difficult to articulate in books which document the deaths of others. Given the uncompromising title of the novel and the fact that readers are cued from the beginning of the narrative to expect that there will be no miracle cure, no last minute reprieve for Tess, this strategy also lends the ideologies of the text an unusual gravity.

At twelve, Tess is diagnosed with leukaemia. By the time she is sixteen, the hospital has "officially [given] up" on her and she has moved so much "further along the line" that she has only a few months to live (47, 53). Armed with this knowledge, and determined to "live properly" before she dies, Tess makes a list of everything she hopes to achieve in the limited time she has left. First on the list is sex: "I want to feel the weight of a boy on top of me", she writes (1). Typical teen transgressions and desires follow (to try drugs, break the law, drive without a licence), but with one difference; as Tess's friend, Zoey, tells her: "'There are no consequences for someone like you!'" (10). If death is the ultimate outcome of risky behaviour (as is clearly articulated in texts such as *The Memory Shell*), then these boundaries have become confused and somewhat irrelevant here because the novel essentially questions what it means for the adolescent subject to operate without such constraints and limitations. For Tessa's father, who objects to her sudden unruly behaviour, it is not so much that he wishes to keep her safe, but that she is "giving the best of [herself] away". "'To be left out of that'", he tells Tess, "'hurts so much'" (80–81). This conversation signals the narrative's preoccupation with female sexual development, and with growth towards self-conscious subjectivity, for it is suggested that, in order for Tess to grow up before she dies, she must, like other characters in adolescent fiction, learn what portion of power she wields "because of and despite such biological imperatives as sex and death" (Trites, *Disturbing* x). It also implies that the authority Tess will need to negotiate with to reach such a goal is patriarchal in nature, and this is made abundantly clear when she reacts to the worry and pain in her father's voice by thinking: "I don't want to spend the rest of my life huddled in a blanket on the sofa with my head on Dad's shoulder" (81).

In psychosexual developmental terms, the exchange marks the point at which Tess's desire will be displaced from her father and onto other males. The ways in which this transference is played out thus has implications for the kind of feminine subjectivity that the narrative constructs for her. Tess's transgressions, her refusal to co-operate with her father's notion of what constitutes acceptable "dying behaviour", and her dislike of the way he "pulls authority, as if it's all sorted because he says so" (228–29), suggests that audiences may be offered a critical feminist position from which to read the text. Yet, in truth, readers are given few opportunities with which to interrogate the gender ideologies promoted by the novel, and there are limited choices made available to Tess in terms of her becoming. Essentially, there are three versions of femininity on offer to her: Either she can look to the free-spirited, unorthodox model represented by her mother; she can choose to be wild and sexually adventurous like Zoey, the only girl at school who is not afraid of Tess's impending death; or she can follow the familiar patriarchal path to maturation in which romantic love is privileged over unconstrained desire and happiness is equated with (hetero)sexual monogamy. It is evident very early in the novel, however, that neither Tess's mother nor Zoey embody appropriate female ways of being. In contrast to her father, Tess's mother is represented as irresponsible, impractical, and flighty since she leaves her family for a nomadic existence with another man (with respect to the psychosexual gender dynamics of the narrative, this is a pivotal event because it coincides with the diagnosis of Tess's disease at puberty). Her inability to cope well with Tess's illness and her slipshod housekeeping also constructs a view of the maternal feminine that is at odds with the mothering objectives of patriarchy. Zoey is constructed pejoratively too; from her "very blonde" hair and savage-looking acne, to the way she wears a skirt that "only just covers her bum", to her casual approach to sex, she is depicted as the antithesis of a suitable role model for Tess (8, 59).

During Tess's rebellious stage (that is, before the desire to transgress is replaced by a longing to fall in love), she nevertheless tries out Zoey's way of being female. After enlisting her friend to help her lose her virginity, the pair hatch a plan to go out dancing and "find some boys to have sex with" (8). Tess's quest for identity is symbolised at this time by her willingness to be made over in Zoey's image. The end result, which sees her "glitter" a little like Zoey, and even smell like her as she puts on Zoey's soft, clingy, red dress, means that she does not quite recognise herself: "When I look at myself in the mirror, it's great how different I look—big-eyed and dangerous [...] Even my hair looks good, dramatically shaved rather than only just growing" (7–8). Stephens argues that makeovers in teen fictions are either transformative or cautionary; they demonstrate to the character concerned that she can "transform her life and thus realize her full potential", or else they constitute a "wrong movement" which comes to be identified as such later in the narrative ("Constructions" 6). For Tess, the exercise implies the latter. The makeover causes her to feel excited, "as if anything is possible" (7), and thus it foregrounds the performative aspect of gendered identity while simultaneously suggesting to readers that, even in the face of death, Tess has begun a process of awakening. However, once the night is over, she feels lonely, constantly on the verge of tears, and baffled by her choices. The same clothes become "unfamiliar shadows scattered on the floor", and the red dress "seems smaller than ever" as she tries to pull it down to cover her knees (26). A scene in the toilets of the club where the girls have gone to dance reinforces this idea. Here, Zoey responds to Tess's apprehension about the two boys they have just met by angrily asking her: "'[D]o you want to have sex or not?'". Tess is more concerned what the girl at the sink next to them makes of the exchange: "I'm not what she thinks. I'm very nice really", she worries to herself (15). "'I want it to be perfect'", she tells Zoey. "'If I have sex with a boy I don't even know, what does that make me? A slag?'" (15–16).

The message that is constructed by these episodes is very obvious; to use Harris's phrase, they act as "a kind of *Struwwelpeter*" for nicely brought up young girls (44). The burning of the "dangerous dress" (48), coupled with Zoey's unplanned pregnancy (which the narrative implies is a consequence of the girls' night out) then adds heavy-handed emphasis to the warning. Thus, although the makeover initially implies that the character of Tess is not yet interpellated within a particular feminine schema, because the experiment has such negative results, and because it functions to affirm her "authentic and essential self", to return her to "a 'natural' [...] subjectivity" (Stephens, "Constructions" 7), in the end, it merely emphasises how little capacity there is for the character to shape a gendered identity that is not based on the normative model. The introduction of Adam at this point, the boy that the narrative constructs as a suitable male partner for Tess, is therefore a defining moment in the story. Unsurprisingly, there are parallels between Adam and

Tess's father. Both are safe, calm, sensible, and protective; Adam lives next door in a mirror-image of the Scott house; and, unlike Jake, Tess's one-night-stand, Adam is the kind of boy with whom she can share childhood memories of her father. He is also emotionally brave, committed, and thinks Tess is "gorgeous" even when she believes she is "ugly and useless" (260). In short, Adam embodies all of the ideals of romantic love.

According to Sandra Taylor, romantic ideology (and the ideologies of marriage and motherhood to which it is linked) is "a key gender ideology implicated in the reproduction of patriarchal gender relations". The meanings associated with romantic love function "to lead women into dependency", she argues, and to "their apparent compliance with their own subordination" (128). In addition to rewarding Tess with an exemplary romantic lover, one of the ways in which the text works to valorise romantic outcomes is through the aforementioned list. As Tess negotiates the transition from childhood to adulthood, the items on the ever-expanding list reflect her growth into maturity so that stock-standard teen desires to flout rules are replaced by simple but profound needs to drink a cup of tea (283), or "to hold [her] brother as dusk settles on the window ledge" (288). Mixed in with the experiences she wishes to achieve before she dies, however, are those she knows that, due to the limited time left to her, will not be realised: getting married to Adam, having children together, sharing a bank account, "singing in the bath with him", and "listening to him snore for years and years" (234).

Another way that the novel draws on such desires and dreams (that is, the kind of romantic but phallocentric fantasies that work to socialise girls into conventional female roles) is by creating a striking contrast between Tessa's sexual experiences with Jake and Adam. During the encounter with Jake, she lies passively underneath him, feeling "mostly silent and small" (25). However, sex with Adam is entirely different: "I didn't know it would feel like this [she thinks]. I didn't understand that when you make love, you actually do *make* love" (212, emphasis original). For Tess, and thus potentially for readers who have aligned themselves with her perspective, sex therefore becomes not "just a way of being with someone", of "keeping warm and feeling attractive" as Zoey believes (33), but a "gift" (212). This is emphasised in a later episode where Tess is thinking of the times in her life when she has known that she is happy in a conscious way. The first occurs when, as a child, she is lying on the grass, holding hands with her best friend, eagerly anticipating the school fair and her mother's promise to buy her a jewellery box. Kissing Adam replaces this as "the best moment of [her] life", and then "making love replace[s] that" (227). There is a particular emphasis in the novel on "moments"; the narrative is interspersed with tiny but evocative episodes—a leaf caught by a gust, a fork whisking against a bowl, cuttlefish washed up on a beach. In the end, these brief periods of time become all that Tess's life is made up of: "Moments [. . .] all gathering towards [the final] one" (327). The passage is therefore a significant one in terms of the ideological thrust of the narrative, not least because it works to suggest that the pleasure and happiness associated with female friendships can be no match for the joys and desires afforded by the romantic, heterosexual relationship.

As the episodes I have discussed so far demonstrate, there a number of messages for young women that can be drawn from such romantic discourses, and these are contained in the self-other interactions that the text sets up for Tess: It is best not to get involved with a boy who doesn't love you; monogamous, romantic sex is preferable to casual encounters; safety and stability afford the teen girl happiness; and nothing should be more important to a mother than her own child. The text's representation of becoming is not quite as straightforward as this reading implies, however, since at times it is complex and imbued with contradictions and tensions. There are many points in the narrative, for example, where Tess is clearly not the perfect sex object promoted by patriarchal models of femininity. On one occasion, when she sees Jake for the first time since their night together, she recognises the fear and pity in his eyes: "He shagged a dying girl and now he's afraid I might be contagious; my illness brushed his shoulder and may lie in wait for him" (65). At another point, she describes herself as "half-robot, with plastic and metal embedded under [her] skin" (106), and as "a pile of bones covered in cling film" (260). These textual moments are then contrasted with others in which she focuses on the particular curve "where [her] spine meets [her] bum" (233), or where Adam "licks the run of her heels" (277) and "gently cups [her] breast through [her] pyjamas" (262). Thus, although such descriptions still operate to establish Woman as the object of the male gaze, as sexual object, they also build up a picture, to borrow Mikhail Bakhtin's phrase, of a "contradictory world of becoming" (149).

Similar grotesque and beautiful, decaying and fertile images are scattered throughout the narrative: Tess imagines that "[e]verything feels volatile" (249), that the sky is "full of something, the clouds low down and expectant" (230); the garden smells "moist and secretive" (241); and Zoey's baby spins a lazy somersault, moving inside her for the first time (247). In the hours before her death, Tess can also "smell [herself] farting" (317), and feel that she has been "dying all [her] life" (316). And when she clutches at a memory to stave off her fear, she focuses on "Adam's hot breath between [her] legs" (318). In this way, the process of death is represented as cyclical rather than linear, and in a manner that recalls the Bakhtinian concept of death, where death is never in isolation from birth, or from the indecencies and scatological aspects of the organic framework of thought to which it belongs. These ideas are summed up nicely by two further episodes; one where Tess desires "to be [the] baby deep inside" Zoey (290); and the second, where she is thinking about her impending death:

> I want to be buried right here under this tree. Its roots will reach into the soft mess of my body and suck me dry. I'll be reformed as apple blossom. I'll drift down in the spring like confetti and cling to my family's shoes.

[Then in] the summer they'll eat me. Adam will climb over the fence to steal me, maddened by my scent, my roundness, the shine and health of me. He'll get his mum to cook me up in a crumble or a strudel and then he'll gorge on me. (205)

Such passages provide an interesting counterpoint to the ones I discussed in *Painted Love Letters* because, even though the novel concludes with Tess's death, they are far more effective in establishing the idea of becoming within the narrative. Rather than the closed ending offered by the Bateson text, *Before I Die* therefore ends with the sense that "anything could happen next" (a notion that is first alluded to during Tess's makeover). If adolescent fiction is often used as an ideological tool to supress teenagers' sexual desire, and if it portrays sexuality more often than not in terms of displeasure rather than pleasure (Trites, *Disturbing* 85, 116), then the novel is, furthermore, also notable for its celebration of (female) sexual pleasure. And yet in spite of such textual aporias—and regardless of the narrative's frequent stress on irresponsible and improper behaviour—it is clear that it works as well to channel sexual desire and ways of being female into culturally approved and thus normative forms. To be blunt, Tess's death occurs at just the point in her development where she has come to an acceptance of patriarchal cultural law, and therefore her demise can be seen as a means to stabilising and taming the female body. The same may be said of Zoey who is similarly fixed into the kind of subject position that is advocated by dominant discourses of (hetero)sexuality. By the conclusion, Zoey has become a happier, softer version of the hard-edged, glittery self she was prior to her pregnancy. In itself, this is not problematic, but the later scenes featuring her character—one depicts her hand-sewing a baby suit, her blonde hair "piled high, her neck at a tender angle" (290)—not only invoke traditional ideas about femininity, but also draw on patriarchal myths which view female sexuality as antithetical to motherhood, and maternity as a joyful state that women should "naturally" aspire to. In this sense, the novel participates in what Trites calls the "paradox of authority" that is at play in much YA fiction because while it employs the sexual potency motif as a metaphor for empowerment, it also suggests that the adolescent subject must "accept a certain amount of repression as a cultural imperative" (*Disturbing* 55, 84). Indeed, this theme is encapsulated in Tessa's own words when she declares just prior to her death: "I was outrageous. Wanting, wanting so much" (307).

In the second group of texts that I referred to earlier, characters undergo a "regendering" process. Here, it is masculinity rather than femininity that is inclined to be the focus of the narrative. In *Elijah Greenface, Deadly Unna?*, and *The Glass Mountain*, for example, death tends to work as a marker of the transition between one model of masculinity and another because, although the protagonists' masculine self-concept has already been disrupted to some extent by other social factors and influences, death is the defining event which, to use Rolf Romøren and John Stephens's term, puts "masculinity under pressure" and stimulates them to choose an alternative way of being male (221). Significantly, this reconstruction is apt to encompass a shift from a traditional, hegemonic form to an alternative mode, a narrative strategy that, it has been suggested, is characteristic of contemporary adolescent fictions which are concerned with masculinity (Romøren and Stephens). In the case of *Deadly Unna?*'s Gary "Blacky" Black, the crisis is precipitated by the death of his Aboriginal friend, Dumby Red, who is killed during an attempted armed robbery at the local pub. The death of Dumby Red (and the racist incidents which follow it) effectively force Blacky to examine the culture of the small coastal town in which he lives—a culture which is heavily influenced by its often violent and misogynistic male inhabitants. Blacky's masculinity is then defined, as Romøren and Stephens argue, by the set of choices he must make: to obey his brutal, domineering father and work on the family fishing boat; to attend a farewell barbecue for Cathy, the beautiful, middle-class summer visitor he is attracted to; or to attend Dumby Red's funeral (229–30). Blacky's choice to take the long, hot walk to the funeral is a difficult one because it involves possible violence on both sides. A potentially hostile reception awaits him out at the Point Aboriginal Reserve, and his father's reaction to such blatant disobedience is encapsulated by Blacky when, thinking about his options, he comes to the following conclusion: "If I didn't go out fishing with the old man, he'd kill me. I'm not joking, he'd spiflicate me" (213–14). Blacky's choice signals his desire not only to embrace an alternative to the hegemonic model of gendered subjectivity represented by his father, but also to engage with a culture that is Other to the ethnocentric one that has shaped him until this time.

Although the use of a first-person narrative positions readers to identify with Blacky, and thus to view Aboriginality through the eyes of a male character for whom Anglo-Australian culture is normative, the text nonetheless works to "contest norms of race and gender that stand in the way of relations between Aboriginal and white people" (Bradford, *Reading* 102). A telling example of Blacky's move away from the racist masculinity associated with the Port occurs at the funeral when a number of incidents in which he becomes "Other to the normative group" jostle against moments where he makes a connection between his own home and that of Dumby Red's (Bradford, *Reading* 205). In one, Blacky sits on the sofa only to find that his "bum [sinks] right down, almost to the floor". "The springs [are] busted", he realises, "just like our sofa at home. Probably for the same reason too. Kids jumping up and down on it, pretending it was like a trampoline" (231). Here, as elsewhere, to use Bradford's words, "the narrative infers that Blacky's self discovery is contingent upon his willingness to understand and empathise with another" (*Reading* 203). This idea is also symbolically encoded in the scene in which Blacky joins other mourners to file past Dumby's casket: "I opened my eyes [and the] first thing I noticed was the inside of the coffin. It was purple, like my tie" (227).

This is not to say that *Deadly Unna?*'s representation of death and its impact on the choices available to Blacky as a gendered subject is unproblematic, however. This same incident can be seen to throw into stark relief the difference between the boys by subjecting the dead Aboriginal body to the (surviving) white male gaze, and thus by bringing into play a set of hierarchical binary oppositions between dead/black/Other/feminine and living/white/norm/masculine. These dynamics of power are also evident in the way that Blacky stands over the coffin, running the back of his finger along it as he describes the physical appearance of Dumby's corpse. The textual focus on Blacky's alternating fascination and dread as he sees Dumby's grave and his dead body only adds to this uneasiness because, although there is little doubt that the scene is intended to invite an empathic response, its treatment of death is quite different, for example, to that of Meme McDonald and Boori Monty Pryor's *The Binna Binna Man*, a text which is situated wholly within Aboriginal culture.[13] Here, it is not the physical details of the suicide of Sister Girl that are the focus, but rather the effect that her death has on the community.[14] Unlike Blacky, for whom the grave and the burial gives him "the creeps" (227), for Sister Girl's cousin, the male narrator of the narrative, the earth around the grave "smells warm like home" (50). The gathering of the extended family for the funeral in *The Binna Binna Man* is also represented, all at the same time, in terms of comedy (such as when Auntie Lill falls into the grave), sorrow, and happiness. The funeral is a source of pain and despair for both the narrator and the whole clan; however, it also becomes a source from which to draw strength as well:

> [My Yarrie popeye] knocks three times on Sister Girl's coffin and talks to her spirit in language. Two of my cus's are there painted-up, too. They dance, bare feet stamping into that wood floor. The sound of those clap sticks scares off the bad spirits. Tears come rolling down m'face. Then they carry her out. I feel happy my people are strong. Stronger even than dying.
> [. . .] Those strong fullas, my cus's, take turns carrying her. I watch that coffin rock from side to side, like a boat. Looks like she's floating out across an ocean. That ocean's all of us. (50)

The movement that is encapsulated in this passage contrasts starkly with the funeral scenes in *Deadly Unna?* which, in comparison, seem static and overlaid with a sense of hopelessness. The point at which Blacky becomes angry because Dumby's body has been dressed incorrectly (that is, in such a way that he is not recognizable as "himself"), is a good example. Although no-one else mentions it, Blacky is horrified that Dumby's hair is "wrong", that he is wearing a suit and tie, and that he is missing his customary basketball boots: "Typical", he muses—"just because you're dead they think they can do what they like" (227). Within this scheme, Dumby is represented, like so many

Indigenous people before him, as the powerless victim of a white regime, in need of a white other to champion his rights.

A further limitation regarding *Deadly Unna?*'s depiction of cross-cultural relations as they relate to masculine subjectivity is evident in the way that the narrative implies that Blacky's growth as a subject is dependent upon Dumby's death. Dumby's death can be seen to function as a narrative device that helps to affirm Blacky's subjectivity because it represents the entry-point for Blacky into the Aboriginal community at the Reserve, and also cements his friendship with Dumby's sister, Clarence (their tentative friendship is developed into a romantic and sexual relationship in *Nukkin Ya*, the sequel to *Deadly Unna?*). As Kate Herd argues, "Blacky is able to complete his transition into subjectivity [not only] in the *absence* of his friend [but] also *because* of Dumby's death" (25, emphasis added). Blacky's development as an individual is a "one-sided quest for white subjectivity", Herd contends; the narrative does not allow Dumby any capacity for "self-representation, disclosure and discovery", and Dumby is constructed as the stable cultural Other against which the white self (as represented by the focaliser Blacky) can "learn to read his own culture and thus, himself" (21, 24, 25). The unequal distribution of power that is created by such a strategy is summed up by Herd when she argues that "Dumby can be considered to be a character who is ultimately literalised in the sense that he becomes that which the racist members of the town would have him become—a dead Aboriginal teenage male" (24–25).

According to Stephens, aesthetic completeness is achieved in children's literature through "representations of symmetries or movements from states of lack to states of plenitude" (*Language* 42). As *Deadly Unna?* demonstrates, this movement can become a problematic feature of a narrative when it suggests that subjective development is dependent not only on the death of an/other, but also an/other who is in some way less privileged in terms of social or personal power. A similar situation is presented in *Walking Naked* which, unlike many of the other texts in this group, is predominantly a story about girls rather than boys. The concern with interrogating the performance of gendered practices is played out here through a conflict between characters who represent different models of femininity. The narrative, which is set largely within a high-school, is focalised through Megan, one of the leaders of the bitchy and self-centred "in-group". It tells of Megan's tenuous and uneasy almost-friendship with Perdita, a girl with a vastly different perspective to her own. Perdita is branded as the school "freak"; this label, coupled with Megan's description of her, positions readers very early in the narrative to view her as abject. From the mocking pronunciation of her name—"*Purdeetah Wigweegan*" (4, emphasis original)—to the references about her ungraceful physical appearance—"she walked [. . .] hunkered down with her shoulders stooped and her chin forward [and she] took long clomping strides like a man" (4)—to her reputation, she is represented as a socially alienated Other:

I heard that she was part of a cult, that she was a witch.

[. . .] I heard that she smelt. I heard that she didn't wash or brush her hair and that once someone had seen a tiny cockroach scuttle down behind her left ear and then disappear again in the hair at the nape of her neck. (8)

The discrepancy between the girls' subject positions is also signalled by the differences in their home-life. Megan is the only daughter of educated, middle-class, and loving parents; by contrast, Perdita's parents have a physically abusive relationship, and although Perdita lives in the family home, she is largely estranged from them.

Perdita commits suicide not long after an incident in which she is cruelly and publicly rejected by Megan, whose friends have delivered her an ultimatum: "'You can't be friends with the Freak and friends with us. You will have to choose'" (150). By this point, audiences have been cued to expect Perdita's death, not only because she is denied a subject position within the narrative and because she is constructed as abject, but also because of the many small moments in the text which suggest that her attempts to reach out to others will only result in her being more isolated than before. The sense of determinism surrounding Perdita is demonstrated by an episode in which the girls have a sleepover. As Megan listens to the "quiet, routine thumping" that Mr Wiguiggan is giving to his wife in an upstairs part of the house, she begins to understand the bleakness of Perdita's life (119). Instead of drawing the girls together, however, the incident only serves to illustrate to Megan how Other Perdita is—that Perdita's world is "so far from anything [she has] ever experienced" (120). The following morning, Megan leaves the house while Perdita is still sleeping. Struggling to understand her reaction, she thinks to herself: "Maybe we are wired to keep away from people who are weak or injured? They attract predators. And while we recognise the need for compassion, something deep down makes us wary" (120).

Like Blacky, Megan's growth as a subject is predicated upon the death of an/other because the suicide acts as a catalyst, forcing Megan to "resign" from the group and to violently reject the behavioural codes that have, until this point, governed her way of being female. Her development as a gendered subject is also illustrated by the changes she makes to her life after this event: She organises a poetry appreciation group in memory of Perdita; she begins new friendships with girls who exhibit a "quiet, respectful kind of camaraderie" (170); and she takes another social misfit under her wing (a boy that she sees as her "second chance"). There are a number of problems that arise from the novel's use of death as a strategy for growth and regendering, however. One is that Perdita is persistently constructed in ways that make it difficult to empathise with her, and this is only reinforced by Megan's position as focaliser, for it is her pain and alienation (from "the group") rather than Perdita's that becomes the focus of the narrative. A further complication is that narrative closure is centred around Megan's empowerment, while yet another is that the choices involved with living and dying are represented as a competition between the girls. This is apparent when Megan writes the dead Perdita a letter and a poem which she calls her "right of reply" (163)—an ironic term given that the poem merely demonstrates that Perdita's voice has been silenced by her death:

> You were the tiger in lamb's clothing,
> You were the thinnest of the thin,
> Prising open my eyes,
> To watch them fill with tears,
> But I'm a survivor,
> And what have you got to say to that?
> Nothing?
> Then I win. (165)

As Megan's final words imply, the letter, the poem, and the episodes which follow it, assign Megan the power that Perdita so clearly lacks throughout the narrative because they construct Megan rather than Perdita as the victim, Megan as a saviour, and Megan as the reference point around which this tragic story unfolds:

> I think [Perdita] gave up on the world, and gave up on me, too soon. [But the] thing that most disappoints me, is that [she] was not around to see that I too have learned the enterprise in walking naked. (171)

Conclusion

As Stephens argues, in teen fictions, abjection is itself "a boundary state from which the abjected will either spiral down to social dysfunction, insanity or death or else turn existence around to wrest some form of agency from it" ("I'll Never" 124). In *Walking Naked*, both Megan and Perdita are represented as abject in that the threat they pose to a particular social order results in them being cast aside. For Perdita, this move has tragic consequences because abjection cannot be overcome, and so it signals her failure to produce an agential subjectivity. By contrast, the struggle between abjection and agency represents empowerment for Megan. Like other texts in this chapter, then, *Walking Naked* suggests that, although death can signify the erasure of subjectivity, it can also function to "reaffirm or reinstate the subjectivity of others who exist both inside and outside the narrative frame" (Mallan, "Fatal" 175). This is clearly articulated by those fictions in which death acts as a psychological and emotional displacement because it removes the subject from their familiar surroundings and thus destabilises, or puts into crisis, their sense of (gendered) identity (McCallum 69). These texts also demonstrate, however, that when gendered growth is associated with death, it is firmly wedded to issues of power. This pattern is perhaps most visible in *Touching Earth Lightly, Deadly Unna?, Settling Storms,* and *Walking Naked,* where death clearly functions as an instrument of power. As these novels suggest, the use of death as a narrative device to allow one member of a friendship to mature and grow is problematic when the surviving subject is already privileged in terms of class, sexual orientation, or race.[15] Perhaps the major limitation of texts which adhere to this pattern is that their desired gender schema is defined too restrictively. As Romøren and Stephens contend, when this occurs, "characters are not able to engage in the kind of code-switching between schemata which many [subjects] in actual world social interactions may commonly practise" (225). The distinct division that is constructed here between pejorated and valorised ways of being also tends to turn the narrative into a form of social advocacy rather than reflection (Stephens, "Always" xv). This is emphasised, moreover, in narratives such as *Touching Earth Lightly* and *Walking Naked* which suggest that the transformation of the gender schema is permanent.[16]

Death can be seen as well to disclose the workings of power and to function as a process of division in those narratives which work to differentiate between normal and abnormal behaviour and practices. The boundary which defines these terms is brutally demarcated by the corpse in *Walking Naked, Touching Earth Lightly, Out of the Shadows, Wasteland,* and *Sleeping Dogs.* Although each of the latter four offers open resistance to orthodox ideas about what constitutes acceptable sexual behaviour and practices, at the same time, conflict surfaces between what the texts represent in the narrative and the processes of representing it. In this way, it is suggested that death is a punishment for transgressing those same social codes and structures. In *The Memory Shell,* death is also a consequence of transgression and risky behaviour; however, in this instance, it additionally acts to curb female (sexual) power since it coerces the protagonist into a way of being female that is heavily influenced by male-derived paradigms. Indeed, this notion that the feminine is unstable, liminal, and disturbing haunts a number of the texts I have examined here. Besides *The Memory Shell,* death acts to stabilise the multiply-coded feminine body in *Touching Earth Lightly, Out of the Shadows, Settling Storms, Before I Die,* and *Painted Love Letters.* At times, the strategy of these texts is to construct a normative heterosexual resolution for the protagonist, and thus to interpellate her into the patriarchal ideal of femininity. Yet, at others, to regulate female sexuality and female desire it is to remove the body from the sexual economy altogether because, to paraphrase Elisabeth Bronfen and Sarah Webster Goodwin, stable object equals stable meanings (14).

Chapter Four
Beyond Consensus Reality:
Death and Fantasy Fiction

Like the ghost which is neither dead nor alive, the fantastic is a spectral presence, suspended between being and nothingness.

(Jackson 20)

[T]ransgression lies at the root of the fantastic, not only as structure but also as content [...] via the fantastic we are enabled to journey beyond limits we would otherwise not dare to cross.

(Armitt 97)

The novels I consider in this chapter all locate their narratives within the realm of the fantastic, a textual space which, like death, can be seen to challenge cultural ideas about order and boundaries, is surrounded by an instability of meaning, and is difficult to articulate or to define. As Rosemary Jackson argues, the fantastic is "preoccupied with limits, with limiting categories, and with their projected dissolution", it "opens on to a region which has no name and no rational explanation for its existence", it traces "the unsaid and the unseen of culture: that which has been silenced, made invisible, covered over and made 'absent'" (4, 25, 48). The intersection between death and the fantastic in this group of texts is, then, to appropriate Julia Kristeva's words, one that involves "borders, positions, rules" (4)—in particular, their transgression or collapse. In the sub-genres of fantasy I examine here, death's role is to blur the boundaries between reality, dream, and the supernatural; to fracture domestic structures; and to separate child from adult, "normal" from "abnormal", disorder from order, self from other—in short, to undermine cultural stability. Each of these texts also tends to focus upon bodies and their margins, or to problematise hegemonic constructions of femininity and masculinity, creating a sense that the boundaries delineating biological sex and cultural gender are shifting or mutable. As a group they therefore embody "implicit criticism of social norms", since by giving readers experiences of social practices and ways of seeing that deviate from the norm, they can be seen to play with or subvert orthodox ideas about sexuality and gender (Searsmith 144). The majority of the texts I discuss function to restore or redefine those limits too, however, working less to push the boundaries and more to maintain them—and perhaps suggesting, as Lucie Armitt contends, that "although the relationship between prohibition and transgression is one of apparent mutual denial, in actuality each necessitates the existence of the other"; transgression "requires the affirmation of the limit in the very act of crossing it" (71, 97).

Fantasy Fiction

The notion that fantastic literature can be involved in undermining received ideas about such subjects as gender and culture at the same time it can be seen to reinforce or even produce them is central to my discussion here.[1] Yet much of the critical work focused on the fantastic to date has paid little attention to its broader ideological implications. At least until the recent past, academic approaches to the subject have been notoriously untheoretical, reducing fantasy's innovations to "the formal fixities of genre theory" (Armitt 2), or concentrating on its thematic features, effects, and terms. Indeed, to use the border motif again, fantasy fiction has consistently occupied a position at the edges of literary culture. A possible reason for this marginalisation is the tendency to use conventions of realism as defining criteria for "great" or "serious" fiction; another is because fantasy is often viewed as frivolous or as pure escapism (Atterby vii). Jackson, for one, contends that literature of the fantastic repeatedly emerges as second best in comparisons with the more "civilized" practices of realistic fiction. She also suggests it is subject to claims that, in providing vicarious gratification, it "transcends" reality, and "'escapes' the human condition" (2, 172). To dismiss fantastic literature as merely escapist, however, is to ignore its potential to act as a space where an array of cultural fears and fantasies can be projected—where the kind of unconscious impulses and desires that are repressed by the social order can be expressed (Jackson). As Brian Atterby argues, fantasy is full of "loaded" images and "concrete emblems of problematic or valuable psychological and social phenomena"—and the ordering of these images into story is an attempt to achieve iconic representation so that the narrative can, like a map, call attention to, or give insight into, the phenomena it references (7). Fantasy fiction is, then, like any other body of texts, never "free" because it is produced within, and determined by, its social context; it may "struggle against the limits of this context, often being articulated upon that very struggle", but "it cannot be understood in isolation from it" (Jackson 3). To quote fantasy writer China Miéville:

> Fantasy is still written and read through the filters of social reality. That's why some fantasies [. . .] are so directly allegorical—but even the most surreal and bizarre fantasy can't help but reverberate around the reader's awareness of their own reality, even if in a confusing and unclear way. (qtd. in Newsinger)

Fantasy Fiction for Children

Despite critical studies such as those that I have drawn upon above, fantasy fiction often still suffers from "the slur of the 'fanciful'" as Armitt terms it (2). Peter Hunt argues, for instance, that many of the traits of fantasy are seen as negative and intellectually unsatisfying—as belonging to "a cruder phase of human development"—thus making them far more "suitable for children" (*Children's* 185–86). Similarly, John Stephens contends that the inclination to polarise fantasy and realism into rival genres by associating realism with seriousness, and fantasy with non-serious or popular literature, means that fantastic fiction has become synonymous with "those audiences, such as children, deemed incapable of complex aesthetic responses" (*Language* 241–42). There are several implications associated with viewing the genre in this manner: Firstly, the ability of young readers to appreciate fantasy literature's often indirect references to transcendent concepts and abstracts is underestimated, and secondly, there is a suggestion that it does not warrant a sustained and serious criticism. This is not to say that the genre is not valued in the field; a large body of quality fantasy novels aimed at children exists as a consequence. The genre has always attracted academic interest too. Rather, theoretical approaches to children's fantasy texts, like those for adults, characteristically demonstrate a lack of focus and sophistication. Hunt's dissatisfaction with the "oceans of ingenious ink" that have been used to classify the genre suggests as much ("Introduction" 11).

As I am largely concerned with the ways in which ideology is inscribed into the genre's discourses, and with its discoursal features, I am therefore going to draw on Stephens's "Words of Power: Fantasy and Realism as Linguistically Constituted Modes" (*Language*) to frame my discussion. Stephens's principal arguments can be summarised as follows. The dominant concern of fantasy, like that of realism, is the nature and operation of power in human societies—particularly the different ways that power is implicated in language (*Language* 287). In contrast to realist fictions which encode this thematic concern metonymically, however, fantasy fictions operate in a metaphoric mode, giving the theme a more mythic dimension by suggesting that "there is a 'real presence' in verbal signs, and that these signs are thus grounded in transcendent meanings" (*Language* 263). The way in which the genre is inclined to construct reader subject positions and to spatio-temporally order its macro-discourse also differs. Whereas realistic texts work to maintain "a simulated transcript of the actual world", fantasy fiction deliberately alters the existents of time and place in order to fracture illusions of verisimilitude. It does not tend to rely heavily on focalisation strategies either; instead, it is apt to create a distance between readers and texts, and thus to comment on contemporary social practice by way of indirections, parallels, symbols, and allegory (*Language* 287–88). In addition, the kinds of truth expressed within the two modes are ideationally different: "Truth" is equated with verisimilitude in realist fictions, yet in literary fantasy "truth" can be seen to signify "a transcendent entity which imparts meaning to human life" (*Language* 242, 287). Children's fantasy fiction also tends to support the ideological position of liberal humanism, implying that all societies are underpinned by a set of "eternal" humanist values. As with other traditional genres in children's literature, the fantasy genre is inclined to be heavily gendered as well. That is, gender is inscribed within the features that constitute the genre (at the level of both story and discourse) in particularly characteristic ways (Stephens, "Gender"). Finally, as much of this chapter demonstrates, because fantasy narrative is at least twice removed from reality, it seems more prone to "a kind of ideological slippage" whereby implicit ideology becomes "interpolated between the desired and eschewed values constructed more overtly in the text" (Stephens, *Language* 288–89).

Strange Bodies, Perverse Appetites: Gothic, Horror, and Death

I am going to begin by looking at the genres of Gothic and horror (the contemporary horror genre owes its thematic and stylistic conventions to the Gothic novel, so I will use the terms "Gothic" and "horror" here interchangeably).[2] Gothic is by no means the dominant mode of fantasy fiction, although it does appear to have a powerful appeal to contemporary adolescent audiences. Indeed, the popularity of the genre is such that it occupies a large part of the YA market.[3] Perhaps it appeals because so many of its key themes— monstrousness, the body, metamorphosis, transgression, anxiety, sexuality, romance—strike a chord with the adolescent subject. David Punter claims, for instance, that the nature of adolescence is integral to Gothic writing. Adolescence, he argues, can be seen as a time when there is a fantasised inversion of boundaries: "[W]hat is inside finds itself outside (acne, menstrual blood, rage)", and "what should be visibly outside (heroic dreams, attractiveness, sexual organs) remain resolutely inside and hidden" (*Gothic* 6). For James B. Twitchell, adolescence is a period "ripe for the experience of horror". The horror text holds a deep fascination for adolescent audiences, he contends, since it is here that the adolescent's inarticulate sexual anxieties are given form: "Like the fairy tale which prepares the child for the anxieties of separation, the modern horror myth prepares the adolescent for the anxieties of reproduction" because essentially, "horror has little to do with fright"; rather, "it has more to do with laying down the rules of socialization and extrapolating a hidden code of sexual behavior" (7, 66, 68).

Critical investigations of Gothic and horror texts have often focused on the centrality of sexuality and gender to the narrative. As Punter points out, Gothic fiction is "erotic at root", and in its fascination with the taboo, constantly preoccupied with matters to do with sexuality (*Literature* 190–91). Fred Botting argues that uncertainties about the nature of such things as power, law, and sexuality dominate Gothic fiction (5, 19); Paulina Palmer's *Lesbian Gothic: Transgressive Fictions* demonstrates Gothic's potential to be subversive by focusing on the genre's tradition of making space for representations of transgressive sexualities (Smith and Wallace 6); and Carol J. Clover draws attention to the horror mode's tendency to be gendered and misogynistic. In the area of children's literature, sexuality and gender also provide an angle for analysis of the Gothic/horror text. It has been suggested, for instance, that many children's texts in the horror genre privilege macho, hegemonic constructions of masculine subjectivity (Christian-Smith)—perhaps, as Paul Gray argues, by positioning readers to view the psychic struggles involved in growing up male in largely violent terms. As John Stephens and Robyn McCallum's study of the *Dark House*—a collection of stories compiled by Gary Crew and inspired by the clichéd Gothic motif of the dark house—reveals, representations of the monstrous-feminine are prevalent: of the twelve stories in the anthology, eight hinge on a monstrous female "who seeks to destroy, devour, or otherwise symbolically castrate one or more of the male characters" ("Ghosts" 170).

What, then, is death's role in the Gothic/horror tale? Barbara Creed argues that horror stories are obsessively concerned with death (*Monstrous* 154). Indeed, it is difficult to imagine a text belonging to the genre without the staple images of corpses, ghosts, and other undead or abject beings. The iconography of the genre is essentially the horror of death made manifest: the axe-wielding murderer; the river of blood; the premature burial; the shattered casket. As Punter eloquently observes, Gothic provides "an image language for bodies and their terrors" (*Gothic* 14). Fears about death and what becomes of the (decaying) body after death are, in fact, central to Gothic/horror fiction, and because bodies are gendered, in many texts these terrors are framed through themes of gender and sexuality. In narratives where death functions to regulate norms of sexual behaviour and/or reinforce dominant sexual subjectivities by killing off the deviant body, the intersection between mortality, gender, and sexuality is particularly clear. As Linda Christian-Smith contends, monsters in horror narratives frighten by "acting out desires, usually sexual, that are feared or taboo and are in turn punished for doing so" (164). These texts suggest that those who threaten the security and stability of the social order—by failing to take up their proper gender roles or by exhibiting signs of abnormal sexual desire—will meet with an untimely end. Victor Kelleher's *Into the Dark*, an overtly erotic retelling of the Dracula myth, works in this way, for instance, largely by juxtaposing the normal with the pathological and conflating aberrance with monstrosity to privilege a particular way of being male. It is clear that the novel proceeds to complicate these constructions of sexual subjectivity too since Ox, the tale's narrator, is represented as Other—as much monster as man. And by submitting to Mina Harker at the novel's conclusion, he also proceeds to break the cultural taboo which maintains "the division between men as possessors and women as possessed" (Hendershot 43). Yet by insisting upon a hetero-normative resolution for the protagonist, and death for the perverse Count, at the same time, the text can be seen to illustrate how the Gothic functions to reaffirm dominant sexual ideologies and ways of being.

To return to Twitchell's argument, it would seem that horror stories involving monsters can be seen as fables of sexual identity because they "carry the prescriptive codes of modern Western sexual behavior" (104). Admittedly, the orthodox sexual ideologies encoded in *Into the Dark* owe something to the text's grounding in the past, because historical fictions and retold stories are inclined towards social, cultural, and political conservatism (Stephens, *Language;* Stephens and McCallum, *Retelling*). However, similar ideologies and outcomes are also evident in Gary Crew's *Gothic Hospital*, Jackie French's futuristic "Outlands" trilogy—*In the Blood, Blood Moon*, and *Flesh and Blood*—and Scott Westerfeld's *Peeps*.[4] Although the vampires end up as the "good guys" in *Peeps*, the novel carries out similar ideological work to the Kelleher text because, to borrow Roberta Seelinger Trites's words, it acts as a "tool [to] curb teenagers' libido" (*Disturbing* 85) by playing on fears about casual sex, AIDS, and other sexually transmitted diseases. Indeed, the narrative plot pivots on an incident in which all of these anxieties are brought together. Cal Thompson, the novel's nineteen-year-old narrator, is picked up by goth-girl, Morgan Ryder, in Dick's Bar, a club that caters predominantly to a gay clientele. The pair have a drunken one-night-stand, during which Cal loses his virginity and becomes infected with a parasite that turns him into an oversexed vampire (or "peep", meaning "parasite positive"). This association between unsafe sex, transgressive sexuality, and pathology is then reinforced in an episode that occurs soon after, where the word "positive" can be seen to take on a double meaning. Hoping to fill in the missing memories of the night he became infected, Cal retraces his steps by returning to the bar. After drinking a couple of Bahamalama-Dingdongs (a cocktail made with a whole banana) and chatting to a few of the leather-clad patrons, Cal remembers his progenitor "giggling and squeezing [his] hand" as they arrived at her building. "'That's where I live!' [Morgan had said], thus marking the exact moment when [Cal] was absolutely *positive* [he] was going to get laid" (52, emphasis original).

While the disease can be managed with medicinal drugs, it is still spread by sexual contact and the transferral of bodily fluids, and thus Cal spends much of the novel in an enforced celibacy. That is, until he begins a romantic relationship with Lacey, a fellow peep, and the pair realise that, together, they can "do anything [they want]" because "even with the parasite's spores in [Cal's] blood and saliva" Lacey is infected, just like he is (274). From very early in the novel, then, it is evident that there are consequences for giving into unconstrained desire outside monogamy, and this is emphasised by the textual focus on "control". Besides Cal's constant self-monitoring, ideas about restraint are apparent in the afterword (a lecture on how to avoid parasites), in the way that the disease is policed by the Night Watch and handled in such a cautious manner, and in the biology lessons that are interspersed between the chapters which trace the main story. Each of these short but graphically detailed essays concerns a different parasitic organism, and almost all of them imply that there are catastrophic consequences for disturbing the "natural order". In spite of the conclusion, where readers discover that without the vampire parasite the human race will perish in the coming apocalyptic fight against a far deadlier epidemic, the narrative therefore acts as a cautionary tale because it suggests that there are abnormal and "normal way[s]" for teens to "[lose] their virginity" or engage in sexual contact (104). Again, a double-meaning is at work here: Leave the parasites alone to do their job because they are "part of nature's balance"— but remember, too, "[w]ithout our parasites to keep us in check, we're all in trouble" (175).

Although the Gothic has been reimagined in French's series through its displacement into a high-tech future, the use of familiar Gothic/horror figures, themes, and effects suggests that the texts share much with the traditional conventions of the genre. A blend of detective fiction, science fiction, and horror, the trilogy is set in a world where the boundaries between technology and the body, and between reality and virtuality, have eroded to the point that genetic engineering, human-computer networking, cloning, and human/animal hybridisation have become commonplace. As the novels' titles suggest, however, the texts are also liberally infused with material bodily images (blood, sex, death, violence, food, excrement, and flesh), demonstrating the tensions that are a particular feature of children's texts about the posthuman future (Ostry). This tension is also played out through the juxtaposition between urban and rural landscapes. In the enclosed City, with its shell of holographs and guaranteed TrueLife sensations and flavours, there are no animals, residents are chipped for identification and Linking (establishing a connection between the mind and the Internet), and their movements are monitored. By contrast, the emphasis in the small communities of the Outlands (called Utopias) is on the physical and the tactile. All are self-sufficient, and only those items that each community cannot produce themselves—grow, catch, make, or farm—are procured by trade.

The trilogy is narrated by Danielle Forest, a Virtual engineer whose genetic modification enables her not only to Link quickly and super-efficiently into any data web she chooses, but also to retain whatever information she has scrolled through. Danielle, and eleven others who were created at the same time, form the Forest, a group who are Linked so closely that each is an extension of the other. In the first novel, *In the Blood*, the Forest becomes a threat to the powers that govern the City, however, and their modification consequently fails to gain formal approval. Proclaimed "non-human" by the City authorities, Danielle is then sent to a house in the Outlands, and her ability to Link is taken away. Amidst the turmoil of trying to come to terms with an existence in RealLife (which includes a sexual romance with a male neighbour called Neil), she therefore finds herself facing an identity crisis: is she Forest or Tree? "'I don't think I can be like other people'" she tells the administrator at the nearby Utopia of Faith Hope and Charity. "'I certainly don't want to be. If I'd wanted to become human I'd have had a brain tissue transplant and stayed in the City'" (36). Yet Danielle has little time to agonise over her predicament because, soon after, she finds a semi-conscious teenage girl, named Doris, at her gate. Slashed across the throat and the wrist, Doris appears to be the victim of a vampire. Doris dies a short time later, and Danielle sets about attempting to solve the mystery surrounding her death.

In the Blood's association with earlier Gothic texts which explore otherness, social exclusion, the monstrous body, identity, and the dangers of science without conscience, are quite obvious. Distinctly Gothic themes and motifs also appear in the second of the series, *Blood Moon*, in which the murder mystery involves a family of werewolves, and in the third, *Flesh and Blood*, where an influenza plague has turned its victims into zombies intent on killing all around them. Given the trilogy's preoccupation with exploring the possibilities of genetic manipulation and interrogating the effects of biotechnology on the body, the Gothic works here as a reminder of the corporeal aspects of existence—in particular of sex/uality, and of death which, regardless of scientific advances, continues to be an unalterable facet of the human condition. This is encapsulated by Danielle in *In the Blood* when she says: "I had never worried about the sight of blood before. But I had never seen it ooze from neck and wrist before either. I had never realised the power blood has. It's our life, and our death" (57). As the presence of the monsters implies, however, the Gothic also gives form to a variety of fears and anxieties regarding these same subjects.[5]

According to Jenny Wolmark, this is a characteristic feature of fantasies of the technologised body. The new forms of embodiment that are envisaged in these texts are "emergent and incomplete" and, as a consequence, "often disruptive, even monstrous", suggesting that, at the same time they are celebrating the erosion of the body's boundaries or new ways of representing the "human", they are also revealing a considerable anxiety about the unstable parameters surrounding such distinctions (79). These contradictions are played out in the series in a very pronounced manner. The texts can be seen to challenge dominant notions of "humanity", and of the human body (especially its differences) in a number of ways. By focalising the narrative through Danielle, the texts position readers to identify with a protagonist whose outlawed modification renders her "non-human". During her detective work in the Outlands, Danielle encounters many other Proclaimed beings—some who are automatically Proclaimed as second-generation modifieds, some with only minor genetic alterations whose bodies thus bear few surface differences, and others, like the part bird/part human creatures in *Flesh and Blood* who are the result of more dramatic tampering. In each instance, the blurring of the categories human/animal/machine and reality/fantasy is such that they are all distinguished by their departure from the "norm", by their corporeal *abnormality*. Over the course of the series, Danielle is also able to move between the two worlds of the Outlands and the City, and often to take what she needs from both, suggesting that the rigid demarcation between the "real" in the Outlands and the virtual in the City—between organic and inorganic—is not as stable as it appears (indeed, by the conclusion of the final novel, Danielle has even had her MindLink illegally restored). However, while the human continually jostles against the posthuman in such a way that allows for alternative ways of thinking about bodies and their material circumstances—and thus about being human—the series can be seen to map orthodox meanings onto these notions as well.

On the whole, the trilogy adheres to a liberal humanist ethic, suggesting at several points that to be human is to possess innate behaviours and traits (such as co-operation, compassion, and loyalty). By privileging monogamous ways of being and thus normalising conventional heterosexist models of desire, it also works to reinforce hegemonic views of gendered bodies and subjectivities. The latter trend is of particular interest in this case because, in order to do so, the texts are inclined, like other Gothic narratives, to create a clear demarcation between the deviant and the normal, healthy, or pure (Halberstam 2). *Blood Moon* functions in this way by representing particular female subjectivities and behaviours as abject or monstrous. Danielle's task in this narrative is to discover the identity of the murderer who is threatening nearby Utopias. The clues point to a family of friendly werewolves (or human-wolf crosses), so that when Len, one of the young and very wolf-like males, ostensibly attacks Danielle, the case appears solved. In the tradition of the Outlands, justice is brutally meted out, and Len is killed. However, the murderer turns out to be Eleanor, the family's lead female, who is so troubled by her wolf genes that she has not only engineered the death of Len, the future alpha male, but also secretly mated with a Truenorm in order to fall pregnant. Eleanor is proud of her wolf self, but aware of the limitations this imposes on both her own ambition to be one of the City's top management consultants, and on the potential ambitions of her children. As Danielle deduces, Eleanor's plan is first to pass baby Mitch off as her husband's, and then to ensure that the child wins when the time comes for him to challenge his father for the position of leader of the pack. In this way, Eleanor argues, the "next generation and the next will not look wolf, no matter what they are inside" (249).

Deconstructing the meanings associated with *Blood Moon*'s monster figures is not a simple process; werewolves are depicted in the text in both positive and negative terms. It is reasonable to argue, however, that because the themes of female ambition and motherhood constitute such a prominent feature of the narrative, monstrousness is largely associated here with a set of masculinist ideologies concerning femininity. Eleanor's embodiment as werewolf reveals much about male anxieties and desires, for instance, because she is represented in what is characteristic of "male constructions of the female body within Western discursive traditions" (Robinson 129)—as both horrific and desirous. She is "extremely attractive" (18) and "compelling" (52), but as her bloodlust suggests, dangerous and terrifying too. Her monstrousness (which is firmly linked to the moon's cycle and thus to Woman) further functions to articulate the kind of tensions engendered within patriarchy by feminism. As an ambitious, working mother, a ruthless killer, and an unfaithful wife, Eleanor challenges orthodox constructions of motherhood and of femininity and thus poses a significant threat to the patriarchy. This threat, which is symbolically enacted in the novel's prologue when she murders a man called Patriarch, means that she is often pejoratively depicted in contrast to other females in the narrative (such as when she is referred to as a "bitch"), and that there are moments when the narrative implies that her desire to succeed at all costs has literally turned her into an animal.

The focus of *In the Blood* is upon sexuality rather than gender roles, although it too demonstrates how representations of monstrous beasts can play on anxieties regarding women as gendered subjects. The strategy in this text is first to depict particular sexual activities as perverse, and then to violently remove those who practise them from the sexual economy. Unusually for adolescent fiction, the narrative gives expression to an array of sexual fantasies and grotesqueries: The text is littered with representations of sexual acts, with naked and sexually aroused bodies (particularly males); it features machine-like beings able to pleasure themselves; and when human-animal bodies are depicted engaging in sexual activity, it hints at bestiality. In one sense, then, the text can be seen to challenge or destabilise orthodox notions of sex/uality; yet it also displays a number of tensions relating to these same ideologies. The death of Doris illustrates this point. At first it seems that Doris is the helpless victim of a vampire, and so she is treated with sympathy and care: The local medic gently administers to her until she suffers a fatal heart attack from blood loss, and then Danielle organises a ceremonial burial for her and a hunt to find the culprit. As the mystery unfolds, however, it becomes clear that, until her death, Doris had willingly participated in numerous acts of vampirism (both real and virtual), and Danielle and Neil suggest that it may be wise to "rethink [their] idea of sweet little Doris". "'She seemed so young and helpless'", Danielle remarks to Neil, to which he replies: "'She was young and she was helpless [. . .] Then, at least'" (226). By the time the pair discover Doris's seduction of a number of elderly "true" (that is, genetically engineered) vampires, and trace her movements to a castle housing the sexually transgressive Uncle Bertie, it is not difficult for readers to associate her behaviour with perversity. Crucially, the text provides little access to Doris's thoughts or her motives since she dies soon after her blood-caked body is dumped at Danielle's door. Her character is thus largely constructed by others in the narrative, and from these small snippets of information, she appears childlike, but sexually indiscriminate—a wanderer who is always on the move in search of "fresh blood" and excitement (130–31), a young girl fascinated by danger (242).

Given her sexual preferences, it is therefore suggested that Doris's death is not unexpected, making her demise a clear warning of the kind of punishment that will be meted out to those who transgress the codes of acceptable sexual behaviour. As I have argued, a number of complexities in the representation of sex/uality illustrate that notions of acceptable behaviour are somewhat ambiguous in the narrative. However, in addition to the representation of Doris as deviant, there are several other features of the text that work to valorise monogamous sexual subjectivities. The first concerns Danielle's relationship with Neil. The conventional trajectory and outcome of their sexual romance equates safety with monogamy, and key moments of its development are interspersed between horrific scenes of carnage, juxtaposing the two in a way that privileges romantic love over unconstrained desire. The conclusion of the narrative is a case in point because the final episode, which involves images of Danielle and Neil walking through "dappled sunlight", grinning happily as they return home together (262), occurs not long after other episodes detailing Doris's erotic but violent murder (257–59) and the death of one of her vampire lovers who is hung, decapitated, and disembowelled "like a slaughtered beast" (235). The second feature is associated with the text's twin motifs of vampires and blood, around which a number of anxieties concerning the dangers of "promiscuity" are manifest. Vampires are sexual predators, simultaneously terrifying, seductive, and dangerous, and they can be seen here to articulate contemporary fears about potentially fatal diseases of the blood—about being killed through the act of sex or the transferral of bodily fluids. This becomes clear when Danielle associates vampirism with pathology by suggesting that a vampire virus might be responsible for Doris's death (70–76). Here, the vampire also poses a threat to monogamy and thus to family (essential features of capitalist and patriarchal ideology) because it is a symbol of aggressive female sexuality. Doris's appetite for sex is bound to fulfilling her desires rather than her potential for reproduction, and so, in her incarnation as vampire, she violates the "contemporary hegemonic ideal of heterosexual coitus"—an ideal which is often "legitimated and reified" through its reference to the sex-for-reproduction myth (Krzywinska 193–94).

The "Outlands" trilogy demonstrates that the connection between deviance and deadliness (which tends to haunt representations of strong or sexually liberated women in Western discourses) is a remarkably durable one. Thus, although the texts' use of Gothic conventions works both to question how subjects are "clothed" in the human (Punter, *Gothic* 11) and to explore the myriad ways in which bodies are marked by difference, they also draw a clear boundary between acceptability and perversion or between normal and abnormal. The series suggests, too, that in fictions where social or psychological problems are distorted to emerge as melodramatic shapes (such as monsters, devils, and hybrid beasts) there is a tendency to reaffirm the dominant ideology of the culture because, as Jackson argues, through this identification, "troublesome social elements can be destroyed in the name of exorcising the demonic" (121–22).

A similar, although less radical, approach to "expulsion" is offered by *Gothic Hospital*. This text is a Gothic pastiche loaded with intertextual references to novels such as *Dracula*, *The Island of Doctor Moreau*, and *Frankenstein*, and littered with stock Gothic motifs (an attic, a castle, corpses, graves, windswept cliffs). In accordance with the Gothic genre's tendency to "dramatize uncertainty and conflicts of the individual subject in relation to a difficult social situation" (Jackson 97), it explores an adolescent boy's grief over his younger sister's death. The narrative is structured as a series of sessions between the boy, Johnny Doolan, and his psychiatrist, moving chronologically from past to present as Johnny details the period in his life which begins just prior to the death of his sister, Jana, and concludes with a counselling session during which the final events of the story unfold. At the first consultation, Johnny discloses that his father, Peter, has left the family home to live with his fiancée, that his mother has begun speaking to the dead Jana, and that he feels as though, in his parents' eyes, he may as well be invisible. This is compounded by the belief that Johnny's parents loved Jana more than himself: "My dad used to call her 'Princess' [and] I'm sure she was Mum's favourite" (9). Attempting to escape the anxiety caused by their arguments and their apparent indifference to his pain, he buries himself in books, including "a pile of musty Gothic tomes, all weighed down with blood-soaked castles and haunted ruins and ghosts and crumbling headstones" (14). Reading soon becomes a kind of bibliotherapy, helping him to cope by forgetting until, as the novel's cover tells it, he not only actually "enters the terrifying world of the gothic novel", but gets lost within its "fantastic world of print and picture".

There is a suggestion here that, like many other Gothic texts for children, the real horror that is hidden by, and discovered within, the Gothic setting is a fear of "adult neglect or hatred, loss of home and support" (Cosslett 96). This is signalled firstly by Johnny's own admissions to the doctor in their initial session: "'I try to tell myself that some kids' dads work on oil rigs. Some work in Antarctica twenty-three months out of twenty-four. Some are in jail [. . .] But I miss him, Doctor'" (19); and secondly when he finds himself inside the Gothic text, travelling on a train towards the infamous hospital which declares on a sign swinging from its heavy, timber gates, that it is "an infir-mary for orphans" (29). As the story unfolds, however, and it becomes clear that the main thread of the narrative is little more than a symbolically-loaded tale generated by Johnny's own tortured psyche, it appears that Johnny's con-flict is bound in several ways to his psychosexual development. This is largely suggested by the tense relationship that is manifest between father and son, the most cogent representation of which occurs when, during his train trip to the hospital, Johnny dreams that he finds his father in the laboratory of an old castle. The monstrous Dr Gorman (who is experimenting with body parts in order to discover what it is that makes a human "human") has harnessed Peter to an apparatus and he is wearing a helmet of silver metal to which a series of wires, catheters, and glass flasks is attached. The machine, which is directly fitted at one place to his heart, is in the process of extracting his body fluids. "'It's not that I think that my father is tied up somewhere having his guts sucked out'", Johnny tells the doctor, "'[b]ut I reckon that deep down these dreams are hinting that I wish he was'" (24).

The rather heavy-handed invocation of the Oedipal drama in this scene suggests that *Gothic Hospital* can be read like a Freudian textbook with Jana's death functioning to fracture the domestic structure of the fam-ily, and thus bring Johnny's unresolved psychological problems to a head. Unable to deal with his anxieties, Johnny has employed a classic defence mechanism to help him cope, distorting reality and transferring his fears onto un/super-natural figures and uncanny situations.[6] His sessions with the doctor therefore represent an attempt to bring those repressed fears and thoughts back to the conscious level of awareness—to heal the conflict between id and ego, between unconscious and conscious self (and, in this instance, between father and son). Under these terms, Peter represents all of the authority that the child must reconcile him/herself to so as to assume a position within the cultural order as a whole. Johnny's neurosis is focused on the moment in which his psychical development had become arrested or "fixated", and as his fantasy of killing Peter suggests, it is analogous to that stage when the subject is "introjecting" (making its own) this patriarchal law (Eagleton). The path to Johnny's recovery, which is played out in the hospital grounds of the text, consequently involves a quest to symbolically reassemble the family. This is achieved in a number of ways in the narra-tive (such as when all the dead orphaned children who were once part of Dr Gorman's experiments rise from their graves), but the most important involves Johnny piecing together a series of keys. The first key (which is associated with the outsider) merges father with monster. The three middle keys represent the various members of a traditional (heterosexual) family unit: mother, father, and child. The final key is the key to the self, but also the key to the heart. The completion of the set signifies a closing of the rift between father and son, but it also suggests that Johnny has grown into an acceptance of the authority of the Father—or in Freudian terms, that he has developed an individual identity and thus "a particular place in the social, sexual and familial networks" (Eagleton 136).

Taming the Child: Supernatural Fiction, Death, and Gender Socialisation

Gothic Hospital illustrates some of the ways in which both Gothic literature and psychoanalytic theory engages with the taboo and the concealed aspects of the psyche; that is, by working in the language of metaphor to speak the "unspeakable" and give expression to an array of repressed dreads and desires. I now want to look at a number of other fantasy texts that function in a similar way. These texts also highlight fantasy's ability to confront distressing issues or resolve emotional crises by exploring them metaphorically, and they also trace these tensions through family or adolescent/parent relationships. More specifically, they work to destabilise the boundaries between psyche and reality, since each of them features some kind of supernatural or paranormal element: alternate realities; ghosts, apparitions and otherworldly beings; or characters who are possessed by an evil entity. Sometimes the appearance of the paranormal seems to be mostly for effect—such as in Lucy Sussex's *Black Ice*; at others—for example, in Isobelle Carmody's *Greylands*—it is obviously psychological at root. In looking at these texts as a group, however, it is clear that, in their treatment of death, they tend to approach the supernatural in very different ways.

Narratives aimed at younger readers generally use these themes and motifs in a therapeutic way; that is, to console the protagonist/s—and, thus, potentially the reader—often by working against the idea of death as permanent.[7] As Trites argues, for this genre, learning about death is likely to be represented as "a stage in the child's process of separating from the parent more than anything else" (*Disturbing* 118). This is evident in Phil Cummings's *Angel* where the protagonist, Shane, is visited by his dead sibling, David. The tension between parent and child is illustrated by the disbelief Shane's parents express when he relates the story, but is then resolved when David, their guardian angel, helps the family to survive a blizzard and to grieve, promising them at the conclusion a "lifetime of visits" (184). Judith Clarke's *Starry Nights*—with a target audience of early teens—is based on a similar premise, although its protagonist, Clem, does not know he is dead until the novel's conclusion (it is suggested that his mother's inability to accept his death contributes to this confusion). Here, the influence of the kind of immortalist themes that are threaded through contemporary popular culture is manifest, first because learning to let go and come to terms with dying is framed as much through the living as the "dead", but, more importantly, because the final departure is restaged, allowing the family one last opportunity to connect with Clem.

Texts for older adolescent readers also suggest that learning about, and dealing with, death is closely tied to the child/adolescent's separation from the parent, although this separation (which at times becomes alienation) is more pronounced. The intersection between death and the supernatural or paranormal tends to have more sinister overtones in these texts too. In Victor Kelleher's *Del-Del*, for example, the central character, Sam, is purportedly possessed—a year to the day after his sister Laura's death from leukaemia—by both a malevolent spirit (the Judaeo-Christian Devil) and an alien being, driving him to be in turn "a wild animal, a mass of struggling limbs and teeth and claws" (21) and a cold, mocking child with "beady, unfeeling" lizard-like eyes (119). Sam's parents and grandparents struggle to cope with his increasingly strange outbursts, but the burden of responsibility largely rests with his older sister, Beth, the story's narrator, who takes it upon herself to solve the mystery, look after Sam, and pick up the pieces when the family falls apart.

It is in texts for adolescent readers that themes of gender and sexuality have a more obvious place too, not only because supernatural figures and events can often signal the child/adolescent subject's identity crisis (a crisis which is usually exacerbated or precipitated by grief and/or the contact with death), but also because it is here that the drama of family conflict is most clearly played out. As Frances Bartkowski argues, the family is "the ideological realm in which sexuality, gender identity, and self-image are framed" (66). To return to *Del-Del*, for instance, the disturbing behaviour exhibited by Sam is given a rational explanation when the presence of the paranormal is revealed to be a displaced representation of his psychosis. As Beth reasons at the conclusion, Del-Del—Sam's alter ego—was created so that he could cope emotionally with Laura's death: "Del-Del was never any of those weird creatures Sam made him out to be. He was merely a part of Sam himself—the hard, brainy part that didn't want to get hurt, that shied away from the painful fact of Laura's death" (194). The narrative is constructed as Beth's account of these events and its purpose, she writes, is twofold: to "remind Sam of *who he really is*", and "to keep Del-Del at bay" in case Sam tries to "open the cupboard and let Del-Del out" again (194–95, emphasis added). The source of Sam's crisis, the text suggests, is emotional repression, and for healing to take place he must learn to express his grief—to cry—and thus to assimilate the cold/rational and warm/emotional aspects of his personality (Schober). That these two halves are coded respectively as masculine and feminine (as is common in Western cultural discourses) is clear when Sam, acting out the Del-Del persona, explains that Laura's death was the catalyst for "his" arrival: "'I [arrived here] using the child's mind as a beacon to guide me [. . .] While [the girl, Laura,] was present, the beacon signal was faint, unclear. But after her departure it gained steadily in strength'" (124). As Adrian Schober explains, "[w]ithout Laura's (warm) heart to balance his (cold) mind [. . .] the beacon signal from Sam's mind becomes perceptibly stronger to Del-Del" (46).

The moment at which Sam begins to cry is when Beth forces him to acknowledge Laura's death. Sobbing brokenly, he lies in Beth's lap "mourning at last for the dead sister he'd loved so dearly" (193). Rather than her mother, Hannah, or her father, Desmond, it is Beth who is instrumental in caring for Sam—and in "pursuing the hermeneutics of his tortured psyche" throughout the novel (Scutter 216). Thus, this episode is a pivotal one, because it creates closure for both of them, and because it so neatly encapsulates the dominant ideology of the narrative; that is, that the crisis in Sam's self-concept and his inability to accept that Laura is gone can be traced to the corresponding lack of "proper" parental (particularly maternal) care in his life (Scutter 216). This is symbolised in one particular incident when Sam deliberately shatters a crystal model of the astrological sign of Gemini that was given to him and Laura by their grandmother, Mimi, and then returns the shards to Mimi at a family gathering (although not the siblings' birth sign, the piece signals their closeness and their shared birthday). This gesture implies that his emotional distress can be located in the figure of the mother, while the fractured state of the model clearly points to the unsteady family dynamics that are such a feature of the story. As Heather Scutter points out, "the novel's subtext bears signs of something wrong at the heart of the nuclear family" (216).

It seems apparent, therefore, that death's presence in *Del-Del* largely acts to allow a number of anxieties related to notions of (gendered) parenting to be articulated. Care has been taken to invert traditional family gender roles; however, in a household where the parents are often negatively depicted (as either absent or self-focused), and where the mothering has fallen to the eldest child, this strategy holds little weight.[8] That Beth is, in Scutter's words, the "superior surrogate" (221) is demonstrated on numerous occasions in the novel. In particular, it is evident at points where the three principal female figures of Hannah, Mimi, and Beth are juxtaposed in a way that clearly privileges the maternal and caring Beth. Hannah is consistently represented as castrating, and Mimi, with her smeared mascara, broken English, and "outdated remedies", as ridiculous. In contrast, Beth is depicted as the linchpin that holds the family together. Hegemonic masculinity is also problematised in the text, yet the character of Desmond is ultimately pushed into a traditional way of being male. As a receptionist at a big hotel who won't leave home until he looks like "one of those perfectly dressed models in a shop window" (12), he has the potential to complicate the conventional model, but he is nevertheless pejoratively constructed both as lacking in authority and as impotent (particularly because he loses his job), traits that have traditionally posed a dire threat to orthodox ideas about masculinity.

Conventional representations of the family in literature for children (including parenting, social structure, and gender relations) have been subject to scrutiny since at least the 1980s. Yet, as is suggested here, there often remains a conservative element at work in these texts (Agee; Beere; Mallan, "Fatal"; Pearce, "Growing"; Scutter). Admittedly, these kinds of contradictions may be attributed to the timeframe in which the narratives were produced: *Del-Del* was published during a period in which it was common for the female protagonists of adolescent fictions to "feel the pull of the domestic" (Pearce, "Growing" 12). As Sharyn Pearce argued in 1991, it was implied that, in order to "prepare for their biological destiny", girls in such novels were encouraged to cultivate a role as "nurturer within the private sphere of the home" ("Growing" 12).[9] Certainly, Laura's death and Sam's consequent emotional crisis allow Beth to assume this traditional role, moulding her into a way of being female that, the text implies, is preferable to that of the emasculating version of the feminine associated with her mother.

Another text (also published around this time) which potentially offers a positive model for the female reader, but which achieves a similar ideological outcome to *Del-Del*, is Deborah Lisson's *The Devil's Own*. While the mother in this text does not have a prominent place (it is the relationship between father and daughter that is central), the protagonist, Julianna Dykstra, is nevertheless also domesticated and encouraged to develop a gendered subjectivity that relies very much on orthodox masculinist values and desires. The narrative follows the rebellious Julie as she is caught for shoplifting, warned off by the law, and finally grounded for the two-month Christmas holiday period by her father, John. Unable to join her friends in their various activities—which include "meeting the boys outside Hungry Jack's" (5)—she is forced to accompany her family on a yacht trip to the Abrolhos Islands. Determined not to enjoy the holiday, she is uncooperative and antisocial, and soon wishing for something to break the boredom of boating. Her wish is granted by way of a time-slip, and she becomes swept up in a three-hundred-year-old nightmare involving the wreck of the *Batavia* and its infamous mutiny. Julie experiences romantic love with a boy called Dirk while she is stranded in the past, but is also subject to scenes of abuse, rape, murder, and justice seventeenth-century style, discovering, in short, that without adult male protection there is little chance of her surviving the ordeal.

At the beginning of the novel, Julie is entirely subjected by the Law of the father, thus suggesting that the narrative may develop into a story about female agency.[10] As it progresses, however, a number of strategies are employed that work against this idea, positioning the audience to view female sexuality in conventional patriarchal terms. The narrative operates in the romance mode, for instance, following the familiar hetero-normative pattern by telling the tale of a quest by the female hero for the "male who will make her complete". At the same time it also tames the wayward female child, first through an "initiation into romantic love" which domesticates her and renders her safe, and second by "supress[ing] oppositional desires in the cause of the patriarchal family" (Rutherford 3). The latter is achieved by juxtaposing law with lawlessness and present with past in a manner that proposes that the present is superior and—especially for the female subject—safer. The present is constructed as a place of security and as familiar, while by contrast, the past is depicted in terms of

violence and restriction, because here women are little more than chattels—
helpless beings that are "tossed like playthings from one brutal pair of hands
to another" (151). As Leonie Rutherford argues, in this predatory world of the
devil's own, the price of womanhood and autonomy is savage violation and
depersonalised subjection, and Julie escapes death only because of the protection of Dirk and, importantly, of father-surrogate Weibbe Hayes. In doing so,
however, she learns to value the childlike dependence she fought against in the
twentieth-century world, concluding, Rutherford contends, that it is "better to
submit to one male lawgiver, whether father or husband [. . .] than become a
prey to all the rest" (9–10).

The conclusion of the novel serves to highlight this idea because the reader
is given a pronounced sense of the relief Julie feels upon returning. During
this episode, the violence of the past and the safety of the present are starkly
emphasised. Huddled on a coral island, alone in her terror with the scarecrow
figures of the dead mutineers creaking on the gallows above her, Julie falls
asleep only to be woken by her father who has come to the rescue. She sobs
"like a three-year-old" in his strong and protective embrace and he rocks her
to "drive away the nightmare". "'I'm sorry,' she gulp[s] [. . .] over and over
again [. . .] 'I'm sorry, I'm sorry. Oh, Dad, I'm sorry'" (166). According to
Rutherford, the narrative bears "traces of adult anxieties about the potentially
uncontrollable female child" (12) so it is pertinent that, at this time, Julie
realises how "stupid—and selfish" she has been. Indeed, that she has "learnt
[her] lesson" (167) becomes abundantly clear on the final pages:

> 'Dad [. . .] I've been a brat haven't I?'
>
> John Dykstra stared at her as if his ears were playing tricks on him.
> A huge smile spread slowly across his face. 'Yes,' he said, 'You've been a
> brat. Now, get your shoulder to that boat and let's go home and face your
> mother's wrath.'
>
> Together they dragged the boat down to the water. Julie's heart felt as
> light as a feather in the wind. Let her mother scold—she deserved it. She
> *had* been a brat. She could see it now and it was as though that insight had
> lifted shackles from her mind. (168–69, emphasis original)

Rutherford's analysis of *The Devil's Own* concentrates largely on the
domestication of female sexuality through the romantic rite of passage, yet it
illustrates how the adolescent subject's confrontation with death in the past
can function to normalise dominant gendered social and ideological systems
in the present. Brian Caswell's *Dreamslip* works in a similar way. It tells the
story of female and male twins, Rebecca and Martin, whose visits to both the
past and the future (which are triggered by traumatic events such as deaths,
wars, and disasters) also construct the present as a much safer place to be. For
Rebecca, trapped in a violent future, this idea is particularly apt (although the
danger is balanced against an intense sexual romance). The narrative, which

hinges on a hetero-normative conclusion for Rebecca—who returns, pregnant, to the twentieth-century after dying in the future—functions like *The Devil's Own* to enable its protagonist to become an adult woman in an alternative setting, while in the process sustaining, to use Rutherford's phrase, "the myth of the mother under patriarchy" (3). It achieves this largely by denying Rebecca a narrative voice (at least until she is safely home and thus locked into her reproductive role), but also by suggesting, as historical fictions tend to, that (gendered) ways of being are transhistorical because, irrespective of the time or the place, the socio-political ideologies informing the societies that the twins occupy are always masculinist.

The final text that I want to consider which uses death to shock its characters (and perhaps, by extension, its readers) into a particular way of being or seeing, is Isobelle Carmody's *The Gathering*. Conversely, it attempts to do so by a turning away from, rather than towards, the patriarchy. In part, *The Gathering* tells the tale of a violent father/son relationship, charting the emotional and sexual maturation of its chief protagonist, Nathaniel Delaney, from a state of subjection to one of agency. While it is heavily influenced by horror chronotopes, the novel's plot is based upon the good versus evil metanarrative of traditional fantasy (Stephens and McCallum, "Ghosts" 173–74). As in *Del-Del*, possession is a key theme, although the evil is an amorphous entity, channelled through a number of authority figures and their minions—a darkness that has infected a patch of earth and its surrounds, ostensibly because of a violent event in the distant past. The darkness periodically returns to this point of origin, forcing the vessels it possesses each time to commit further acts of violence, and leaving in its path any number of dead or scarred individuals. The narrative follows a group of five psychologically damaged adolescents (the Chain) who band together in order to fight these negative forces. Its setting, a town called Cheshunt, is associated with death by the stench that blows into the area from the nearby abattoir. Cheshunt seems to magnify the potential of its citizens to be either good or evil: The members of the Chain represent those who are summoned to heal the tortured earth, while those who are drawn to the dark are the corrupt of the area, exercising control over others wherever possible.

The operation of power is a central theme in the novel because Cheshunt is a totalitarian community, organised in conformity with Foucault's panopticon (Stephens and McCallum, "Ghosts"). The exercise of discipline in the town is carried out primarily by men who hold positions of power, such as the policemen and the school vice-principal, Mr Karle (also known as the Kraken), while male members of the Gathering (a vigilante committee made up of the town's youths) work to physically coerce those who do not conform. Because fantasy "presupposes a continuity between the social and the personal" (Stephens and McCallum, "Ghosts" 176), as the narrative progresses and the personal demons of the Chain are revealed, it becomes clear that, for most of them, their battle also involves confronting an abusive male from either the past or the present. Seth's father represents a source of personal angst: As the quintessential patriarch, it is he who wields the power in the father-son relationship by subscribing to the belief that, like his mother, Seth requires "a firm hand". Nissa's confrontation occurs when, by chance, she meets her mother's predatory ex-boyfriend, the man who is responsible for her homelessness, while for Nat it is the return of repressed memories of his father, a violent man who once attempted to strangle him, that triggers the challenge.

In accordance with the horror genre, the text deploys the present everyday chronotope and then disrupts this sense of everydayness with uncanny moments, working to implicate the reader in mental states based on "primitive" superstitions and irrational fears, and inviting them to view familiar places, customs, and objects "not as different but as signifying differently" (Stephens and McCallum, "Ghosts" 165–66, 177). An episode in the text which demonstrates these ideas occurs in the prologue when Nat first returns to Cheshunt (the scene of his childhood abuse) and experiences the same "watery horror" in his gut that he felt when standing over his father's coffin—the sense that something is "wrong and unnatural". The association between his father's corpse and the town signals a nascent awareness of his father's evil nature and this is made clear by a familiar nightmare which seems to simultaneously hover over him. The dream involves running from a monster through a dark, wild forest with a bloody, full moon riding high in the black night above him—a "shambling, leering [monster] with a shark's smile [and] reeking breath" that, Nat divulges, is sometimes his father (xiii). This is hardly a subtle warning of danger, but because it occurs in an ordinary moment when Nat and his mother are driving into the town, and because it pivots on the kind of macabre and malevolent images that have traditionally induced horror in audiences, its effect is to imbue both Nat's relationship with his father and the landscape with a special significance.

This sequence of events also draws attention to the dominant messages in the narrative; one, that "[p]ower corrupts and absolute power corrupts absolutely" (151), and two, that patriarchal institutions and figures are the sources of that power in its most dangerous form. Like other fantasies which foreground the good/evil polarity, these messages are laid on with a heavy hand. Nevertheless, they have the potential to be coercive because readers are encouraged, through the use of first-person narration (a strategy not typical of fantasy), to share the narrator's view—and thus the ideologies constructed in and by the text. As Scutter suggests, the emphasis on "the stinking danger of the town, its bestial abattoirs [and] its power-mongering" make it difficult for audiences to fail to identify with the Chain and with Nat who is "penetrated, assailed, assaulted and battered with fear throughout the text" (233, 235). One graphic episode in particular illustrates this point. It is also, I would suggest, the most horrifying event in the text because Nathaniel's beloved dog, The Tod (a character in his own right), is set alight by Buddha, the hateful leader of the Gathering, burning to his death while an impotent Nat is forced to look on:

I screamed in utter horror, helpless. The match landed in his tail and flames swept forward up over him. Devoured him.

He arched and coiled, yelping in pain and fright, and then he screamed, a long inhuman howl of agony and terror. For one terrible second, his eyes looked at me from out of the flames, bulging and pleading.

And then there was nothing but the crackling sound of burning meat. (214)

The dead pet is such a staple feature of the teen horror genre that, according to author R. L. Stine, "[i]f the kid has a pet, he's going to find it dead on the floor" (qtd. in Gray 54). As this passage demonstrates, however, The Tod's death is no cliché. Rather, it enhances the sense of dread that pervades the novel since readers have been cued to expect it, both at the beginning of the narrative when Nat dreams of it, and then just prior to the incident when The Tod howls at Nat's departure—"as if he knew what was coming to get him", Nat thinks later (215). At the same time, it serves to emphasise the depths of the evil haunting Cheshunt, and to mobilise the Chain in a way that nothing else in the narrative—including the pain and deaths of others—has managed to do. It is at this point, then, that the text's outcome seems assured because if good does not triumph over evil, The Tod's death is rendered pointless. Indeed, the evil is defeated in a final showdown between its disciples and the Chain, and significantly, the Kraken howls like a wounded animal during the battle, suggesting that The Tod's death has been revenged (256). In this way, the torture and killing of the dog can be seen to drive home the novel's message about the potential tyranny of patriarchy.

The effectiveness of this message is complicated in a number of ways, however. The narrative's construction of female subjectivity is aligned with masculinist agendas, in that female roles are few and restricted, Nat's mother is "a classic victim figure" (Stephens and McCallum, "Ghosts" 177), and the female members of the Gathering hold little power. Nat's relationship with his mother also creates a tension. At the opening to the novel, the path of Nat's life is dictated by his mother: She chooses when they must move house (a frequent occurrence), where they will move to, which school he will attend, whether she will answer his questions, listen to him, or even believe his version of events once he gets into trouble with the law and the principal. Nat's frustration is always evident, but at several points this is represented in terms of violence—once, in particular, when Nat feels like "smashing her in the face" (60). As Scutter argues, "the text transgresses its own codes alarmingly" (233), and nowhere is this more apparent that in the conclusion, when the power differential between Nat and his mother is reversed, a move which effectively reinstates patriarchal authority. The character of Nissa creates a textual aporia as well. Nissa is strong and assertive, but according to Stephens and McCallum, these traits are narratively constituted as her weakness. The frequent references to her sexual desirability, they argue, also "align her with the female as object of gaze typical of horror" ("Ghosts" 177).[11]

Redefining Gender: Death and the Quest Hero(ine)

Although it seeks to interrogate the kind of hierarchical and sexist power relationships that are embedded in patriarchal discourses, *The Gathering* therefore displays a number of contradictions in its narrative that work against such ideas. Perhaps this occurs because the assumptions of the horror genre, to which the text belongs, are usually patriarchal. As Stephens points out, "generic discourses readily evoke gender stereotypes because characters are caught up in events which tend to have gendered forms and outcomes" ("Gender" 19). Gendering is a prominent feature, for example, of hero narratives. For a number of reasons, the heroic quest tale (one of the most common and enduring narrative patterns in children's fantasy fiction) tends to be heavily gendered at the level of both story and discourse: It draws on, and is already shaped by, a substantial set of pre-existing narrative patterns, ideas, and values pertaining to quests and to heroes, all of which are inclined to be patriarchal; it is likely to relegate female characters to passive or background roles and to address an implied male audience (thus potentially positioning female readers to identify with a selfhood that is male); and, moreover, since it traditionally traces the transition from boyhood to manhood, it is "often overtly concerned with the question of what it means to be a man" (Hourihan, *Deconstructing* 69).

Irrespective of the perennial concerns surrounding issues of gender representation in literature for children, critical interrogations of the conventional gendering of the quest-narrative genre have occurred only in recent years.[12] Furthermore, the number of texts available to children which seek to deconstruct, disrupt, or expose the conservative masculinist discourses associated with the hero paradigm remains limited (Stephens and McCallum, *Retelling* 117, 124). Nonetheless, a striking feature of the quest-narratives that I have examined in the course of my reading is that many make a point of attempting, in some way, to reconfigure the genre and its gendered representations. The foremost strategy is the use of a female hero; however, a few texts also explore the subject from a comedic perspective. At several points in C. D. Francis's *Three Realms* (which employs the latter approach), for example, the narrative attends to resisting the hero stereotype by parodying both the genre and its male hero, Griff. The novel tells the story of Griff's adventures at the "Academia Gentium", a boarding school that is focused on the philosophy of science, religion, and magic, and to which Griff has been sent in order to discover the mystery behind his mother's apparent terminal illness. One such incident occurs when Griff's pre-conceived notions of heroism are complicated (ideas which have been gleaned from popular texts including *Star Wars* and *Harry Potter*). Expecting to be mentored by a Zen Master on his quest or, at the very least, to have a wise, "elegant and extremely articulate" companion for the heroic journey, he is disappointed—and quite deflated—to find instead that he has been partnered with Ludic, an "odd little man" who looks and sounds like "an overdressed parrot with a bizarre speech impediment" (22).[13]

The reader is positioned here to view Griff as self-important and his attitude towards Ludic as rude and patronising. Indeed, Griff is constructed for much of the novel as a distinctly unheroic character. On the whole, however, the success of this approach is quite modest since any potential these kind of strategies possess to modify the genre or to give it a different gender inflection is always limited by the narrative's adherence to the traditional male hero paradigm. Quests are typically built around "a male career pattern" which follows a structure of "anxiety, doubt, conflict, challenge, temporary setback, then final success and triumph", Stephens argues ("Gender" 29), and the story closely follows this trajectory. Griff often doubts his ability to be heroic, he has numerous conflicts with the evil being that is responsible for much of the narrative's mayhem (and also his mother's illness), he is almost killed during the penultimate meeting with this being, yet at the conclusion he overcomes it to emerge from the challenge victorious. On the path to the goal, the hero is often involved in the rescue of a virtuous (usually female) prisoner and may be rewarded as a mark of this success with a "trophy bride" (Hourihan, *Deconstructing*). This occurs when, on a school excursion, Griff is instrumental in releasing a number of children from imprisonment, including the grateful Brit (the girl who has, over the course of the narrative, been constructed as a likely romantic mate for Griff). Heroic narratives also hinge on "the hero's active engagement with events and experiences, leading to the discovery of positive self-identity as masculinity" (Stephens and McCallum, *Retelling* 116). During his time at the academy, Griff learns a variety of lessons about strength, courage, tolerance, healing, reasoning, and logic—lessons which prove useful in overcoming the fears and anxieties he has about death but which also contribute to his formulation of a (masculine) heroic sense of self.

Griff's role as the only focalising character also works to privilege the masculine bias associated with the genre. As the following example demonstrates, this is particularly evident in episodes where Brit is involved:

Griff, where are you? I need help.
 Griff sat upright. *Brit? Brit, is that you?*
 Yes, you ignoramus, the voice said more loudly. *Where have you been? I've been calling to you for ages!*
 Yep, that's Brit all right, he reassured himself, smiling as he jumped to his feet. Typical. She needs help, and I'm here to help, but she's mad at me again. Can't win. (250)

The gendered stereotype that is invoked here depends on a humorous viewing of females as unfathomable and males as subjected to their (ever-changing) whims. However, there is no corresponding access to Brit's point of view that allows readers to assess the underlying stereotype. Furthermore, this is only one of a number of ways in which Brit is constructed pejoratively, suggesting, as Stephens contends, that there is "a tendency for traditional stories and genres to devolve always back into patriarchal discourse" ("Gender" 20).

Making a difference to gender representation, then, is not simply a matter of "reformulating gender schemata in relation to participants' roles or actions"; rather, gendering must be considered at the level of both story and discourse (Stephens, "Gender" 29). In order to explore this idea in more detail, I wish to focus now on two texts which interrogate the conventional gendering of the quest-narrative by allotting the hero's role to a female. Garth Nix's *Sabriel* and Paul Collins's *Dragonlinks* make an interesting study not only because they both have the potential to reconstruct versions of the male hero paradigm (and thus critique the patriarchal discourses it draws upon), but also because they engage so closely with woman/death, that twin "enigma" which Western culture posits as what is "radically other to the norm, the living or surviving masculine subject" (Bronfen and Goodwin 13).

Sabriel (the first in the "Old Kingdom" series), provides a useful starting point, not least because the work has been commended for its positive representation of female subjectivity.[14] Like *The Gathering*, the novel is a hybridisation of genres, blending high fantasy with horror. It is set in a world which is divided into two by a heavily-guarded wall. The southern area, called Ancelstierre, has much in common with early-twentieth-century Britain as its references to public boarding schools, tea ("the universal comforter" of the society), modern—if antiquated—armies, and various inventions of the Second Industrial Revolution suggest. Here, bureaucracy and science are society's organising principles, and most of the citizens do not believe in magic nor come into contact with the spirits of the dead. Yet, to the north of the wall in the Old Kingdom (which by contrast is an anarchic and pre-technological civilisation), magic and necromancy are commonplace, and the dead can make a diabolical and murderous return to the land of the living. The story, which utilises the good versus evil metanarrative of traditional fantasy to explore themes such as grief, death, growth, and power, follows the age-old quest pattern. Its protagonist, Sabriel, is the daughter of the Mage Abhorsen, a necromancer whose job it is to maintain the proper boundaries between the realms of Life and Death. Schooled in Ancelstierre, where magic can be worked only in close proximity to the wall, Sabriel possesses just a rudimentary knowledge of necromancy and its workings. However, when her father's spirit is trapped in Death and his body in the Old Kingdom, she is forced to cross the wall in search of him and thus begin the familiar quester's journey that will propel her from adolescence into adulthood.

The narrative can be seen to revise elements of the male paradigm in a variety of ways. The masculine quest pattern is complicated, for instance, by reversing the characteristic gender roles: In this version, a female hero takes centre-stage, is assisted by a male, brings a prince back to life with a kiss, slays the monster, and then succeeds the "throne" (Mills, "Fixity"). The outline of Sabriel's story correlates closely with others in the female hero paradigm. Her father is of mage stock and her birth is surrounded by unusual circumstances, for it is not only her mother who dies during the birth, but Sabriel too (she is rescued, however, before the First Gate of Death by Abhorsen). As an infant, an attempt is made to kill her, so she is taken from her home in the Old Kingdom to be raised in Ancelstierre. On becoming an adult, she returns to her home in order to succeed her father as the next Mage Abhorsen. To do so, she completes a quest during which: her innate talents are recognised; she rescues the principal male character in the narrative (a young royal named Touchstone); she is supported by a network of female-helpers; and she performs tasks that are characteristically ascribed to the masculine domain.[15] Sabriel also functions to define femininity in the novel as much by vulnerability and dependence as aggression and power. Moreover, the instruments she uses to wield her power are both yonic (bells) and phallic (sword). Like other contemporary demon-hunters such as Buffy the Vampire Slayer, she embodies a form of action femininity that, Kerry Mallan argues, typifies the current wave of popular feminism promoted to youth audiences: She is capable and strong, rarely hesitating to use her powers to banish the evil dead back to Death; she inhabits the kind of dark and dangerous spaces that are traditionally encoded as masculine; and with her "curiously pale" skin and fashionably cut "night-black" hair, she draws on the appeal of teen goth culture ("Hitting" 139, 142).

On the surface, then, Sabriel appears both to reconfigure the heroic narrative around a female hero paradigm, and to offer an alternative to horror fiction's traditional female victim-hero tale. However, a closer reading demonstrates that the narrative's affirmative account of female agency and subjectivity is undermined by a number of tensions and contradictions: the aforementioned use of gender reversals to appropriate the traditional quest pattern; an emphasis on binary oppositions; a repeated representation of the feminine as abject; and a denial of true agency for the female hero. It is widely recognised that the first of these factors, the reversal of gender roles, is a problematic strategy. As Stephens and McCallum argue, it is an obvious point, often made, that simple gender reversals cannot but fail to transform the masculine paradigm. This is because the influence of the male heroic narrative is so pervasive that, by allotting the hero's role to a female character, in all probability "she" will merely be assimilated into the socially and politically conservative discourses associated with the traditional paradigm (Retelling 117). Indeed, there are several episodes in the text which serve to illustrate the difficulty of constructing positive versions of female subjectivity from within the kind of phallic systems of representation that characterise the genre. In one—the final confrontation between Sabriel and her arch-enemy Kerrigor—Sabriel finds that no matter how expertly she wields her sword, it has little effect since it can only punch through the wicked prince's chest to project out the other side. The sword becomes instead the instrument by which Kerrigor demonstrates the perverse power he has over Sabriel, and by which he eventually impales her, sending her into Death:

> Irresistibly, Kerrigor drew her towards him [. . .]
>
> [His] blistered lips moved towards hers [. . .] His breath was overpowering, reeking of blood, but she had long gone beyond throwing up. She turned her head aside at the last second, and felt, dry, corpse-like flesh slide across her cheek.
>
> 'A sisterly kiss', chuckled Kerrigor. 'A kiss for an uncle who has known you since birth—or slightly before—but it is not enough . . . '
>
> Again, his words were not just words. Sabriel felt a force grip her head, and move it back to face him, while her mouth was wedged apart, as if in passionate expectation [. . .]
>
> Swiftly as a snake, arm and sword went out, striking through Sabriel, through armour and flesh and deep into the wooden floor beyond. Pain exploded, and Sabriel screamed, body convulsing around the blade in one awful reflexive curve. (321–22)

This passage—which has obvious sexual overtones since it obscenely mimics the act of intercourse—not only works to reinscribe the image of the tormented (sexualised) female body that is such a staple of the horror genre, but it also suggests, as Stuart Hall argues, that the very concept of the female hero would seem to "operate on decisively masculine terrain" ("Editorial" 116). In this instance, the reference to terrain, particularly gendered, is quite apt given that *Sabriel*'s preoccupation with territory, its boundaries—and their collapse—is perhaps the defining feature of the novel. The inspiration for the setting came to Nix from an image of Hadrian's wall which appeared to show two different seasons operating on either side of the barrier: green lawn on the southern side and snow on the northern side ("Interview"). These binary oppositions are part of a larger scheme within the text: south/north can also be seen to correspond in the narrative with life/death, father/mother (and thus male/female), good/evil, order/disorder, and, as the pairing of Ancelstierre with the Old Kingdom illustrates, with civilised/uncivilised. The conceptual centre of the hero story consists of this kind of dualistic thinking (Hourihan, *Deconstructing* 15), but as feminists such as Hélène Cixous point out, its effect is always to privilege one set of concepts and terms over another (Tong 199). Within this scheme, then, all that signifies the masculine in the narrative (south, life, father, good, order, civilised) is defined as the norm while that which is associated with the feminine (north, death, mother, evil, disorder, uncivilised) becomes the deviant Other.

Under these terms, Sabriel's quest can be seen to conform to the traditional male paradigm by playing out a masculine fantasy of power in which the hero restores order by subduing the unruly (and thus dangerous) cultural Other. The dichotomous conceptual order informing the text functions, as well, to realign the familiar (pejorative) association between death and Woman. Death takes on a territorial identity in the narrative, and it is an identity that is clearly marked as female. Death is consistently conflated with the maternal, for instance: It can be seen to operate metaphorically as the maternal semiotic element of the social realm, the element that "seeps in from the 'territory' of the pre-Oedipal" (Tong 205), and, as Alice Mills argues, at several points it is rendered as "a monstrous birth canal whose current flows the wrong way" ("Fixity" 21). The waters of Death into which Sabriel and Abhorsen venture recall other images in Western literature of rivers that transport the dead. However, the "flowing", "leaking", "gushing", "gripping", "slippery", "black" channel that is depicted here is aligned instead with a grotesque maternal body—a body from which long-dead corpses can "squirm triumphantly" into Life (58). The figure of the mother also finds a prominent place within Death's landscape. In one episode, Kerrigor, leader of the evil dead, is represented as a monstrous mother-substitute when a newborn Sabriel wriggles towards him as though searching for her mother's breast (Mills, "Fixity" 21). In another, Sabriel enters Death (significantly when she first begins to menstruate) "in fear and desperation", summoning a spirit guide to answer her questions about puberty and sex—a "blurred, glowing human shape, its arms outstretched in welcome" that she sees as her mother (59–60).[16]

The source of horror in the narrative is clearly the Kristevan abject—those polluting objects and images that "stand for the danger to identity that comes from without: the ego threatened by the non-ego, society threatened by its outside, life by death" (Kristeva 71). The Abhorsen's duty to maintain the borders between the living and the dead thus represents a ritual of defilement—a method of keeping the abject at bay so as to contain the threat it poses to the symbolic order. As Creed contends, the modern horror narrative "brings about a confrontation with the abject (the corpse, bodily wastes, the monstrous-feminine) in order, finally, to eject the abject and redraw the boundaries". It works to "separate out the symbolic order from all that threatens its stability, particularly the mother and all that her universe signifies" ("Horror" 257–58). Admittedly, Sabriel somewhat complicates the masculinist agenda that is manifest here for she is able (as Kristeva suggests the liberated subject is) to "play" between the maternal, semiotic pre-Oedipal realm and the patriarchal Oedipal realm—"between the 'feminine' and the 'masculine', chaos and order, revolution and the status quo" (Tong 205). This movement is countered, however, by the way the narrative persistently frames Sabriel's subjectivity through that of her father, and by the limitations it imposes on her heroics and her quest for agency. The inscription in

Sabriel's almanac and also in *The Book of the Dead* reads: "Does the walker choose the path or the path the walker?" (37), suggesting that the quest for agency is indeed central to the text. Yet, at crucial points during the narrative, Sabriel lacks the power to perform her role as Abhorsen and must rely on the support of the principal males to achieve her objective. In many ways, Sabriel is defined by her dependency on the masculine. As Mills argues, in *Sabriel* and also in *Lirael: Daughter of the Clayr*—the second in the series—there is a pattern of daughters operating as replacements for the father, of "assuming the father's functions", which in Sabriel's case, amounts to her being unable to "find an identity of her own in the novel" ("Fixity" 22).

The final problematic factor working against a feminist reading of female subjectivity in the text concerns the novel's romantic sub-theme. According to Stephens and McCallum, in order to reconstruct the traditional heroic paradigm in a way which affirms and celebrates female experience, it is important that the hero is not entirely interpellated by conventions of romantic desire, and that she can achieve an identity which is not reliant on orthodox female ways of being (*Retelling* 119–24). It could be argued that Sabriel's character works within these parameters. As the daughter of Abhorsen, she is free in ways other girls her age are not; moreover, she approaches her hereditary duty to return the demonic enemies of Life to their proper place in Death with a single-minded determination. However, there is also a persistent suggestion in the text that there is really only one gendered subject position and one maturational path available to her, both of which are expressed in conventional patriarchal terms. The episode in which Sabriel, Touchstone, and Abhorsen confront Kerrigor in the reservoir is a good example. After ringing Astarael, the bell that calls everyone who hears it into Death, Abhorsen dies, leaving Sabriel to fulfil his role as the new Mage. At this same moment, Sabriel and Touchstone share a violent kiss—a kiss that acts to stave off the bell's magnetic pull into Death, but also to mark the point at which Sabriel is effectively passed from the hands of her father to that of her lover. This incident functions to undermine Sabriel's strength and independence by suggesting that being female is to conform to a hetero-normative model of sexual subjectivity. At the same time, it also reinforces the (masculine) code of order that is woven through the narrative.[17]

Like *Sabriel*, *Dragonlinks* (the first in the "Jelindel Chronicles") also seeks to destabilise the conservative discourses associated with the male hero paradigm. From the outset, the novel's hero, Jelindel dek Mediesar, struggles against the patriarchal ideologies which govern the medieval-like world she inhabits, suggesting something of the feminist agenda that is such a prominent feature of the narrative. When she alone escapes the massacre of her whole family and the burning of their home, however, this struggle is brutally emphasised because, not only is she without the protection of her father the Count and his guards, but she is dressed as a boy and must learn to operate in a world that, as a girl of noble birth, is largely foreign to her. The narrative follows Jelindel as she becomes the male Jaelin, finds employment as a scribe's assistant, and befriends Zimak (a streetwise youth who is also a courier at the local market). Jelindel, Zimak, and a warrior named Daretor, then get caught up in the same evil plot that is responsible for the death of the Mediesar family. Outlawed and on the run, the three embark on a quest to find the magical, power-bestowing links of the chainmail shirt that is behind the plot.

Through the adventurers, the narrative constructs a dialogue between a number of versions of masculinity. The somewhat clichéd male subject positions occupied by Daretor and Zimak work in a way familiar to many adolescent fictions; that is, by juxtaposing two quite different masculine models (McCallum and Stephens). Daretor represents the traditional hero—the romantic knight in shining armour who is bound by honour and a strict moral code. Zimak, by contrast, is the macho male—a bragging, unprincipled, uneducated brawler who would rather "get a leg over" a girl than make conversation (297). As the subject who belongs to both masculine and feminine categories, Jelindel/Jaelin acts to disrupt the dialogue, however, because, through her cross-dressing behaviour, she provides a rather unorthodox twist to this textual strategy. According to Victoria Flanagan, since they occupy "a unique gendered niche which is not grounded within a single gender category, but incorporates elements of both", female-to-male cross-dressing characters like Jelindel/Jaelin can work to "create a gendered realm outside conventional expectations and stereotypes" (79, 80). When disguised as a boy, Jelindel/Jaelin is accepted absolutely as a male, even attracting sexual attention from other females. Yet her female corporeality is emphasised in a number of episodes too, thus destabilising conventional notions of the ways in which females and males "should" behave, and suggesting to audiences that the factors which are often used to determine masculinity and femininity (such as visual cues) are arbitrary. One incident, in particular, highlights this tendency. Here, Jelindel/Jaelin has spent weeks on the run after murdering an evil mage. She is mounted on a horse, and wearing the mailshirt for safekeeping:

> '[. . .] I'm not in the mood for a fight', grumbled Zimak. 'I've got saddle sores. Its hard to feel like a heroic warrior on a dangerous quest when you've got saddle sores.'
>   Try having saddle sores with Rucelmoon in the wrong phase, Jaelin thought to herself, rubbing her abdomen. (141)[18]

Admittedly, Jelindel/Jaelin's path to sexual development is marked by several conventional and gendered rites of passage—after mastering the sword and slaughtering the mage, her induction into the hero warrior's world is assured and, at the same time, she learns how to harness her power to perform magic (a common strategy in fantasy fiction to signal a female character's maturation from girl to young woman). Yet, in bringing these rites together like this, the boundaries which typically divide masculinity and femininity become blurred and something of the artifice of gender constructions is exposed. In contrast to Sabriel, Jelindel/Jaelin is also not interpellated by conventions of romantic desire, nor is the conclusion to her story predicated upon a normative heterosexual resolution. She is assisted by the principal male/s in the novel as is often the case in heroic narratives that are written against the male paradigm, but neither becomes her partner or consort (Stephens and McCallum, *Retelling* 118–19). In fact, Jelindel/Jaelin's companions turn out to be traitors, seduced by the power of the mailshirt and the weapons associated with it, and so she sends them to a parallel world—a move which does not mean death for the two, but is "as final as death" since they can never return (361). Moreover, rather than becoming a ruler herself, working within institutions which rely on the familiar dominance and submission power binary, Jelindel/Jaelin chooses a life of relative anonymity, becoming a neophyte priestess and renouncing her royal title. In this way, female autonomy is privileged over heterosexual romance, and the romantic quest narrative is rewritten from what I think is a more persuasive and positive feminist perspective than that offered by *Sabriel*.

This is not to say that *Dragonlinks* is wholly successful in redefining the masculine meanings associated with the term "heroic" since it is clearly based on the linear (male) career pattern associated with traditional quest-narratives. And, yet, while the novel leads its audience along a familiar path by encouraging them to identify with the hero(ine), at several points it nevertheless reassesses conventional gender codes. The narrative works by positioning readers first to approve of Jelindel/Jaelin's actions and choices, and then to privilege her/him above the other questers in the novel. Crucially, this occurs when Jelindel/Jaelin kills her brother for his part in the family massacre. It is then that Zimak and Daretor discover that she is biologically female and, from this point, they do not readily accept her as equal (even though, prior to this, the three worked together in a way that made use of their individual strengths and allowed for their weaknesses). If readers accept that the judgement of the men is skewed by their narrow-minded attitude to gender, at the same time, they are positioned to accept the fluid notion of gender offered by Jelindel/ Jaelin and all that it entails. This has especially interesting possibilities in the episodes which detail the friendship between Jelindel/Jaelin and Kelricka, a priestess whom the trio meet several times during their journey. Because of the confusion surrounding Jelindel/Jaelin's gender, the scenes between them become erotically charged and take on a number of unorthodox sexual meanings. Much is made, for instance, of what appears to others as the (sexual) pairing between a boy of sixteen and a much older, more experienced woman. And the moment at which Jelindel/Jaelin is first naked after a year in the saddle (that is, when she transforms from "male" back to "female") is, pointedly, when both she and Kelricka bathe in tubs which, though separate, are also side-by-side. As Flanagan explains, "gender is never quite what meets the eye" in the context of these kind of narratives since "feminine becomes masculine [and] heterosexual attraction becomes homosexual" (88).

Looking Both Ways: Dead-Narrator Tales and the Transition from Innocence to Experience

As I have argued, *Dragonlinks'* challenge to prevailing gender assumptions and categorisations is largely contingent upon the ways in which it employs the female-to-male cross-dressing model to imagine an alternative to the traditional binary division between masculinity and femininity. The novels I look at in this section also use narrative strategies that allow them to play with and deconstruct conventional ideas about (gendered) identities and sexualities. Indeed, they seek to explore such notions in a particularly dramatic manner because they belong to a recent genre of what has been coined "dead-narrator tales".[19] The perceptual point of view in these texts typically belongs to a character who has died and is telling their story from "beyond the grave". Thus, Laura Whitcomb's *A Certain Slant of Light* begins: "Someone was looking at me. A disturbing sensation when you're dead" (1).

Several characteristics mark YA dead-narrator novels. Like other narratives of metamorphosis, they are, to borrow Clare Bradford's words, "always metaphorical, always located within the realm of the fantastic, so that the trope of bodily transformation stands for a range of meanings typically centred around identity, gender, and sociality" ("Possessed" 150).[20] Whether tragic, comic, or serious, the transformations represented in these texts are also, like other YA texts about metamorphoses, apt to symbolise the physical and psychological changes involved in adolescence, and to destabilise orthodox ideas about personal growth and development. As with so many other YA novels dealing with death, dead-narrator tales are overtly concerned, too, with life, grief, love, and other such existential issues. However, soul-searching takes on an especially profound meaning here because what is represented is not the death of an/other, but the death of oneself. The protagonists of these fictions therefore tend to express an intense regret for what they did not achieve or could not do, as occurs when Jesús (or Chuy), the teen narrator of Gary Soto's *The Afterlife*, thinks shortly after his murder:

> I rose out of my body [and] I realized that the pain was gone. But so was my last year in high school. So was the fall dance, my time with Rachel, who was not yet *mi novia*—my girl—but might have been if I could have brought her into my arms and convinced her that I was one marvelous thing. (4–5)

Lastly, YA dead-narrator stories often contain a sexual or romantic relationship. As the character of Chuy demonstrates, death interrupts what is typically perceived as a continuum of psychosexual development which, according to the general aims of adolescent literature, must then be resumed if the character is to grow up or come of age.

In essence, then, the protagonists of adolescent dead-narrator novels are "looking both ways" since, to paraphrase Maria Lassén-Seger, the ambiguity of a metamorphic event lies in its ability to point back to what the subject was and forwards to what s/he may become ("Child-Power" 159). Transmigrations are dissimilar to "traditional" metamorphoses, however, in that rather than tracing the process of alteration from human to animal, animate to inanimate, or from one human to another, they address the change from mortal to immortal—from the *em*bodied to the *dis*embodied. Unlike many metamorphs, dead-narrators also rarely undergo a change by choice, and it is usually impossible for them to return to their anterior body. One of the central "problems" facing authors of dead-narrator tales is thus the question of how to represent a subject who is no longer corporeal but is housed in a "body" made different by death. As Kai Mikkonen argues, it is now quite commonly accepted that literary metamorphosis "tests the limits of a 'character' and thus of representing a subject in writing" because on the one hand, the metamorphic event suggests that the human body is no longer capable of encoding a stable identity, yet on the other, for the change to be represented as a metamorphosis, it "requires a presupposition of the original form" (Mikkonen 309, 310). In *A Certain Slant of Light*, it is this very issue that drives the plot because the narrative is largely concerned with the ghostly protagonists' quest to "climb into flesh again" (4). Between them, Helen and James have been dead for around two centuries; yet, in order to fulfil their carnal desires, to sleep together "all night, every night [. . .] reaching into forever" (169, 190), they must both come to inhabit contemporary teen bodies. By comparison, the relationship between Chuy and Crystal in *The Afterlife* is one that involves only their spectral selves. Here, bodies travel "where the slightest wind [blows], kicking along with little control" (18). Thus, while the couple also meet and fall in love after their respective deaths, the novel is more concerned with their partnership as "soul mates" who decide to experience together what happens once their dead bodies, which are fading limb by limb, have disappeared altogether.

Needless to say, dead-narrator tales can be seen to construct shifting views of subjectivity and to resist a number of fixed and stable meanings regarding embodiment. In this respect, *A Certain Slant of Light* is particularly complex because notions of subjectivity and identity are made strange by both historical and material factors. Firstly, the age at which James and Helen die does not correspond with the age of the host bodies they come to occupy, so there is a discrepancy in experience between their "outer" and "inner" selves. Secondly, the pair belong to different eras and thus different cultural milieux, so although they have spent time accumulating new knowledge about the material world since their death, their corporeal developmental trajectories were halted at some time in the past, the effect of which is also to create a discrepancy in experience. The displacement produced by this split in identity, between one body and another, between past and present, is keenly felt when the pair initially have sex. At one point, James asks Helen whether it is her "first time". His question is not for Helen but for Jenny (or the "shell" of mentally disassociated Jenny whom Helen occupies). Misunderstanding, Helen replies in the negative on behalf of herself, but then she acknowledges that it is possible that Jenny is a virgin; without access to Jenny's consciousness, it is difficult to tell. Even then, the experience is altogether new for Helen because her way of being female belongs to a different era, and thus she is not used to being a sexual "aggressor" (139–40).

Nonetheless, for the most part, A Certain Slant of Light promotes a unitary and essentialist view of the human subject. Notwithstanding the narrative's unorthodox approach to embodiment, it says more about ontological anxiety than it does about fluid concepts of identity. The potential for reconceptualising ideas about gendered bodies is not challenged, for instance, because whether material or immaterial, Helen and James retain a stable sense of their selves as, respectively, female or male. Both the happy ending and Helen's moral justification for giving into desire "without shame" suggests, too, that the novel is largely a romantic love story, and thus it aligns itself with conventional, humanist (and heterosexist) ideas about subjectivity: "As far as I know [. . .] we are the only two of our kind in the whole world. Who could be more mated in God's eyes?" (139). As Catherine Belsey explains, true love as romance novels portray it "transcends the dualism of passion in conflict with morality", and through unification "dissolves the anxiety of division in the subject" replacing such unease with "a utopian wholeness" (Desire 23).

In contrast to A Certain Slant of Light, the metamorphic event in John Larkin's Cyber Payne functions to displace the novel's dead male protagonists into an alternate reality where they are given both a new body and a new gender. Offering a slight variation on the model, the narrative of Cyber Payne is humorous, involves a parallel Earth world, and is aimed at the younger end of the teen scale. It opens with the maiden voyage of a flying trike, home-built by Phil Payne and Paul "Larry" Larwood. Something goes wrong during the takeoff, however, and the trike crashes, leaving the boys hovering over an accident scene featuring a number of concerned neighbours, an ambulance, and what seem to be their own dead bodies. In the parallel world the pair find themselves in, phallic symbols and structures have been replaced with feminine alternatives, male and female genitals have been exchanged, and males not only menstruate and bear children, but their monthly cycle is a cause for celebration. The potential in the novel for questioning various ideas about gender—and about death—is therefore immense, particularly as Phil is dead in the alternate realm (albeit residing in a cyber-governed version of heaven), and there are two of Larry (the first male Larry, and Pauly, the paraworld "she-male" as s/he is called in the text). Rather than subverting gender norms or reconstructing gender into something new, however, the text works from conventional ideas, basing its model on differences, divisions, and "proper" ways of being. Moreover, it plays these kind of situations for laughs in a way that is both misogynistic and homophobic. A telling example of this approach occurs when Phil finds himself dreaming about kissing Kim Wilton (a girl from school that he is attracted to). During the dream, which is channelled by his alternate "dead" self, he wakes to find himself in the midst of a sexual encounter with Larry, but then spends the next two hours brushing his teeth, dry-retching, and dousing his hand in hot water. Certainly, much is made in the narrative of the inequality of orthodox gender constructions. At the same time, hegemonic versions of masculinity are parodied, and the concept of transgender is explored. Yet, regardless of these surface-level messages (and the conclusion which makes it unclear whether the boys' urgent quest to find the wormhole that will enable them to get back home is as successful as it first seems), the text ultimately reinstates the status quo since it is very clear that the dominant hetero masculinity embodied by the boys in the "real" world is the original from which any departure is, at best, derivative.

Although *Cyber Payne* encourages readers to question the norms of heterosexuality and its associated sexual practices, in the end it effectively sidesteps an in-depth interrogation of such issues because, to borrow Linzi Murrie's words, it falls prey to the "inherent tensions between the need and desire to remake masculinities in a contemporary world and the relative 'security' for [males] of dominant gender ideologies" ("Changing" 178). The novel's carnivalesque metamorphic event can therefore be seen as a temporary transgression—a narrative device for staging the kind of "time-out" scenario that Lassén-Seger argues can be "paradoxically both affirmative and subversive" because it provides authors of metamorphosis narratives with the means to play with unorthodox subject matter within a safe framework (*Adventures* 169).[21]

The ambiguity that is produced by the circular/carnival plot pattern is also a feature of Gabrielle Zevin's *Elsewhere* which chronicles the experiences of a fifteen-year-old hit-and-run victim—"a girl who forgot to look both ways before she crossed the street" (142). The narrative follows Elizabeth Hall as she negotiates an afterlife in Elsewhere, a realm where people age "backwards", getting younger until they are reborn. When she first arrives in Elsewhere, Liz has yet to come to terms with the idea that she will "never go to college or get married or get big boobs or live on [her] own or fall in love or get [her] driver's licence or anything" (48, original emphases not inc.). "'How the hell [can] it get any worse?'", she asks her grandmother, Betty (who died before Liz was born): "'I'm fifteen, and I'm dead. Dead!'" (48). Liz is horrified that she will never get the chance to grow up or "to do anything fun" (48), but as she soon learns, while she will get progressively younger, living out her fifteen years in Elsewhere until her infant self is swaddled up and sent back to Earth, she will still develop mentally and emotionally, still acquire memories and experience, still have the potential to form new relationships or resume old ones that were interrupted by death.

In fact, "life" in Elsewhere is so like existence on Earth that, bar the inverse ageing process and the body's inability to perish, there is little to distinguish between the two. As a consequence, the narrative is able to destabilise conventional ideas associated with growth, and with social roles and behaviours. On several occasions, for instance, the hierarchical child/adult dichotomy is problematised, such as when "children" (who are really mature subjects housed in child bodies) are given adult responsibilities, or when retirement occurs because an employee has become too young rather than too old. At other times, the disparity between chronological age and experience leads to questions about what constitutes a "proper" relationship. This occurs when an apparent age difference renders one of the novel's many romantic partnerships unorthodox, but also when the use of seemingly irregular labels creates confusion. A good example of both the former and the latter can be seen in Betty's relationship with Curtis Jest, the lead singer of the band Machine, who arrives in Elsewhere after dying of a heroin overdose. At the time of their respective deaths, Betty is fifty and Curtis thirty. When the two finally meet, however, Betty's Elsewhere age can be calculated as thirty-three–seventeen (33–17), and Curtis's as twenty-nine–one (29–1). (The first number corresponds to age at death minus the second number, which represents the years spent in Elsewhere.) Although it should be clear to audiences that the pair are now similar in body-age (or biological years), there is likely to be a discrepancy between the terms and the images that are evoked by discussions of their partnership, because Grandma Betty—as she is called in the narrative until Liz becomes comfortable with her—seems an unlikely match for a thirty'ish teen idol.

Despite these anomalies, however, the similarity between the two worlds also acts to bring about a normative (and, I would argue, repressive) gendered developmental path for Liz. Since Elsewhere "looks like almost any other place on Earth" (47)—or, at least, any other place in the United States of America—her journey is based on the prototypical or dominant female pattern, as illustrated by a dream she has early in the narrative. In the dream, her life continues on as if she has never died: she turns sixteen, gains her driver's licence, receives a new car, graduates with a degree in biology, becomes a veterinarian, and then one day meets a boy "with whom she can imagine spending the rest of her life" (56). Significantly, the dream is interrupted at this point by Betty (an *in loco parentis* figure), signalling that there will be no real or radical alteration of the adult-adolescent power dynamic in the novel because, like other adolescent female characters before her, Liz will only be allowed to progress so far. As the captain of the SS *Nile* (the ship that transports the dead to Elsewhere) informs her, there are still rules: "'If you think your death gives you free rein to act as you please, you are wrong'" (42).

Indeed, the restrictions that are imposed on Liz's development are encoded in the text in a number of ways, several of which involve the novel's strong romantic theme. The novel essentially belongs to the romance genre in that it is a narrative containing a central love story and a mode of fiction that "addresses the human impulse away from realism", allows for exploration of the human psyche, and engages with the "universals" of human experience: kinship, love, loss, and death (Saunders 540). One of the defining features of romantic fiction is the desire for movement away from contingency towards unity (Wetherell 132). This closing off of emotional ambivalence is implied by the circular pattern of the narrative which sees Liz returned to Earth as an infant—a baby girl who dreamed she "was lost at sea but one day found the shore" (269)—and by the textual emphasis on the romantic concept of the lifelong (heterosexual) partnership. This insistence on partnering is evident in the narrative as a whole, but as Liz's dream implies, the theme is primarily played out through Liz's desire for, and attainment of, a male other with whom she can spend the rest of her life (at least in Elsewhere). Liz meets Owen, a detective with the Bureau of Supernatural Crime and Contact (and a metonym for patriarchal law) when he detains her after she tries to illegally communicate with her family on Earth. The relationship then develops as Owen agrees to help Liz with her goal to acquire a driver's licence. The subsequent driving lessons become synonymous with their courtship; as Liz is schooled in the art of three point turns and parallel parking, she is simultaneously taught about love and relationships, and inducted into a particular way of being female.

Vehicles are often used metaphorically to symbolise the individual self; the way they are controlled or operated is thus analogous to the self's ego development or journey in life. In *Elsewhere*, driving is representative of agency; learning to drive is used to mark Liz's growth in self-awareness, but it also becomes a code for the various stages in her sexual development. The accident that she orchestrates on her first day in Elsewhere is indicative of her impotence, of the rage she feels because she did not choose to die, as is her refusal to drive from this point on; if she is only going to get younger, she tells Betty, she might as well "get used to being a passenger" (61). Once Liz is reconciled to the rules and regulations of Elsewhere and is granted a (limited) degree of personal freedom, however, she becomes tired of Betty driving her around and Owen takes over. Owen has already reached adulthood and experienced marriage—has already "been there before" (181)—so he makes "an excellent driving teacher" (230). Yet his tutoring of Liz is curiously devoid of carnal elements. Given the novel's setting in an afterlife, it is not surprising that there is an emphasis on the spiritual rather than the corporeal, but herein lies the crux of the novel's ideological message: Growing up for Liz entails a getting of wisdom, but not a chance to sexually mature beyond a certain point that, in conventional terms, is considered appropriate for fifteen-year-old adolescent girls. Thus, although her body "feels the same as it always has" (29), and although she expresses a desire to be involved in a sexual relationship, when she wonders after numerous trips to a local drive-in theatre why she and Owen have not "naturally" progressed to the back seat of the car, he informs her that "intimacy doesn't have all that much to do with backseats of cars" because "[r]eal intimacy is brushing your teeth together" (181). Even though the novel explicitly states that "dying is just another part of living" (76), in this sense, Liz's quest for maturity is one-dimensional, and thus the setting and the metamorphic event can be seen as a means to regulate sexual practices or contain adolescent (sexual) power. In Elsewhere, Liz can be a bridesmaid (as she is when Betty marries Curtis), but never a bride. She can live with her grandmother, but not alone or with Owen. She can experience sex, but only vicariously. In fact, where sexual relations are concerned, the belief that she is only "getting everything secondhand" (205) is especially pronounced, evident when she visits the observation decks that allow Elsewhere's residents to look back at Earth and sees her friend Zooey "lose her virginity in a fancy [hotel] room" (103), and, on another occasion, watches her parents brief, anguished coupling.

For Liz, the movement between innocence and experience is therefore firmly linked to what she learns about death, but not about sex. She is allowed to begin the transition, the text implies, but it will be conditional; one day she will turn "sweet sixteen" (in the Western world, traditionally the age of consent for lawful engagement in sexual conduct)—but not just yet. This notion that Liz is positioned at the threshold of adulthood, but still "safely" contained within the bounds of adolescence (and childhood) is also borne out by the narrative's temporal aspects. As the novel is largely concerned with a period of about one year in Liz's Elsewhere life, the concluding chapters cursorily trace her remaining years up until rebirth. In this way, the discourse of the narrative acts as a kind of textual authority too, because the duration of the different story strands are weighted unequally making it difficult not only to connect the adolescent Liz with the child and baby versions—particularly the new Liz "who is Liz and not Liz at the same time" (271)—but also to convey the associated changes in her perception. The effect of this strategy is to create the impression of a stable rather than a fluid identity, which is then reinforced by the repetitive declaration that concludes the section dealing with her adolescent self: "For better or worse, this is my life [. . .] This is my life. My life" (252). Liz is also fixed in childhood by the circular nature of her journey. The narrative traces a temporal arc that begins at fifteen years and finishes at zero, and thus it completes a circular trajectory that began "offstage" with her birth. Regardless of her rebirth, the aesthetic and thematic completeness that is created by this pattern imposes such a sense of final order on the text that, to use Stephens's words, "the end resumes the whole structure" (*Language* 43).

Conclusion

Elsewhere upholds Trites's contention that both characterisation *and* narrative structure are "wedded to adolescent literature's function of communicating to adolescents about cultural power and repression" (*Disturbing* 55). Here, the afterlife setting acts to foreground the power transactions that occur between the adolescent and the structures of authority with which s/he must come to terms, because while Liz learns to engage her own power, she also comes to an acceptance of her place within the power structure. This is neatly summed up in a conversation Liz and Curtis have about agency. For Curtis, "there's always a choice", but when Liz argues that she "didn't choose to die", he tempers his statement with "there's always a choice in situations where one has a choice" (113–14). *Cyber Payne* operates similarly in that while it enables a transgression of limits and boundaries, at the same time it works towards restoring them too. Death is used here as a plot device to enable the novel's protagonists to occupy a space in which conventional notions of gender have been overturned; the bodily metamorphosis that they undergo allows them to experience shifting subjectivities and thus to explore the supposedly fixed categories of male and female, heterosexual and homosexual. However, by imagining that death is not absolute, the narrative also allows them to escape the situation when it becomes too confronting.

If, as Lassén-Seger argues, metamorphosis in YA literature can be interpreted in general terms as "a trope for the physical and sexual changes that adolescents both fear and embrace" (*Adventures* 49–50) then I do not think it is too much to suggest, at least in the texts that I have examined here, that the motif reveals as much about adult anxieties as adolescent ones, particularly those concerning the potency of teenage girls. As *Elsewhere* and *A Certain Slant of Light* demonstrate, one of the ways that such power can be defused is through the use of romantic themes and plots, because the predictable endings of romances stifle alternative interpretations and impose authority over other accounts (Wetherell 132–33). Like the majority of the fantasy fictions in this chapter, then, these texts treat the figure of Woman not only with unease, but also with ambivalence since at the same time that there is an obvious attempt to construct positive accounts of female agency and to critique existing cultural practices concerned with gender, they disclose a pronounced tension regarding female power. Besides *In the Blood*'s graphic warning about the consequences for girls of transgressing the codes of "acceptable" sexual behaviour, for instance, *Sabriel*, *The Devil's Own*, and *Blood Moon* each works in their own way to shore up the patriarchal order. In *Sabriel*, this is played out through the ritualised abjection of the maternal or the feminine. Here, the distinct boundary between life and death is analogous to that between male and female, meaning that what is aligned with life/male in the narrative is defined as the norm, and as "what it means to be human", while death/female is Other: "deviant, different, dangerous" (Hourihan, *Deconstructing* 68–69). The strategy in *The Devil's Own* is to domesticate the potentially uncontrollable adolescent girl. This text proposes that female sexuality is threatening by using death to coerce the protagonist of the narrative into accepting both patriarchal authority and a masculinist way of being female. While *Blood*

Moon uses images of death to point to the fragility of the symbolic order, it too asserts masculine power by suggesting that females who operate outside the boundaries of the patriarchal order are monstrous. Finally, *In the Blood* works to privilege sex for reproduction over female sexual desire in a particularly violent manner; that is, by erasing the "promiscuous" female from the sexual economy.

These latter two texts not only highlight the horror genre's moral conservatism, they also point to its problematic view of Otherness. As Judith Halberstam argues "[b]y making monstrosity so obviously a physical condition and by linking it to sexual corruption, such fictions bind foreign aspects to perverse activities" (23). Nonetheless, as I have argued, the horror novel (and its attendant images of the abject or the disgusting) has a particularly powerful appeal to teen audiences. Perhaps this is because it acts as a form of transgression—as a "silent protest against the strictures of adult society with its socially sanctioned forms of behavior and codes of politeness" (Mallan and Pearce xviii). As studies of transgressive literature have demonstrated, however, because it functions as a "licensed safety valve", its ability to challenge entrenched systems of meaning and dominant ideologies is questionable. Jackson warns, for instance, that while fantasy fiction threatens to transgress social norms by permitting an articulation of taboo subjects, in simultaneously supplying a vicarious fulfilment of desire it can also neutralise the urge towards transgression, and thus re-confirm the institutional order (72). Halberstam makes a similar point when she argues that the violence of representation in the horror narrative does not always lie in bloody scenes of carnage or in images of monstrosity; rather, it more often works "through well-meaning and sincere humanist texts that feel compelled to make the human into some earnest composition of white, bourgeois [...] heterosexuality" (188). The "Outlands" trilogy can certainly be viewed in this way because while it subjects the gendered and monstrous body to a variety of violations—and thus, to borrow Elaine Ostry's words, "push[es] the envelope in the subject matter and grotesque imagery"—it also plays it safe by showing the posthuman body as "comfortingly familiar, human despite appearances" (243). As Botting contends, then, by crossing the social and aesthetic limits, transgression also serves to reinforce or underline the seeming value and necessity of such limits (7).

Chapter Five

Imagined Futures:
Death and the Post-Disaster Novel

The end is never the end [. . .] The end itself, the moment of cataclysm, is only part of the point of apocalyptic writing. The apocalypse as eschaton is just as importantly the vehicle for clearing away the world as it is and making possible the post-apocalyptic paradise or wasteland.

(Berger 5–6)

Just as the experience of time forces individuals to ponder the meaning of death and decay [. . .] so too does a historical and social consciousness of time force members of any society to imagine and anticipate its end.

(O'Leary 32)

Speculating on the future of the human race is not a new practice, nor is the tendency to set that future in a world irrevocably altered by a cataclysmic event. In the last few decades or so, however, the number of post-disaster scenarios appearing in Western cultural discourses has increased significantly. M. Keith Booker argues, for example, that this period has seen the rise of a dystopian mood in popular culture as a whole (*Literature* 7), while Veronica Hollinger notes that it has been an extremely fertile time for the apocalyptic imagination: Encouraged by the "confluence of a calendar system that situates us on a millennial cusp" and by a series of "apparently unprecedented epistemological and technological ruptures and transformations", she contends, we have been persistently canvassing the idea of a catastrophic, near-future end to the present world order (160–61). This latent anxiety about such issues as environmental pollution, nuclear war, and rapid advances in technology is especially apparent in literature written for child audiences. Indeed, in the 1990s, the post-disaster genre became one of the most prominent in British, American, and Australian children's fiction (Nikolajeva 167). Critical studies point to the prevalence of this theme in YA novels in particular: Carrie Hintz argues that YA readers have been sensitised to dystopian writing through popular works by Lois Lowry and Monica Hughes (255), and John Stephens's analysis of contemporary post-disaster novels for children is almost wholly concerned with adolescent texts ("Post-Disaster").[1] For several reasons, the genre is an important one for this study: Firstly, because of the gendered nature of the genre's ideologies; secondly, because the future societies imagined in post-disaster fictions are built upon the ashes of others and thus engage at a fundamental level with notions of life and death; and, thirdly, because post-disaster literature for YA readers tends to conflate the personal with the political in such a way that broad social issues are addressed within the (sexual) developmental narrative of adolescence (Hintz).

Post-Disaster Fiction

Post-disaster fictions can be used to make a comment on a vast number of topics ranging from world politics (Crawford), to gender (Inness), to history (Baccolini), and to the very "meaning" of life and of death. Peter Fitting's "You're History Buddy: Postapocalyptic Visions in Recent Science Fiction Film" demonstrates that portrayals of mass disaster can function as a critique of a form of government; act to contextualise themes and stories illustrating the eternal qualities of the human condition; highlight the power differentials in traditional gender representations; and "manage" various socially produced angers and frustrations. Furthermore, Fitting points out, because the post-disaster setting is a future world without a state—that is, outside the boundaries of the law—like the classic western, it can also operate to sanction violence through its tendency to privilege a social Darwinist view of life in which only the toughest survive.

The futuristic setting is the hallmark of the post-disaster novel; it begins with the known and extrapolates some part of it into the unknown future, imagining what life may be like "if . . .". As such, it is an exploration of social possibility, but since it invites readers to examine the contrast between the present world and a world which might be, it is also a critique of the existing social order. While these fictions may be set in the future, they are therefore not really about "tomorrow", but rather about "today" because they are effectively a statement regarding the particular historical moment that produced them. Visions of post-holocaust landscapes speak volumes about present-day societies, for instance, where issues relating to the production and trade of nuclear weapons are prominent. In the same way, narratives depicting a future world in which epidemics have killed vast numbers of people can reflect contemporary desires to discover cures for deadly diseases such as tuberculosis, hepatitis, and AIDS. Contemporary theories of dystopia therefore offer a useful focus for analysis of post-disaster texts because they are consciously concerned with social and political ideologies, and hence with social criticism (Baccolini and Moylan; Booker, *Impulse;* Moylan). As Tom Moylan so eloquently observes, the dystopian text "invites the creation of alternative worlds in which the historical spacetime of the author can be re-presented in a way that foregrounds the articulation of its economic, political, and cultural dimensions" (xii). For Booker, the primary function of dystopian literature *is* social criticism; by focusing their critiques of society on spatially or temporally distant settings, he argues, these fictions "provide fresh perspectives on problematic social and political practices that might otherwise be taken for granted or considered natural and inevitable" (*Impulse* 19).

Post-Disaster Fiction for Children

Stephens argues that apocalyptic themes have been present in children's literature since about 1970, occurring as a response to *fin de siècle* concerns regarding urban decline and the perceived meaninglessness of modern existence ("Promised" 16). Yet the post-disaster genre did not really come of age until about the 1980s when anxieties about the environment, nuclear holocaust, and rapid accelerations in technology were prominent themes in Western society as a whole (Bull; Saxby; Stephens, "Post-Disaster"). Fictions pervaded by this "sense of an ending" were initially concerned with scenarios involving nuclear holocaust. Recent novels have tended to focus more on the possible effects of genetic engineering, global-scale pollution, and the finiteness of resources, however, projecting cultural unease into narratives that forecast bio-plagues, climate shifts, massive earthquakes, and changes in sea level. It is inevitable, then, that the ideological orientations of the post-disaster novel are quite explicit, but because children's literature is already didactic to some degree or another, this effect is magnified in texts aimed at child audiences. According to Geoff Bull, writers of this kind of children's science fiction are attracted to the genre because it allows "alternative societies to be proposed and possible solutions advanced for contemporary problems" (161). Carrie Hintz and Elaine Ostry's focus on the readers of children's utopian and dystopian literature reveals similar ideas since they argue that it teaches young people about social organisation, governance, and the possibility of improving society, and encourages them to "view their society with a critical eye, sensitizing or predisposing them to political action" (1, 7).

As with children's literature in general, YA post-disaster novels also tend to offer their readers hope for the future. Thus, although innocent children *can* die in order to bring attention to "the negligence and corruption of the adult-created world they have inherited", the outcome of the narrative is inclined to be optimistic (Sambell, "Carnivalizing" 250). The genre is, therefore, not truly dystopic in its world view or pessimistic about the future of the human race; indeed, Kay Sambell contends that fictions which do not provide some measure of reassurance for the adolescent reader are frequently met with critical condemnation ("Presenting" 165). The perceived need for hope in children's fiction informs Millicent Lenz's arguments on the selection and teaching of youth "nuclear literature", for example, in which she advocates texts that treat nuclear conflict as avoidable and denounces those that evoke "total despair and nihilism" (*Nuclear* 161). This attitude also frames Monica Hughes's discussion of her own writing: "I may lead a child into the darkness, but I must never turn out the light" (160).

The emergence of the genre largely coincided with the development of YA fiction itself. Perhaps, as Elizabeth Braithwaite argues, this occurred because of the close correspondence between the nature of the post-disaster scenario and the genre expectations of adolescent literature as a whole (45). Post-disaster fictions set up a variety of narrative situations, she argues, in which "the tasks of Western adolescence can be played out at both a personal and a public level". This includes scenarios which force the adolescent protagonist to: rebel against parents, cope without them, or live with them in a situation where the power balance has changed; to find a sense of identity; or to leave childhood behind them for good (48). According to Braithwaite, this process is often mapped onto a journey through a wasteland. Here, the wasteland functions as a psychological or physical place which must be successfully negotiated in order to find the "self" (48)—it is "a gateway for physical and emotional transitions" (Stephens, *Language* 174). In its post-disaster form, the image of the wasteland evokes a range of binary meanings: Both a threat and a promise, the infernal and the paradisal, it is a place of spiritual possibility, but also of sterility, conflict, and death. This dichotomy is clearly articulated in post-disaster fictions for adolescents. "The Promised Land" in Victor Kelleher's *Red Heart* is depicted by turns as a rich land of milk and honey, and as a kingdom tainted with death, for instance, while in Catherine Bateson's *The Airdancer of Glass*, where a massive war has released wave after wave of contaminants into the world's ecosystems, the difference between the "haves" in the glittering, enclosed city of Glass and the "have-nots" in the smelly, shanty town of Tip, is vast.

A Return to Arcadia?: Rewriting the Myths of the (Masculinist) Past

In order to explore these politics of spaciality further, I want to examine, to varying degrees, three post-disaster novels which engage with ideas about territory, community, and history. My discussion is framed by several of the arguments concerning national history that I made in Chapter 2. Again, I am going to refer specifically to Australian narratives and contexts, but I believe that some of the patterns I identify here are equally applicable to other Western national literatures (particularly those of settler societies). Whether overtly or implicitly, these texts are preoccupied with the past; in their constructions of imagined futures, each bears traces of old world orders and systems of meaning, and each plays out some aspect of Australian history within a landscape that, although vastly different to that of contemporary Australia, is nonetheless recognisably Australian in that it is a place where the "meanings of a plurality of cultures are being contested, reworked and renegotiated" (Pearce, "Messages" 247). In the first, Kerry Greenwood's *The Broken Wheel*, the warring groups occupying the post-disaster landscape represent an Australia of old that is heavily divided by its ethnically diverse population.[2] The second, John Marsden's *Tomorrow, When the War Began*, situates its story in a dystopic and violent near future but also has links to various periods in Australian history, particularly those times when the relations between Asia and Australia were a prominent political and cultural issue. The setting of *Red Heart*, the third text, replaces deserts with rivers and thus disrupts many of the familiar cultural meanings associated with the Australian landscape; however, it is nonetheless also a place that is, to use Clare Bradford's term, "imbued with memories of colonisation" ("Memory").

In this discussion, I draw on Raffaella Baccolini's theories about dystopian fiction and its application to history. According to Baccolini, all utopias and dystopias are "dependent on their historical context for understanding", but because the dystopia is "usually located in a negatively deformed future of our own world", it appears as a critique of history. The extent to which it can "promote historical consciousness", however, depends on whether it reveals a "critical or a nostalgic attitude toward the past" (114–17). *The Broken Wheel* is firmly aligned with the latter. Set around the Melbourne area in a time soon after a malfunctioning satellite has "striped" the earth with laser beams killing most of the Australian population, the text is a cautionary tale about the destructive tendencies of human behaviour and the potential dangers of technology. This is made quite clear by the narrative's opening words: "We must tell you, the children born after the disaster, that the earth our home is a sphere, ringed with metal satellites which humans launched into space [. . .] They were, and always will be, war machines" (1). Survivors of the disaster are scattered in tribal groups across the dusty landscape and the narrative follows one of these nomadic groups (the Travellers) as they move south to Thorngard, the permanent settlement with which they are affiliated. The setting is similar to others in the genre in that this medieval-like pastoral settlement is contrasted with images of the ruined city, but the twist that is devised for the narrative is that its members are not fighting against an old order, wishing to exercise power by reinstating the destructive past, but a band of Luddites (called the Breakers), intent on destroying past technologies and ultimately, the world.[3]

As John Stephens and Robyn McCallum argue, the thematics of quasi-medieval post-disaster fiction "parallels that of historical fiction insofar as both are apt to be fables about the nature of modernity", and "both pivot on a struggle between civilization and barbarism" (*Retelling* 129). This struggle is played out between the Luddites (who hunt down and murder those using machines) and the medievalists; however, the danger that is posed to the Travellers as they move around also comes from the various bandits and other "uncivilised" tribes they meet along the way. A series of confrontations and meetings between the groups highlights the differences in lifestyle and values that characterise each of them. The group known as Tribe comprises a band of largely male hunters and fighters whose cannibalistic and misogynist ways are abhorrent to the Travellers, and the Tree People are a group of dangerous, territorial tree-dwellers who, as their name suggests, are represented as ape-like and thus "less than human". In comparison, Thorngard is peopled by peace-loving, medieval role-players from the pre-disaster era (those who were already dissatisfied with the technology and the pollution of the previous world), and it is run in accordance with the romantic ideals of the Middle Ages (chivalry, courtesy, honour, graciousness, etc.).

The stark divide that emerges from this dialogical contrast is repeated in various ways throughout the text, positioning audiences to view Thorngard as a version of utopia. The narrative implies that, when combined with other present-day, liberal humanist ideologies, these resuscitated codes of honour create a foundation from which to build a better society.[4] Gender equality is promoted in the text, for instance, and thus another strategy used to privilege the utopian claims of the Thorngard society is to juxtapose a number of incidents in which the issues of gendered power relations are prominent. Many of these episodes revolve around the principal character (and eventual saviour of the world), Sarah. In one such sequence, Sarah is captured in order to become the sexual partner of Ade, a male member of the Tree People tribe (Ade is later killed by Simon, a fellow Traveller, and Sarah is rescued); in another, she becomes involved in a romantic, monogamous sexual relationship with Wulf, a gentle, intelligent, and kind knight from Thorngard; and in a third, she becomes a prophet to the post-disaster survivors after she outwits The Luddite Fathers.

A problematic feature of *The Broken Wheel* is that, although females like Sarah have an agential role, the future society that is privileged by the narrative reinstates in its entirety a conservative, patriarchal social order from the past. Another limitation of the narrative is that it suggests that the blueprint for a better society is already in place, leaving little space for readers to interrogate the ideological positions which inform the book. At points where the narrative engages in a revision of the past, this becomes particularly problematic. A telling moment occurs when, on the Travellers' return journey to do battle with the army of the Breakers, they must decide how to approach the Tree People (who are clearly associated with Australia's Indigenous peoples). The group reaches the conclusion that: "If [they] kill rather than trade [they] are no better than the original colonists of this country" (105). Not only is this enunciation of their dilemma somewhat ironic given that they have already killed Ade in the battle over Sarah, but it seems pointless when instead the group introduces bread (flour) and sugar to the tribe, a primary cause of Aboriginal diet-related diseases and deaths in Australia since white settlement. This episode, which firstly implies that Aboriginal people are a race of savages, and secondly that European culture and practices are inherently superior to that of other societies, represents just one of many instances in the narrative in which the assumptions that govern colonial discourse are manifest.

Heather Scutter argues that many of the post-disaster novels produced for children in Australia over the past few decades involve a retreat to a pastoral haven, and thus, rather than offering "truly radical ways of reconstructing the world", they imagine real progress as "a going back" (30, 34). *Tomorrow, When the War Began*, the first in the "Tomorrow" series, tends to follow this pattern too, although perhaps because it shares so much common ground with realist rather than fantasy genres, in a slightly different way. Since the series, which is set in the fictional rural town of Wirrawee and its surrounds, begins with the military invasion of Australia, ostensibly by an Asian power, it reanimates old anxieties and fears about the apparent economic and social threats posed by the mass immigration of Chinese in the 1800s (the "yellow peril"), and the potential occupation of the country by the Japanese in World War II. It therefore presents more overt associations with aspects of Australian history than *The Broken Wheel*. However, it can also be seen to draw on imperialist and nationalist assumptions, ideologies, and practices in its "retelling" of the past. The narrative follows seven teenagers who know nothing of the invasion until they return home from a camping expedition in the bush to discover their homes abandoned, livestock dead, and the townspeople incarcerated in the local showground. Retreating in the face of this aggressive colonisation into a section of wild and apparently uninhabited land they call Hell, the group fashions a small farm settlement in a clearing. Hell quickly becomes home, but it also acts as a base from which to wage a guerrilla war against the enemy.

Besides the obvious story associations with colonial-era Australia, the text positions its readers to make links between the present and the past by structuring the narrative as a "truthful" and reliable (that is, factual) account of history. As Ellie, the narrator and focaliser of the narrative, remarks after the group has decided that they do not want to "end up as a pile of dead white bones, unnoticed, unknown, and worst of all, with no one knowing or appreciating the risks [they've] run", it is important to record what has happened to them: "There's only one way to do this [she writes], and that's to tell it in order, chronological order" (2).[5] Even so, the narrative is compromised in its capacity to explore and reflect on the historical issues it raises. Firstly, although the text advocates an understanding and valuing of cultural differences, this is problematic when, at the same time, the narrative strategies it employs to demonise the enemy mirror the anti-Asian rhetoric that was used in the past. According to Adrian Caesar, not only does the narrative show a clear connection to the invasion scare novels of the 1890s and 1900s, but a crude "militaristic and implicitly racist" nationalism is also invoked to justify the deaths of the enemy who are described as "scum", "filth", "vermin", and "a cancer" (47, 49).[6] Ellie's glib comments after she kills several soldiers similarly represent a strategy to dehumanise the enemy by rendering them faceless:

> I had no real sense of [the soldiers]. I hadn't even seen their faces properly [and because] I didn't know any of the things you need to know before you truly know a person, [they] hardly existed for me as real people. (96)

The nationalist sentiment which runs persistently through the narrative creates another tension because it evokes the monocultural hegemony of the old Anglo-Celtic order. As Bradford argues, the ideologies informing these texts constitute "a reconfiguration of the 'White Australia' of Federation", since the protagonists "produce a sociality built upon fantasies of a homeland protecting its racial purity through fair play, hard work and martial prowess" (*Reading* 32). Maureen Nimon argues that the narrative creates popular heroes from the "webs of Australian myth"; it constructs a link to the Australian tradition of the bushmen—those men "who went to war as ANZACs and whose experiences became the basis of the most potent of all Australian legends" (9, 16). The parallels that are manifest between the novel and the adventure romances that were highly popular forms of fiction in Australia during the colonial period also limits the narrative's engagement with the issues surrounding Asian-Australian historical relations. The "fictional history" that is constructed by the text is analogous to the boys' adventure books that were in demand in the late nineteenth century—"simple and direct" accounts of adventure that were set in imperial locations and fed off narratives about real soldiers (Dawson 146)—while Ellie's skill as a warrior and her manner of addressing the reader recalls many other narrators of male adventure romances. As Nimon suggests, she "is not only as good as a boy, but actually reaches the status of an honorary male" (11, 12).

Ellie's role as "pseudo-male" is problematic for a number of reasons, however. Like other female killers in post-disaster texts (and in the "Tomorrow" series), she is sexualised, thus affirming the patriarchal view of Woman as sexual object, and limiting her power. Moreover, as I argued in Chapter 4, because gendering is an aspect of both story and discourse, by simply allotting the male hero's role to a female, "she" inevitably becomes assimilated into the kind of phallic systems of representation that characterise the hero genre. This is apparent once Ellie becomes involved in her first sexual relationship with Lee. A second-generation Asian-Australian, Lee is viewed from Ellie's perspective in the tradition of Orientalism as a fascinating, seductive, and exotic Other—that is, "in a mirror image of the stereotypical way in which Australian authors have traditionally dealt with Asian women in their texts"

(Caesar 47). In the same tradition, Lee is also portrayed later in the series as threatening, immoral, and aggressive where the others in the group are not—a factor which costs him the relationship with Ellie because she rejects him after becoming sickened by his bloodlust (Caesar 47). Here, the text's ability to instantiate cultural difference is not only weakened by subjecting Lee to the gaze of the white Anglo-Australian "male" protagonist from whose perspective the story is told, but the tradition of the adventure story "as a form coining violence into pleasure and expressive of male power" is also upheld (Dawson 17). In addition, by making Lee the repository of those aspects of herself that she does not choose to acknowledge, Ellie becomes firmly aligned with the text's characteristic racist and Eurocentric values.

Ellie's progress towards self-knowledge, and thus her growth, is traced through a loss of innocence theme, because what she experiences sexually is framed through what she concurrently learns about death. Thoughts on her sexual experimentation with Lee, and her feelings for him, are interspersed with ruminations on the ethics of murder, the cruelty of "human nature", and the harsh reality of death. Two of these incidents, in particular, highlight the metaphorical "death" of her childhood as a secure and knowable state, because they are both centred around ideas about loss. The first occurs just prior to the novel's final explosive conflict when she and Lee come close to "[losing their] virginity simultaneously". Here, she describes herself as being "lost somewhere in the rapids of her feelings". "If life is a struggle against emotion", she writes in the diary, "then I was losing" (237–38). In the second, she has just returned to the group after setting off an explosion that causes the death of several soldiers:

> I felt that my life was permanently damaged, that I could never be normal again, that the rest of my life would be just a shell. Ellie might walk and talk and eat and drink but the inside Ellie, her feelings, was condemned to wither and die. (95)

Nonetheless, as Caesar observes, this kind of agonising is "never allowed to stop the action or the killing"; rather, the continual triumphs of the group, the lack of any lasting negative effects, and the implication that they are changed for the better, demonstrate that the war is "full of positive values for the youngsters" (47–49).[7] In this way, death functions to signify transformation and growth, but it occurs at the expense of Others—significantly, Others who have been marginalised or demonised in Australia's Anglo-Celtic-dominated cultural and political past.

Tomorrow, When the War Began therefore fulfils the ideological task of the masculine adventure and romance novel; that is "to resolve contradictions in the lived experience of imperialism" by inscribing the reader in "tales of regenerative violence on the colonial frontier" (Dixon 1). *Red Heart* is similar in that it too can be seen to perpetuate the Western metanarrative of heroic masculinity; however, it differs in its re-imagining of history because, while it uses narrative strategies which function to erase the past, it also opens the way for social critique (Mallan, "New"). The narrative is set in a post-Greenhouse future. Annual deluges have swept away precious farmland, and as each year grows wetter, the prospect of survival becomes bleaker. Much of the land is under water, and boats on river highways tens of kilometres wide are the main form of transport. "Old" Australia has died, taking the rules and traditions with it: Farming as a way of life is increasingly fragile, and much of the settled continent is owned by the powerful Company. According to the money collectors of the Company, the organisation is the "only real law" because it "takes orders from no one, the government included" (5). Located far along the flooded Darling River, however, lies the beginnings of a new regime—the Promised Land. A watery territory, rich in deposits of gold, but quite unlike the iconic red heart of Australia's desert, the Land is depicted by its self-appointed, despotic ruler, Jack Curtis, as the country's new heart: "*This* is the new order. The new heartland. It's here that the future takes hold. Here, where a braver, more lasting world begins" (119, emphasis original).

Both of the regimes that are represented in this dystopic state are oppressive in the extreme; the downriver community that is governed by the Company is characterised by its merciless but ostensibly "progressive" capitalism, while Jack's absolute power over the upriver colony makes the Promised Land into a brutal dictatorship. Jack's system of government relies on old ways—"a hybrid mix of old colonial treacheries and nativism" that "keeps 'otherness' at bay by imposing exclusion through violent measures" (Mallan, "New"). His followers are a disenchanted group of nomadic youths calling themselves the Feral Nation. Dreadlocked and pierced, with their skin darkened by hormone pills to protect them from the harsh Greenhouse-era sun, they are not only marked by their physical difference to the largely white population, but also by their rejection of old values. For the Nation, "families are finished" (19) and they are in search of a new belonging. For Jack, however, they are "just a tool to [his] hand, a lowly means to a far greater end", because, upon their sporadic arrivals into the territory, they are assigned at his bidding to one of two groups—a band of armed warriors called the Tribe (Jack's "chosen few") who act to police the borders of the Land, or the labouring workforce who bear the pejorative label of "Pigs" (119).

The narrative follows Jack's nephew, Nat Marles, on a journey between these two contrasting worlds, from his family's downriver farm—which the Company is attempting to repossess—up to the Promised Land. Nat's mission is to save the farm by reclaiming the money Jack borrowed from the family in order to fund his expedition into the heartland. Like everyone else, Nat believes the stories about his uncle's upriver paradise, but he is quickly disillusioned when the *Phoenix* (the paddleboat he is travelling on) runs aground on a sandbank and he discovers a number of dead bodies on a nearby shore. Apparently killed by a new outbreak of haemorrhagic fever, the corpses are nonetheless dressed in combat clothing and located near the shell of a downed Company chopper. Thus, Nat soon comes to an understanding of the drastic strategies that Jack has employed to keep the Land "safe and secure" (55).

Although he is subject to the Tribe's violence, Nat's familial relationship with Jack grants him—and his Feral Nation companions, Pete and Irene—a certain degree of immunity as he travels to his uncle's home at Central Station. Once he arrives, however, he too becomes a victim of Jack's dark heart when he is given a test: whether to kill on command or to disobey the orders of "the Man" and be killed himself. The episode featuring the test recalls an earlier one in which Nat asks Clarrie, the skilful Indigenous skipper and navigator of the *Phoenix*, how Jack divides the Feral Nation peoples into law enforcers or slaves:

> 'Why don't they all join [the Tribe]? It'd be better than rotting away in these crummy settlements.'
>
> Clarrie pursed her lips. 'How'd you fancy shootin' someone, white boy? [. . .] How would you go if I told you to aim a gun at someone and pull the trigger? Would you do it?'
>
> [Nat] shrugged. 'No way.'
>
> 'Not even if I promised you somethin' big in return?'
>
> 'Not a chance.'
>
> 'You sure about that?'
>
> 'Dead sure.'
>
> 'Well then, there's your answer. Not everyone's cut out for the Tribe. You have to be a certain kind to join up.' (87)

As this episode suggests, an allegorical reading of *Red Heart* associates the narrative with colonial-era Australia. The story tells of the violence and conflict between the "natives" and the coloniser, because, regardless of Jack's resistance to the hegemony of the Company, his subjugation of the marginalised Feral Nation group represents an exercise in imperial power. Jack's use of the Tribe as a physical force to subdue others of the Nation also recalls the "pacification" strategies of the Native Police who were deployed by the colonial government to open up areas of Australia for permanent occupation. Although the Aboriginal police occupied a far more complex position during colonisation than the Tribe (who are "pretenders"—white people taking on Indigeneity), like the Tribe, the Aboriginal police force became known for its brutality towards various Indigenous clans, and it was implicated in a number of massacres. Nat's refusal to carry on as his uncle's "natural heir" can be seen, therefore, as an act of resistance against the ideals and practices of imperialism. The narrative's final chapters function similarly because they follow a series of incidents leading to Jack's downfall and death. First, Jack contracts a deranging and deadly fever, then he narrowly escapes being eaten by the Tribe in a ritual act of cannibalism—so that he will "never really" die, but live on through them (194), until, finally, he becomes part of a crocodile feeding frenzy and is "devoured" instead by the "harsh" river, the symbol of his power (216). As the novel's closure is informed by notions of reconciliation and forgiveness, it engages with some of the political issues that have arisen in response to the often brutal practices of colonisation. Nat forgives Jack for the harrowing trials that he has been subjected to by helping his uncle to escape the Tribe, and, after discovering a stash of hidden gold, the four disparate protagonists—Nat, and his friends Pete, Irene, and Clarrie—join together aboard the *Pheonix* to contribute to the re-establishment of the Darling River transport and trade network:

> 'The four of us could really make a go of running this boat' [Clarrie tells the others]. 'And with Greenhouse goin' gangbusters, it's the river traffic that'll count in Australia. Specially here on the Darlin'. Jack messed up, I know, but pretty soon someone else'll start in on the old heartland, and we'll be ready an' waitin'.' (221)

Although *Red Heart* seeks to expose the hierarchical power relationships and the imperialist ideologies that are embedded in colonial discourses, even so, there are a number of contradictions in the narrative that work against this idea. Like other post-disaster texts, the options available to the adolescent protagonist hinge on an either/or choice, a strategy which weakens its potential to offer a critique of the ideas associated with these ideologies. As a hazardous enterprise, offering "a trial of chance—a soliciting of good fortune with uncertain outcome", it also replicates the traditional adventure quest story and thus participates in the masculinist agendas that are tied to this narrative form (Dawson 53). Another limitation of the text is that it suggests that "being black" is a reversible choice for the Feral Nation people (the hormone pills that Pete carries imply that, by foregoing his skin-darkening medication, he can easily revert to "being white"). Under these terms, all of the cultural conditions that have contributed to racial inequity and oppression over time are trivialised. Moreover, Clarrie, the narrative's token Indigenous character, is represented in much the same way as her forebears were; that is, as a resource to others (Mallan, "New").

The novel has obvious connections with its pre-text, Joseph Conrad's *Heart of Darkness*. Its setting is a transposed version of the Congo, replete with the dark imagery that is characteristic of Conrad's tale (tropical disease, a landscape littered with debris and rotting animal carcasses, threatening crocodiles, torrential rain, clinging vegetation). And because it too associates "going native" with pathology, insanity, and death, it tends to resurrect the stereotyped and racist notions of black culture that were prominent in nineteenth century Western societies. Indeed, Kerry Mallan argues that at the level of intertextuality, the text's borrowing from *Heart of Darkness* "engages with a certain determinism which sees history repeating itself and a resignation to an ongoing colonialism" ("New"). At the same time, however, the narrative can be seen to offer an alternative response to the historical issues it implicitly addresses (particularly when compared to the previous two novels I have considered here). Although it suggests that life in the post-disaster future is dependent on a survival-of-the-fittest scenario, for example, it differs from many other post-disaster texts in that it does not insist its protagonists participate in violence and murder in order to establish the new order. Rather, strength is not equated with the traditional (masculine) ideals of physical power and aggression, but with resourcefulness and a commitment to pacifism. Undoubtedly, several of the humanist ideologies informing the text cluster around the familiar nationalist concept of mateship, and the model of racial unity that is presented at the closure seems somewhat contrived (Mallan, "New"). Nevertheless, the text resembles the critical dystopia described by Raffaella Baccolini and Tom Moylan, which by "rejecting the traditional subjugation of the individual at the end of the novel" works to open up a space of "contestation and opposition for those collective 'ex-centric' subjects whose class, gender, race, sexuality, and other positions are not empowered by hegemonic rule" (8). As Mallan also argues, the narrative works against the territorialising strategies of colonialism because it resists "a locatedness in either the designated downriver or upriver territories in favour of the fluidity of movement between these extremes that the river offers". In this way, it therefore destabilises the fixity of place by re-locating the utopian community to "the heart of no-where" ("New").

Action Femininity: Tough Girls and Women Who Kill

The rise of the post-disaster narrative has coincided with the increasing prevalence of warrior women or "tough girl" figures in Western popular media over the past three decades. Indeed, as texts such as *Tomorrow, When the War Began* demonstrate, in recent years, tough girls have not only become common characters in post-disaster texts themselves, but they often occupy central roles (Inness 121). In *The Terminator*, for example, it is Sarah Connor who must defeat the Terminator in order to save herself and her unborn son, and thus prevent the impending holocaust. Dressed in fatigues, a cigarette dangling from her lips, and sporting a formidable arsenal of guns, she also plays a crucial part in the attempt to destroy the T-1000 in *Terminator 2*.[8] In these films, Sarah represents the quintessential action hero: tough, aggressive, physically strong, and displaying no apparent emotion. At the same time, she illustrates one of the reasons why the female warrior can make such an intriguing study; through her use of physical violence and her obvious intent to murder, she is an extreme example of a woman usurping a role that is traditionally considered the province of a man (Inness).

Gender plays an important role in post-disaster fiction, not least because of the genre's capacity to offer a space where the "normal" rules of behaviour have changed. Clearly, Sarah and women like her are an embodiment of this potential since, as Sherrie A. Inness notes, they call into question what it means to be a woman (136)—and perhaps more importantly, what it means to be a woman who kills. Popular culture's fascination with the woman-killer, or, to use Christine Holmlund's term, the "deadly doll", is manifest in a number of YA post-disaster novels; as Mallan notes, youth is a key consumer group for the female action genre ("Hitting" 140). There is a distinct uneasiness surrounding representations of the female as killer, however: Like other texts depicting girls who "kick butt", these texts are marked by contradictions and tensions because, while they offer females new roles, they also tend to demonstrate that these roles are bound within a patriarchal framework. Inness argues, for instance, that because killer-women can pose a threat to the male hegemony, they are repeatedly depicted in a way which either undermines their strength and independence, or tears down their tough and aggressive image to reveal the "real" woman underneath. These women thus do little to disrupt the stability of the patriarchal order, she stresses, because the danger posed by their strength and independence is diffused during this process, or sometimes even erased altogether (67, 81–82).

Inness's argument may be applied to *The Airdancer of Glass*, the narrative of which details the conflict between two polarised communities that exist in a future world ravaged by human mismanagement. The story is centred around a revolt which occurs after the oppressed residents in the ramshackle town of Tip rise up in protest against the privileged inhabitants (called "Fatters") of the nearby city of Glass. Tired of living in squalor amid the stench of decay and disease, and tired of foraging through the detritus of Glass, the Tippers decide to wage a battle against the Fatters to restore equality. The wandering circus-flyer, Lulianne (the protagonist of the novel), represents the Tipper's best chance at success; joined by the idealistic Egan from the utopian community of Clan and members of her newly-adopted family in Tip (including ruthless tomboy, Burr), the group pulls together to help Lulianne scale the faceless dome of Glass, setting the revolution in motion.

The revolutionaries are successful; however, a number are killed in the process. Burr's hard, violent, and wild displays of toughness come to an abrupt end at this point, denying her the better life and new beginning that would have been within her reach after the victory, and also cutting short her growing relationship with Ned, another revolutionary. This occurs soon after she has fatally wounded several of the inhabitants of the city of Glass, demonstrating the kind of unease that Inness suggests typically surrounds such aggressive expressions of female sexuality: If women insist on being too tough and masculine, she argues, they will be punished for their gender-bending transgression (67, 81). In fact, Burr suffers a particularly harsh punishment; she is killed by a flying piece of shrapnel which "mashes in" one side of her head, and her body is left behind in the mayhem which surrounds the explosion of the city. This unease is magnified, moreover, by the juxtaposition between Burr's ruthlessness and the revulsion that Lulianne suffers during the battle:

> Lulianne didn't think she could touch the dead Fatters, not even to get the much needed guns. It wasn't so much the blood, though that was bad enough. Burr pushed her to one side, heaved one of the corpses over, grabbed the gun, wiped it on the Fatter's shirt and gave it to Lulianne.
>
> 'You do what you have to,' she said. 'I'm crazy, but I'm not killing crazy. I just want to bring my kids up with full bellies and something to live for. Do you understand?'

Lulianne nods, so Burr asks her: "'Can you use it?'", to which she replies: "'I don't know'" (147).

Holmlund points out that popular culture worries so much about why women kill that female assassins are often given multiple motives for murder (129). In this episode, it is made clear that the welfare of Burr's future family is the motive. In another instance, she kills in self defence (146), and, as her role as one of the leaders of the revolution illustrates, she also kills for political reasons. In all of these cases, Burr is given a justification for killing, demonstrating that violent women are rarely portrayed as murderers without "legitimate" grounds (Holmlund). Killing in order to protect the family is especially characteristic. Besides Burr's argument in the passage above, this is demonstrated by her conviction that "[y]ou do what you have to", and also by Lulianne's instruction to the tiny, "doll-like" Lovie as they attempt to rescue the imprisoned children of Tip from the Fatters: "'We go in and get them any way we can. If we have to kill them, we kill them'" (135). Here, the patriarchal social order has been unbalanced by the aggressive stance of the girls who will not hesitate to employ extreme tactics in order to ensure the wellbeing of "their" children. However, because their aggression is channelled predominantly through the traditional feminine role of motherhood, there are limitations to the effectiveness of this disruption. In Mallan's view, these kind of ambivalences are a feature of the female action hero genre: Girls who kick butt do not necessarily pose "a serious threat to 'real' men", she argues, and thus "to assume that the [. . .] genre will guarantee 'empowerment' for young women [can be] to adopt a naïve position" ("Hitting" 151–52).

Another insidious way to diminish the toughness of girl killers is to construct female aggression as a pathological condition by portraying such girls as insane or psychotic (Inness 74). Burr herself admits to a kind of insanity on several occasions: in the earlier exchange with Lulianne where she professes to be unhinged; and also at one point when she picks up an automatic gun and, aiming it at the Security men guarding the imprisoned children of Tip, tells them: "'You'd better know [. . .] I'm crazy'" (141). In Burr's words, her wildness does not extend to being "killing crazy". However, in one incident she must be dissuaded from killing for pure pleasure, and in another she cannot hide her glee as she opens fire on the Fatters (140, 146). While Burr is posthumously celebrated as a hero of the Revolution, living on as future generations recount her story, she is the only one of the key female characters to lose her life. As Inness argues, in order to warn women that being too tough is socially unacceptable, and to contain the threat posed to the male subject, females in killer-women narratives who perform indiscriminate acts of violence, or are so out of control that they appear insane, often "get their just rewards" (69, 72).

A clear example of this thesis is *Red Heart*'s trigger-happy and aggressive Del, a member of Jack Curtis's Tribe. Del is an extreme embodiment of the tough girl; as an actively sexual, aggressive, violent, and ruthless woman she also completely inverts traditional paradigms of femininity. Soon after her character is introduced in the narrative, for instance, she punches Clarrie's boss, Gus, across the mouth several times, wildly shoots at a number of crocodiles on a nearby sandbar, and with her "hard-knuckled hands", drags Nat across the deck of the *Phoenix* by his hair in order to toss him over the side (77–80). Unlike Burr, who fights for freedom from oppression, as a warrior in the vicious Tribe, Del is motivated by power, using violence and intimidation to enforce Jack's supremacist Law. Her demise, like that of other Tribe soldiers, Serge and Tone, is therefore not unexpected. It *is* complicated by the way in which her sexuality is represented as monstrous and deviant, however, because this suggests that her death occurs not purely because she is a ruthless Tribe warrior, but also because she has wholly transgressed the hetero-normative construct of female sexuality. As an aside, Kelleher has created a similar character in *Taronga*. Here, a number of post-disaster survivors are living in a warrior-like community within the walls of the Taronga Zoo. They are ruled by the aggressive, cat-like Molly who, like Del, also dies a violent death. Molly's death occurs ostensibly because she is a despot; however, there are also tensions surrounding its representation. For instance, even in the act of dying, she cannot relinquish her hold upon her gun, "the destructive [and phallic] symbol by which she [has] lived", suggesting that she too is being punished for her transgression of gender codes (188).

Del is no ordinary female action figure; rather, she is yet another example of Barbara Creed's monstrous-feminine—a fantasy of woman as castrator, an imaginary Other who must be repressed and controlled in order to secure and protect the patriarchal social order ("Horror" 265). Depictions of woman as an agent of castration take various forms, Creed argues (such as vampire, witch, possessed monster), and are often associated with recurring images and motifs including knives, axes, teeth, spiked instruments, and the deadly *vagina dentata*. Del's monstrosity is encoded in her predatory attempts to seduce Nat, and by her disruption of the boundary between the human and the animal. During several encounters with Nat, her flickering tongue is represented as almost reptilian, while in another incident she fingers his cheek with a "purple-tipped" fingernail, a gesture he finds "strangely intimate" because it makes him "feel uneasy—scared almost—like being wooed by a tiger" (79). Del's monstrosity is most obvious, however, in the conclusion to the scene where the two first meet. Here she is simultaneously depicted as castrator, voracious seducer, and vampire:

> Del was amongst the last to leave. One foot already on the rail, she changed her mind and sidled back to Nat's side.
>
> 'Here,' she said softly, 'a present for you.'
>
> Before he could stop her she drew the blade of her knife across his forearm. He gasped with pain—a thin line of blood in the cut—and she stooped towards it, her tongue flicking out.
>
> 'Yum!' she said, and gave him a sly smile. 'You're mine now, lover. Mine.'
>
> Then, still grinning across her shoulder, she leapt for the bank, a trace of his blood clearly visible on her lower lip as the boat drifted from the shore. (83)

Nat's fascination with, and fear of, female sexuality in this episode is clear. This is a horrifying image of Woman, but it is also a seductive one as the association between death and sex suggests; Nat finds Del attractive, but physically repulsive at the same time. Del's abjection is signified by her lust for blood and her disregard for the dictates of the law which sets down the rules of proper sexual conduct (Creed, *Monstrous* 61). While she challenges the view that femininity, by definition, constitutes passivity, her aggressiveness is, therefore, not represented in positive terms; rather, it is depicted as out of control and even perverse. Accordingly, not only does she die a violent death when a shattered cable from the *Phoenix* lashes into her and her canoe, dumping her into the water to be devoured by crocodiles, but her power is often shown to be limited by patriarchal law. For example, she discovers that she cannot harm Nat unless Jack allows it, and it is often Tone who makes the decisions about who (and when) she can and cannot kill. From this perspective, instead of a display of power, her pot-shots at the crocodiles appear somewhat ridiculous. To appropriate Inness's words, then, Del is "tough, but not as tough as the boys" (74).

Action femininity also has a central role in Simon Higgins's *Beyond the Shaking Time,* which speculates on a future where the world has been devastated by a sudden tilt in the earth's axis. Regular flashbacks to the "shaking" event depict passenger jets plunging into the ocean, vast cracks in the earth's surface swallowing cars, collapsing high-rise buildings, and a coastal landscape inundated by swirling seawater. Some fifteen months after the disaster, survivors are scattered atop the high ridges and peaks of an extinct volcano caldera in basic island villages which have been cobbled together from floating debris. The narrative tells of the interactions between two of these remnant societies: one a disparate community called Fort Necessity, whose small population live in a shared space but are somewhat divided by the social groups they belonged to before the disaster (e.g. townies, farmers, city-dwellers, and hippies), and the other a male band of raiders headed by "General" Darius, a despotic prison escapee. The marked opposition between the two communities can be seen most clearly in the novel's representation of gendered subjectivities. Darius's group of barbarians live by the commandments of violence, ruthlessness, and power. As he tells his followers and his female prisoners: "'Nature puts life on our planet, then lets it freely fight for survival'" (113). In this overtly dystopic society, weak or disobedient subjects are executed, men are viewed as physically superior (and, hence, better survivors), and women are regarded as property. By contrast, Fort Necessity appears to be a community-based, democratic, and largely pacifist village, ostensibly favouring equality and working towards an acceptance of cultural difference. On the surface, neither spaces nor tasks are gendered, and even the battlefield—a domain almost exclusively regarded as masculine—is open to women.

The narrative begins with the death of a crazed drifter (the lone survivor of a bloody attack by Darius and his followers), who floats to the shore at Fort Necessity in a boat, badly sunburned and emaciated but with enough energy to threaten the novel's protagonist, Cass Marshall, and her friend, Jadzia Petersen. The arrival of the madman provides the rationale for the peaceful village's newly formed militia, and it signals Cass's potential to be a valuable member of this force as she gamely tries to fend off the attacker prior to the man's collapse. "'[T]hanks heaps'", Jadzia says to her, afterwards, "'I felt like you were really protecting me'" (6). Unfortunately for Cass, this incident proves little to her father, Eddie, who opposes her plan to join the militia by claiming that Cass is not built to be a warrior, and that an armed force is unnecessary: "'What's to come? Savage goannas out of the forest?'", he asks (10). The tension between Cass and Eddie is reflected in the general community; although the entire village has deemed the militia essential for their protection, there is still an uneasiness amongst many of them about putting this into practice. Once Jadzia and another young woman, Sarah Kline, go missing, and a family is murdered on a nearby atoll, however, look-outs are doubled and soldiers are assigned to those moving outside the village boundaries.

It is evident soon after this that Jadzia and Sarah have been captured by Darius's men. While she is out searching for them, Cass is abducted too, although not before she is almost murdered herself. Unlike the confrontation with the drifter, however, at this point Cass actually kills her would-be assassin. Killing is a traditional rite of passage in the heroic warrior society, and this incident clearly marks her as the action hero; here, she is strong, assertive, and brave, and even able to question her attacker about the whereabouts of the other girls as he lies dying at her feet. These qualities are further stressed upon Cass's arrival at the barbarians' camp as she is the only one of the prisoners to stand up to the men; the remaining girls—the two from Fort Necessity and a number of others from nearby areas—are portrayed as passive and helpless victims. Even though the girls know they will be held at the camp only until they have been fattened up enough for sale as slaves, Jadzia asks: "'How can we escape? We take enough risks just starving ourselves [to delay them]'", to which Cass replies: "'That's crazy. To fight or run, you've got to keep your strength up!'" (127).

As these episodes demonstrate, readers of *Beyond the Shaking Time* are strongly positioned to reject the kind of femininity that Darius and his followers envision for this new world, and thus to value the action hero persona embodied by Cass. This is emphasised in a later episode where Sarah, failing to escape the barbarians, commits suicide by throwing herself off a granite outcrop of the mountain (137). Violence is foregrounded in post-disaster narratives, and this is especially apparent when life in the future is depicted as a competition for survival as it is here. The representations of violence in the narrative are also framed by traditional notions of femininity because they imply that female subjectivity is defined in terms of power and powerlessness. At the extreme, this is expressed in a very limited way: to kill, to be killed, or to kill yourself. This message is made very clear by Sarah's death which, disturbingly, is mentioned only once in passing, suggesting something of the worth that is accorded in the text to young women who are unable to protect themselves. Undoubtedly, the valorisation of the female action hero represents an attempt to construct an empowered form of femininity. However, this is a problematic feature of the text, firstly, because it denies any other way of being female, but also because it insists on the same relations of dominance and submission that already characterise everyday Western societies (Mallan, "Hitting" 151).

Nevertheless, despite these restrictions, there is much to recommend the novel's depiction of the female action hero since the narrative frequently works against more familiar representations in which the tough girl's toughness is diminished by an emphasis on her femininity and gender. According to Mallan, this is a common strategy in youth fictions featuring action femininity: Female heroes are often represented as white, heterosexual, and beautiful, and in ways which emphasise their desirability and sexuality ("Hitting"). Inness makes a similar claim when she argues that, although alternative ways of being a woman can be explored in the post-disaster future by challenging typical gender roles, paradoxically, these fictions can also operate to support them by stressing the tough girl's sexual desirability or by implying that she will never be as tough as the boys. The sexual appeal of female action heroes draws on the eroticised association between violence and women that is prevalent in popular culture—a connection which works to suggest that despite their tough self-presentation, these women are more sex objects than warriors (Inness 69–70). However, neither Cass nor Natty Ferguson (the fierce but gentle woman who is Cass's role model) is constructed in this manner. While Cass, with blue eyes, blonde hair, and a slight physique, is the embodiment of the Western ideal woman, and thus a precious commodity to her captors, in her own community these attributes have little merit. Furthermore, the accounts of Cass and Natty's kills are not eroticised and, significantly,

Cass's warrior identity is not shaped through, or in conjunction with, any kind of romance. Regardless of her lack of physical strength—a signifier of the action hero's power—her credibility as a fighter is also rarely questioned. Nor is Natty's, even though she has begun a tentative relationship with Eddie by the novel's conclusion. Indeed, on the whole, the pair are shown as both vulnerable and tough, and as both the rescuer and the rescued, avoiding the simple inversion that often accompanies attempts to redefine traditional gender schemata.[9]

Beyond the Shaking Time culminates in a war between Fort Necessity and the barbarians, which begins when members of the militia raid the greenhouse where the abducted girls are held. Although Brian Laylor, a Fort Necessity villager, is killed in the ambush, the girls are freed and the militia learn of an impending attack on Fort Necessity, allowing them to prepare their defences in advance. It is at this point that the warrior ethos underpinning the narrative is at its most prominent. The preparation for war unites the village in a way that no other event (even the Shaking Time and its dangerous climatic after-effects) has managed to do. Symbolically, this occurs when the militia leader, Lucas Carrick, brings the community together beneath a flag made from Brian's shirt, neatly tying together some quintessentially nationalist ideas pertaining to freedom, democracy, and war which are further emphasised by the idea that Fort Necessity is "earning its life" through this battle (177).

These episodes also highlight some of the contradictions in the novel's treatment of the female warrior, however. Cass's emotional reaction to Brian's death, a stereotypical signifier of her femininity, is contrasted with Lucas's calm and cold assessment of the event, while several references to the heroic virtues of warrior manhood work to suggest that armed combat *is* a gender-specific activity. In calling on such familiar nationalist rhetoric, perhaps it is difficult to avoid the associated masculine meanings, and yet other ambivalences can be found in the text's representation of the battlefield too. On the one hand, Cass and Natty's presence in this domain draws attention to the disparity typically displayed in representations of mixed-gender combat units. While the girls are positioned as valuable assets to Fort Necessity's militia—it is Natty who finishes the war when she fires a bolt from her crossbow into Darius's ribs—as two of the few female fighters in this action-adventure team, they are clearly outnumbered by their male counterparts. As Inness argues, "the relatively rare women who appear in such teams uphold the ideology that tough women are something of an oddity" (190). On the other hand, their presence, to use Mallan's words, "invert[s] the traditional paradigm of the action genre which delineates masculine and feminine spaces as separate and exclusive" ("Hitting" 147). This presence is, moreover, accepted without question by other militia members, offering an alternative to the familiar female action hero narrative in which, to gain entrance to a territory coded as masculine, women must first assert their strength or prove their physical superiority to the men. Admittedly, Cass faces opposition from her father, but, as the privileging of warrior masculinity in the narrative suggests, more passive males like Eddie hold little power in the community.

Like other post-disaster texts featuring female action heroes, *Beyond the Shaking Time* foregrounds the connections between women and violence by working through ideas about toughness and femininity.[10] This is made most explicit by the stark divide between the two communities; each is distinguished in terms of its vastly different gender ideologies and by its approaches to "girl power". Such a contrast leaves little room for the reader to reflect on, or to question, the gender ideologies addressed in the text because it is quite obvious which model readers should prefer—not least from the narrative's mawkish conclusion, where hand in hand Cass and Eddie watch the return of a pod of Humpback whales (animals that have not been sighted since the Shaking Time) to the seas around the atoll. This strategy functions to justify the community's violent solution to the threat posed by the raiders, as does the narrative's tendency to privilege Fort Necessity's militia over the pacifists, irrespective of the dialogue between them which suggests that there are alternative ways of approaching the problem. In this way, I would argue that the text sanctions violence by suggesting that social change (ostensibly here a move towards an empowered or resistant form of female subjectivity) cannot occur without brutality, destruction, and the loss of life.

Conclusion

As *Beyond the Shaking Time* demonstrates, in order to drive the message home about humanity's capacity for violence, and the will to power, post-disaster fictions persistently use representations of tragedy and death to evoke fear and horror in the reader. Yet the trajectory of each of the novels I have considered here also follows a path from nightmare towards new beginnings, implying that, in the end, these negative capacities can be overcome (and thus offering a life-affirming view of human nature and human society). From this discussion, it is clear, then, that the co-existence of themes of hope with those of suffering, death, and despair has implications for the ideological outcomes of the text. Fitting contends, for example, that the post-disaster setting is often used as a pretext for the spectacle of violence, and while I hesitate to apply this argument to the texts I have discussed in this chapter, the majority of these same texts are nonetheless apt to suggest that war and violence are the most effective survival strategies for dealing with life in the post-disaster world (123). In Fitting's words, these kind of texts imply that "a different society will not grow 'naturally' out of the present". Rather, they make clear "from collapse through rebuilding efforts to the brief glimpse of a utopian society [. . .] how painful that struggle will be" (125). According to Stephens, the post-disaster narrative's tendency to "take the form of an heroic narrative moving towards an optimistic outcome" can also result in an overly simplistic construction of the future that may, at times, act as "a dangerous palliative" ("Post-Disaster" 126, 129). As Sambell argues, not only do didactic approaches which supply hope within the text itself often have the effect of compromising the dire warning contained within the text, but when characters in dystopian texts are represented as emblems of hope for a better future, they reinvoke Romantic conceptions of childhood by depicting childhood as "an antidote to corrupt adulthood" ("Carnivalizing" 252).

This trend is manifest in both *Red Heart* and *Tomorrow, When the War Began* where the overriding message is that, to borrow Mallan's words, "it is up to youth to destabilise the existing hegemonic order" ("New"). It is significant, however, that, unlike *The Broken Wheel* and *Tomorrow, When the War Began*, in *Red Heart*, readers are positioned to view this movement not as a nostalgic desire for an Arcadian past, but as a desire for a more liberated, new social order that is based, at least in part, on a "culture of memory" (Baccolini; Mallan, "New"). The first two texts demonstrate how the genre is inclined to affirm traditional social structures or draw upon a romanticised past in its depiction of a better future after the disaster (Stephens, "Post-Disaster"). These are not necessarily undesirable attributes; nevertheless, as I have argued, this strategy becomes problematic when the reinstallation of old (masculinist) orders simultaneously recreates the cultural conditions that have contributed to the oppression, disempowerment, and death, of "ex-centric" subjects in the past. In *The Broken Wheel*, for example, the image of the autonomous and assertive female is held in acute tension with the female who is subject to the normative codes of patriarchy. As Inness argues, then, gender plays an essential role in post-disaster fiction by contesting present gender roles, but it also helps to perpetuate them (123). Like *The Broken Wheel*, both *The Airdancer of Glass* and *Beyond the Shaking Time* are undoubtedly marked by such contradictions in their representation of female subjectivity, because while they offer a resistant version of femininity in the form of the female action hero, they also fall back on traditional ideas about women as killers, thus suggesting, as Stephens contends, that post-disaster texts for children are "endemically [. . .] patriarchally gendered" ("Gender" 27).

Conclusion
Mapping the Landscape:
The Unknown Country

[T]he narratives we give [to our children] to make sense of cultural experience constitute a kind of mapping, maps of meaning that enable [them] to make sense of the world.

(Watkins 4)

Perhaps the most salient point to emerge from any discussion on mortality is that death is "less the undiscovered country than it is the unknown one" (Charmaz, Howarth, and Kellehear vii). Regardless of the extent to which death is subjected to analysis, it will always remain an enigma; there is no key to unlock its mystery, no way of knowing what it feels like, no concrete answer to that age-old question: "What is death?". As I suggested in the introductory pages to this book, death is also a notoriously difficult topic to pin down; to assign meaning to something that is essentially meaning*less*, to attempt to create order out of *dis*order, is at the same time to be subject to a diverse and often complex range of symbols, signs, and ideas. Nonetheless, my aim here has been to sketch onto that map of the "unknown country" at least some of the understandings of death that have shaped Western culture and, specifically, Western adolescent literature, over the last twenty or so years. I have attempted to do so without a "mandate for conquest", to appropriate Toni Morrison's term (923), but rather with an eye to opening up a space (in what is a largely unexplored area) for further critical discussion. In this sense, I make no claims for definitive or absolute conclusions since, inevitably, my own representation of death experiences has been selective and, moreover, the texts that I have examined represent just a fraction of those produced for adolescents during this period.

In the course of presenting my own arguments and readings, and integrating them with theories about death, I have, however, reached a number of general conclusions regarding the recurrence of key points and patterns. A thread common to these concerns death's inviolable relationship with power because, as I have repeatedly demonstrated, to represent death is also to participate in the production and distribution of power. Elisabeth Bronfen and Sarah Webster Goodwin contend, for instance, that in order for a culture to define its own boundaries, it needs "images of alterity and sacrifice", which, at the extreme, can be understood as "those it chooses to kill, literally and symbolically" (15–16). This idea is manifest not only in the texts in which death functions as a way of "defusing or erasing female power" (Mallan, "Fatal" 175), but also in those which demonstrate that death has been, and continues to be, a marker of disadvantage for Indigenous peoples. In the texts that I have examined here, representations of death can be seen, as well, to "regulate" sexual behaviour, and to reinforce dominant ideas about sexuality and gender, a trend that is especially clear in narratives which construct particular sexual practices and behaviours as "illicit". As these latter fictions suggest, "the benign and sterile-sounding word 'normal' has become one of the most powerful ideological tools" of the contemporary period (Hacking 169).

This brief summary paints a negative picture of the workings of power, yet power does not solely work to repress or control people. Power is also a productive and positive force that produces resistance to itself, and thus "grants" individuality to people and other agencies. As Judith Butler argues, it "not only *acts on* a subject, but in a transitive sense, *enacts* the subject into being" (13, emphases original). At one level, this process is evident in the way that every representation of death in the corpus invariably engages with ideas about transformation or change. At another, it is rendered more overtly, such as in those narratives which consciously conflate experiences of death with the theme of growth. Both treatments support John Stephens's argument, however, that fiction "offers models of socialization by presenting experience as a dynamic, enmeshed in processes of conflict, or moments of crisis or transition" ("Always" viii).

Individual knowledge of death is necessarily conditioned by social environment, and, without doubt, fictions for adolescents represent one medium through which experiences and observations of death are negotiated. Yet despite death's "great discursive presence" in adolescent literature (Trites, *Disturbing* xii), and despite the thesis that cultural criticism is instrumental in assisting subjects to understand the various representational codes and practices that shape their perceptions (Rivkin and Ryan, "Politics" 1026), to date, there exists little critical engagement with the ways in which death has been represented in the YA novel in either iconic or rhetorical forms. My concern here, therefore, has not only been to address some of these methodological and contextual gaps, but also to make a contribution to death studies which have, until now, tended to focus largely on general literature texts. I would hope that this book constitutes more than a gap-filling exercise, however, since it suggests that a critical examination of death in adolescent fiction has the capacity to yield complex insights, not only into a culture's attitudes towards death, but also into the systems of order, governance, value, and meaning of the culture itself. That every representation of death appearing in this book can be seen either to embody, to interrogate, or to respond to prevailing social and cultural ideologies is itself a case in point, but because the use of story as "an agent of socialization" for children is a conscious and deliberate process, these insights may well be unusually clear (Stephens, *Language* 9).

Like any academic project, this one nevertheless has a number of limitations. Firstly, I am aware that my own set of socio-political beliefs and assumptions has undoubtedly influenced the findings of this study. Secondly, as I mentioned earlier, I am mindful that by limiting the scope of the study to adolescent literature and to gender/sexuality, I have not engaged with a number of other prominent meanings that death has for, and within, Western culture. In order to provide detailed analyses of individual novels, and of the patterns which have emerged from the fictions as a group, there are, thirdly, several issues and themes that I have not addressed comprehensively. As an example, the prevalence of YA texts which thematise suicide implies that it is an issue that is of great concern to the Western community at large, and yet it is not a particular focus of this project.[1] There may be value in exploring the representation of suicide in adolescent literature from discursive and rhetorical angles, however, because a suicide is "a site of social reconstruction"; it "both sets a limit and opens up a gap" and, thus, "it enables a certain number of questions about how we construct a self, and about how we construct a narrative" (Higonnet 229, 241).

As I make the argument about the potential of children's literature to communicate with particular clarity some of the ways in which meaning is created and shared within a society, I am conscious too that the social and ethical ideologies pervading children's fiction are, as Stephens contends, not always overt nor "a product of deliberate policy" since they can reflect "beliefs and assumptions of which the author is, or may be, unaware" (*Language* 9). Indeed, working through the contradictions between the explicit and implied ideologies inscribed in the novels that I have examined here has presented a considerable challenge. In light of the multifarious nature of the subject under investigation, I am also aware of the irony in attempting to reduce many of these conflicts or aporias to stable or singular meanings. Where possible, I have endeavoured to highlight the tensions and contradictions that have emerged in the meanings that each text has constructed for death. With a view to emphasising the differences between the texts themselves, I have similarly juxtaposed contrasting readings. Nonetheless, by concentrating on the common or dominant sets of meanings, and on the points of convergence between the texts as a group, finally, it is inevitable that I have glossed over a number of dissonances and differences in the ways that death has been represented.

In a book that is so bound up with the theme of "endings", and with subjecting others' representations of endings to detailed analysis, at this point it feels somewhat incongruous—and, dare I say, perilous—to attempt to create one myself. *Looking for Alaska*, which I referred to in the opening chapter, concludes with Miles's exam paper for his world religions class, in which he is asked to "fit the uncontestable fact of suffering into [his] understanding of the world" (215). Alaska's death acts as a catalyst for both the essay topic and Miles's response, which is summed up in the final paragraph when he writes: "Thomas Edison's last words were: 'It's very beautiful over there.' I don't know where there is, but I believe it's somewhere, and I hope it's beautiful" (221). The audience that I write for here is a different one, however. I need not be concerned (as those who are writing about death for adolescents are likely to be) with the idea that readers require certainties and fixed boundaries, with maintaining the balance between gravity and hope. But I am still plagued by doubts. How do I conclude in a way that is interesting, but, at the same time, does not give in to sentimentality? How do I avoid a neat closure that reduces the complexity of an (irreducibly complex) topic to a handful of lines? It is here that I come to an impasse—another aporia. And yet with that caveat, I will choose to end with the same few words I began: "death loves to be represented".

NOTES

Notes to the Introduction

1 Unless I refer specifically to "adolescent literature", I use the term "children's literature" to refer to texts produced for audiences aged between infancy and late adolescence.
2 See, for example: Alderman; FitzGerald; Hollindale; Mordue; Nieuwenhuizen; Nodelman ("Other"); Scutter; and Trites (*Disturbing*).
3 Although the term "adolescent" is traditionally employed by psychologists and that of "young adult" by the literary community, they are used here interchangeably.
4 The argument in favour of young adult literature as a marketing ruse is offered, for instance, by both Craven and Sorensen in Mordue (13). With respect to defining and historicising the genre, see also: Nimon and Foster; and Trites (*Disturbing*; "Theories").

Notes to Chapter 1

1 I am referring here to symbols and meanings predominantly associated with Western cultures.
2 As an example, Bronfen and Goodwin point out that the French publication of *The Hour of Our Death* (*L'homme devant la mort*) translates as *Man Before Death* thus aligning itself "too easily, and dangerously, with man/life before woman/death" (5).
3 For discussions about general literature texts, see, for instance: Barreca (*Sex*, "Writing"); Bassein; Bronfen (*Over*, "Risky"); Critchley; Dever; Doherty; Gilman; Goodwin; Higonnet; Martin; Mason; Rajan; Schleifer ("Afterword", *Rhetoric*); Stewart (*Death*, "Valediction"); and Tanner. For children's literature, see: Beere; Bradford ("Embodied"); Cockshut; Mallan ("Fatal", "Just"); McCarron; McKenzie; Reynolds; Reynolds and Yates; Scutter; Trites (*Disturbing*); and Wilson.

4 An ideal type, Walter takes care to explain, is a simplified idea "about social life that [has] a logical coherence but that [does] not exist in pure form in reality". And the aim of the sociologist, he argues, "is not to force complex reality into sociological pigeon-holes, but to use ideal types to identify themes and tensions in (in this case) the revival of death" (*Revival* 49).

5 The literal translation of *ars moriendi* is "(the) art of dying". It is the name given to two related Latin texts dating from the 1400s which consisted of literary and visual instructions for the dying individual to prepare the soul for impending death. According to the Christian precepts of the time, the texts offered advice on the protocols and procedures for a good death—on how to "die well".

6 This argument is also made by: Bauman; Bronfen (*Over*); Guthke; and Kearl (*Endings*, "You Never").

Notes to Chapter 2

1 See "Contemplating Otherness: Ideology and Historical Fiction" in Stephens (*Language*).

2 See Morling (11–12).

3 After writing the initial draft of this paragraph, I had to re-choose certain words to describe the event in a more objective manner, disclosing how this process can be unconscious, and the workings of ideology pervasive.

4 I am indebted here to Clare Bradford for pointing out that my position as a white Australian has influenced both my reading of Kellehear and Anderson's work, and my own analyses of "Australian" ways of death.

5 Rose's argument is drawn from Griffiths.

6 Although they are intended for a slightly younger audience, Judith Arthy's *The Children of Mirrabooka*, Allan Baillie's *Secrets of Walden Rising*, and Gary Crew and Peter Gouldthorpe's *The Lost Diamonds of Killiecrankie* could also be added to this list.

7 I have taken Bradford's argument out of context since it was made in reference to James Moloney's *Angela*. However, as the analysis of *No Such Country* demonstrates, this representation of race relations in Australian children's texts is a common one.

8 For further discussion on this topic (with regards to Crew's *Strange Objects*) see Bradford (*Reading* 32–35).

9 For an insightful discussion on Aboriginalist discourses I refer to the chapter "Speaking for the Aborigines: Knowledge, Power and Aboriginalism" in *Reading Race: Aboriginality in Australian Children's Literature*. Here, Bradford argues that in Australian children's literature, "the dynamics of Aboriginalism, knowledge and power operate by positioning child readers to assent to the versions of Aboriginality proposed by knowledgeable and sympathetic experts, who speak about and for Aborigines" (110).

10 This is also the case when Sam describes the strength he can feel from the earth in sexually possessive terms: "a woman bedded-down deep in coals of fire [. . .] the one who is mine, with her warmth and closeness here beneath me" (96).

11 I refer to Stephens and McCallum's use of the term "hieratic" to describe texts whose register is "apt to be figurative, especially metaphorical or allegorical" (*Retelling* 10–11).

12 The following list of texts suggests as much. This selection is not limited to adolescent texts (and Anthony Hill's texts have often been described as "biographical novels" and thus classified as non-fiction); however, see: Barnes; Crew and Tan; French (*Soldier*); Hill (*Soldier, Young*); Jorgensen and Harrison-Lever; Mulligan; Palmer; and Tucker. For a comprehensive selection of Australian children's literature dealing with war and the ANZAC soldier, see also Meiklejohn.

13 Mallan is referring here to Robert Cormier's *Heroes*.

14 See Mallan ("Challenging") for a comprehensive exploration of "phallic" masculinity and its associated terms.

15 Clarke's "His Natural Life" first appeared in the *Australian Journal* from March 1870 to June 1872. The revised book form, *For the Term of His Natural Life*, was first published in 1874.

16 This is Hooper's term for Point Puer in *Prison Boys of Port Arthur*.

17 Turner argues, for instance, that the characters of Dawes in *For the Term of His Natural Life*, and China in the motion picture, *Stir*, are "solitaries" (64).

18 Interestingly, Moore notes how the firmly heterosexual mateship legend of today is at odds with its origins in colonial Australia where, due to the preponderance of males, male-to-male intercourse was a valid sexual option (47–48).

19 Given the arguments I have made in this chapter about masculinity, historical fiction, and heroism, it is interesting that the text which provides an alternative to this version of the bushranger myth—Sophie Masson's *The Hand of Glory*—is female-authored. Indeed, *The Hand of Glory* is one of the few historical novels in the corpus to be written by a female, and to have a female protagonist. I do not look at it here, but Deborah Lisson's *The Devil's Own*—a historical time-shift which also has a female protagonist and a female author—is discussed in Chapter 4.

20 I owe these insights to Kerry Mallan, and I wish to acknowledge that several of the phrases I use here have been taken directly from her perceptive assessment of this chapter.

Notes to Chapter 3

1 The term "Being-towards-death" appears in Heidegger's *Being and Time*. In Trites's words, it "represents the moment of maturation in which the

subject defines himself in terms of his own death, in terms of his own not being" (*Disturbing* 159).

2 In this paper, Wilson also discusses Judith Clarke's *Night Train*, a text which offers an interesting examination of the degenerative effects of abjection on the development of male subjectivity. Here, the narrative implies that, like Janey, the protagonist, Luke, dies as a result of "society's inability to deal with individuals who do not conform to the majority's construction of 'normal'" (29). As an aside, Luke is one of only a few characters in the body of texts I have considered who acts as a focaliser but also dies (another is Tessa, the protagonist of Jenny Downham's *Before I Die*, which I discuss at length in the latter part of this chapter). Although he is granted a subject position within the narrative, he does not really have any agency, however, because, as Wilson points out, the narrative opens with his funeral, thus suggesting that his fate has already been settled (25).

3 Mallan's ideas for this argument are drawn from Bronfen's *Over Her Dead Body: Death, Femininity and the Aesthetic*.

4 Cormier's comments about *Sleeping Dogs* are quoted on both the back and front cover of the Viking/Penguin edition.

5 I find the use of the word "waste" here to be problematic since it echoes the comment made just a few pages prior to this about Steve's death being "a dumb waste of a life". Taken together, and framed through the themes of suicide and homosexuality, these two phrases can be seen to take on a pejorative meaning.

6 For an insightful discussion of the pleasure/pain dynamic as it is associated with homosexuality in YA novels, see the analysis of Aidan Chambers's *Dance on My Grave* in Trites (*Disturbing* 104–07).

7 I am indebted here to Kate McInally for her insights into *Tumble Turn*.

8 While *Angel's Gate* is of interest to this study because, like many of Gary Crew's novels, it clearly demonstrates a pervasive connection between death and sexuality, I do not discuss it here. However, a useful starting point for an examination of these themes can be found in Scutter's *Displaced Fictions: Contemporary Australian Fiction for Teenagers and Young Adults*.

9 Although *The Family Tree* is aimed more at the pre-adolescent audience, I include it here because it is such a clear example of this model.

10 Makeover has a very different function in Philippa Burne's *Fishnets*, however, where the main character, Sophie, blames herself for her younger sister's death. Rather than affirming a sense of selfhood, Stephens argues, here makeover is "metonymic of absence" because it works to "paper over" the cracks in Sophie's fractured subjectivity ("Constructions" 8).

11 According to Stephens, a narrative becomes limited in its capacity to locate the subject in "a position of potentiality" when access to knowledge is articulated in this way (*Language* 283). For more on "words of power", death, and subjectivity, see Stephens's analysis of Lois Lowry's *A Summer to Die* in Chapter 7 of *Language and Ideology in Children's Fiction* (280–87).

12 Kate Benchworth from Valerie Sherrard's *Kate* is another.

13 My thanks go to Clare Bradford for her suggestions regarding the difference between the two cultures' treatment of Aboriginal death.

14 By focusing on physical details, James Moloney's *Gracey* treats the suicide of Raymond, an Aboriginal male jailed for his assault on a police officer, in a similar way to *Deadly Unna?*. In passing, I think it is interesting that, although the deaths of Raymond, Dumby Red, and Sister Girl are framed through the themes of crime and punishment (Sister Girl's suicide occurs after she is released from jail), the details of the crime are not mentioned in *The Binna Binna Man* whereas they are a key aspect of the white-authored *Deadly Unna?* and *Gracey*.

15 Melina Marchetta's *Looking for Alibrandi* has the potential to offer an alternative to this pattern because, although it also equates subjective growth (or "emancipation") with death, the novel's working-class, Italian-Australian protagonist, Josephine, is not privileged in terms of gender, ethnicity, or class. Rather, it is her wealthy, Anglo friend, John, who suicides.

16 A novel that would thus make a useful comparison with others in this section is David Metzenthen's *Gilbert's Ghost Train*. It not only offers a far more subtle depiction of gender under pressure than say, *Deadly Unna?* or *Walking Naked*, it also provides no neat "answers", firstly because it suggests that the processes of growth and grief are ongoing, and secondly because it does not rigorously advocate one way of being male over another. Undoubtedly, the narrative represents an attempt to intervene in masculine behaviours. However, its depiction of the father/son relationship does not suggest that growth and change are limited only to the adolescent, nor is it centred, like many other YA fictions which thematise masculinity, around an Oedipal struggle in which the son's performance of his own masculinity is reliant on the symbolic overthrow or murder of the father (Romøren and Stephens 223).

Notes to Chapter 4

1 This is Botting's argument in *Gothic*.

2 As Bloom points out, although "there are gothic tales that are not horror fiction and horror tales that contain no real Gothic elements", "horror" and "Gothic" are "often (if not usually) interchangeable" because there exists "a multiplicity of apparently substitutable terms to cover the same thing: Gothic tale, ghost tale, terror romance, Gothic horror" (155).

3 The genre is a relatively recent phenomenon for young readers, however. Traces of Gothic and horror—themes, motifs, stock features—are evident in both classic and contemporary children's literature, yet it was not until the early 1990s that Gothic/horror narrative conventions appeared in children's fiction to the extent that they created an identifiable genre (Cosslett; Nodelman, *Ordinary*).

4   The "Outlands" trilogy also belongs to the post-disaster genre (which I examine in Chapter 5), but I have included it in this chapter because its Gothic conventions interest me the most.

5   According to Halberstam, while "[t]echnologies of monstrosity are always also technologies of sex", monsters are "meaning machines", representing such things as gender, race, nationality, class, and sexuality all in one body (19–20, 88). My focus here is obviously on sexuality; however, almost any of these markers of identity could be applied to a reading of monstrousness in the series.

6   The term "uncanny" is used here in a Freudian sense, which at its simplest can be explained as that which is "related to what is frightening [. . .] what arouses dread and horror" (Freud, "Uncanny" 219).

7   For a discussion on death, trauma, and (narrative) therapy in several of David Almond's novels (which, due to their implied pre-teen audience, I do not include here), see: Brennan; Bullen and Parsons; and Latham.

8   See Scutter for a comprehensive discussion of this point.

9   See also Kortenhaus and Demarest for a discussion on gender role stereotyping during this period.

10 For an extensive discussion on the narrative's patriarchal law motif, see Rutherford.

11 Incidentally, the moment at which the attraction between Nat and Nissa is sexualised is also the point at which they first come into contact with death because it occurs straight after the killing of The Tod.

12 Recent studies include Hourihan (*Deconstructing*), Jones and Watkins (*Necessary*), and Stephens and McCallum (*Retelling*).

13 The naming of the guide "Ludic" is also an example of the narrative's tendency to be playful (that is, with language and with genre).

14 See, for example, Page (although even a cursory online search for reviews of the novel is enough to suggest that Sabriel is typically viewed in this way).

15 Here I call on those traits which Stephens and McCallum argue are characteristic of the female hero paradigm in contemporary heterocosmic children's fiction (*Retelling* 118–19).

16 It would be possible to focus entirely on the figure of the archaic or monstrous mother and her relation to death in *Sabriel*. See, for instance, Creed's discussion of horror and the monstrous-feminine (*Horror*), or, for an analysis devoted specifically to *Sabriel*, see Mills ("Fixity").

17 Given the similarities between Sabriel and Lyra in Philip Pullman's "His Dark Materials" series, it would be interesting to compare the two. How does Lyra's quest to release the dead in *The Amber Spyglass* differ from Sabriel's quest to confine them, for instance? For a useful starting point in terms of the series' potential to vary or upset the heroic quest pattern, see Lenz ("Philip").

18 Interestingly, Jelindel/Jaelin's male name is used at this point, although for the remainder of the narrative, she/he is always referred to in the third

person as "Jelindel". Whether this is intentional or not is unclear; however, it does serve to further destabilise orthodox notions of gender and gender difference.

19 Strictly speaking, not all dead-narrator tales are told in the first-person. As yet, there is not a more suitable term, however, so I have adopted it here.

20 As Lassén-Seger's comprehensive study of metamorphosis suggests, endeavouring to make a distinction between the terms associated with the subject is not without its problems (*Adventures*); nonetheless, I take "metamorphosis" to mean "an extraordinary change in form, structure, or substance".

21 While Lassén-Seger's study of child metamorphs primarily addresses the transformation from child to animal, plant, insect, mineral, object, or monster, I nevertheless find her conclusions regarding plot patterns to be especially useful here (*Adventures*).

Notes to Chapter 5

1 See, for example: Braithwaite; Bull; Hintz; and Stephens ("Post-Disaster").

2 *The Broken Wheel* is the first in the "Three Days" series. The others in the set are not discussed here, although they too have much to offer an examination of death in the post-disaster novel.

3 This brief outline of the genre's characteristic features is drawn from Stephens ("Post-Disaster" 128).

4 Isobelle Carmody's *Scatterlings*, which opens with a particularly graphic representation of death, provides another example of this pattern.

5 See Nimon for other techniques Marsden employs to convince readers of the series' reliability as "history".

6 See Meaney for an examination of invasion scare novels and Australian political culture.

7 For further discussions about death in the series, see: Caesar; Nimon; and Scutter.

8 As Inness points out, the *Terminator* films are not strictly post-apocalyptic works since they are largely set in a pre-apocalyptic world. However, they do share many similarities with other post-disaster texts, and, thus, in order to provide background material for my argument, I will include them here.

9 The disfigured Hester from Philip Reeve's *Mortal Engines* would make for an interesting comparison here. As Sambell argues, Hester "redefines the role of the heroine in dangerously masculine, destructive, and tragically self-destructive ways" ("Carnivalizing" 259).

10 See also *Tomorrow, When the War Began* (and other texts in the series) where there are clear tensions evident in the construction of female characters as both women and as warriors.

Notes to the Conclusion

1 For an examination of suicide in YA fiction (and for critical references and suggested novels), see McKenzie, "The Representation of Suicide in Adolescent Literature as a Site of 'Crossing Boundaries'".

Bibliography

Children's Texts

Aaron, Moses. *Elijah Greenface*. Sydney: Hodder, 2000.
Arthy, Judith. *The Children of Mirrabooka*. Ringwood, Australia: Penguin, 1997.
Baillie, Allan. *Secrets of Walden Rising*. Ringwood, Australia: Penguin, 1996.
Barnes, Rory. *Night Vision*. Sydney: ABC, 2006.
Bateson, Catherine. *The Airdancer of Glass*. St Lucia: U of Queensland P, 2004.
———. *Painted Love Letters*. St Lucia: U of Queensland P, 2002.
Block, Francesca Lia. *Wasteland*. New York: Harper, 2003.
Brugman, Alyssa. *Walking Naked*. Crows Nest, Australia: Allen, 2002.
Burne, Philippa. *Fishnets*. St Leonards, Australia: Allen, 1997.
Calder, Charlotte. *Settling Storms*. Port Melbourne: Lothian, 2000.
Carmody, Isobelle. *The Gathering*. Ringwood, Australia: Penguin, 1993.
———. *Greylands*. Ringwood, Australia: Penguin, 1997.
———. *Scatterlings*. Ringwood, Australia: Penguin, 1991.
Caswell, Brian. *Dreamslip*. St Lucia: U of Queensland P, 1994.
Chambers, Aidan. *Dance on My Grave*. London: Bodley Head, 1982.
Clarke, Judith. *Night Train*. Ringwood, Australia: Penguin, 1998.
———. *Starry Nights*. Crows Nest, Australia: Allen, 2001.
Collins, Paul. *Dragonlinks*. Camberwell, Australia: Penguin, 2002.
Cormier, Robert. *Heroes*. London: Hamilton, 1998
Crew, Gary. *Angel's Gate*. Port Melbourne: Heinemann, 1993.
———, ed. *Dark House*. Port Melbourne: Mammoth, 1995.
———. *Gothic Hospital*. Port Melbourne: Lothian, 2001.
———. *No Such Country*. Port Melbourne: Heinemann, 1991.
———. *Strange Objects*. Sydney: Hodder, 1990.
Crew, Gary and Peter Gouldthorpe. *The Lost Diamonds of Killiecrankie*. Port Melbourne: Lothian, 1995.
Crew, Gary and Philip Neilsen. *Edward Britton*. Port Melbourne: Lothian, 2000.
Crew, Gary and Shaun Tan. *Memorial*. Port Melbourne: Lothian, 1999.
Cummings, Phil. *Angel*. Milsons Point, Australia: Random, 1997.
Disher, Garry. *The Divine Wind*. Sydney: Hodder, 1998.
Downham, Jenny. *Before I Die*. Oxford: Fickling, 2007.
Eaton, Anthony. *Fireshadow*. St Lucia: U of Queensland P, 2004.
Francis, C. D. *Three Realms*. South Melbourne: Lothian, 2004.
French, Jackie. *Blood Moon*. Sydney: Harper, 2002.
———. *Flesh and Blood*. Sydney: Harper, 2004.
———. *In the Blood*. Sydney: Harper, 2001.
———. *Soldier on the Hill*. Sydney: Harper, 1997.
Fusillo, Archimede. *Sparring with Shadows*. Ringwood, Australia: Penguin, 1997.
Gardner, Scott. *Burning Eddy*. Sydney: Pan, 2003.
Gleitzman, Morris. *Two Weeks with the Queen*. Sydney: Pan, 1989.

Godwin, Jane. *The Family Tree*. Ringwood, Australia: Penguin, 1999.
Green, John. *Looking for Alaska*. New York: Dutton, 2005.
Greenwood, Kerry. *The Broken Wheel*. Sydney: Harper, 1996.
Gwynne, Phillip. *Deadly Unna?* Ringwood, Australia: Penguin, 1998.
———. *Nukkin Ya*. Ringwood, Australia: Penguin, 2000.
Hartnett, Sonya. *Sleeping Dogs*. Ringwood, Australia: Penguin, 1995.
Higgins, Simon. *Beyond the Shaking Time*. Sydney: Hodder, 2000.
Hill, Anthony. *Soldier Boy: The True Story of Jim Martin, the Youngest ANZAC*. Ringwood, Australia: Penguin, 2001.
———. *Young Digger*. Camberwell, Australia: Penguin, 2002.
Hines, Sue. *Out of the Shadows*. Sydney: Random, 1998.
Jorgensen, Norman and Brian Harrison-Lever. *In Flanders Fields*. North Fremantle, Australia: Sandcastle, 2002.
Kelleher, Victor. *Baily's Bones*. Ringwood, Australia: Penguin, 1988.
———. *Del-Del*. Milsons Point, Australia: Random, 1991.
———. *Into the Dark*. Ringwood, Australia: Penguin, 1999.
———. *Red Heart*. Ringwood, Australia: Penguin, 2001.
———. *Taronga*. Ringwood, Australia: Penguin, 1986.
Lanagan, Margo. *Touching Earth Lightly*. St Leonards, Australia: Allen, 1996.
Larkin, John. *Cyber Payne*. Sydney: Random, 2000.
Lawrinson, Julia. *Bye, Beautiful*. Camberwell, Australia: Penguin, 2006.
Lisson, Deborah. *The Devil's Own*. Glebe, Australia: McVitty, 1990.
Lowry, Lois. *A Summer to Die*. Boston: Houghton, 1977.
Lucashenko, Melissa. *Killing Darcy*. St Lucia: U of Queensland P, 1998.
MacLeod, Doug. *Tumble Turn*. Camberwell, Australia: Penguin, 2003.
Marchetta, Melina. *Looking for Alibrandi*. Ringwood, Australia: Penguin, 1992.
Marsden, John. *Tomorrow, When the War Began*. Sydney: Pan, 1993.
Masson, Sophie. *The Hand of Glory*. Sydney: Hodder, 2002.
McDonald, Meme and Boori Monty Pryor. *The Binna Binna Man*. St Leonards, Australia: Allen, 1999.
Metzenthen, David. *Boys of Blood and Bone*. Camberwell, Australia: Penguin, 2003.
———. *Gilbert's Ghost Train*. Gosford, Australia: Scholastic, 1997.
Moloney, James. *Angela*. St Lucia: U of Queensland P, 1998.
———. *Gracey*. St Lucia: U of Queensland P, 1994.
———. *The House on the River Terrace*. St Lucia: U of Queensland P, 1995.
Mulligan, David. *Angels of Kokoda*. South Melbourne: Lothian, 2006.
Nix, Garth. *Lirael: Daughter of the Clayr*. Crows Nest, Australia: Allen, 2001.
———. *Sabriel*. Sydney: Harper, 1996.
Palmer, Tony. *Break of Day*. Camberwell, Australia: Penguin, 2007.
Pullman, Philip. *The Amber Spyglass*. London: Scholastic, 2007.
Reeve, Philip. *Mortal Engines*. London: Scholastic, 2001.
Ridden, Brian. *Whistle Man*. Port Melbourne: Lothian, 2000.
Schembri, Jim. *The Jay Beans Guild*. South Melbourne: Addison, 1998.
Sherrard, Valerie. *Kate*. Toronto, ON: Dundurn, 2003.
Soto, Gary. *The Afterlife*. Orlando, FL: Harcourt, 2003.
Stewart, Alison. *The Memory Shell*. Sydney: Hodder, 2000.
Sussex, Lucy. *Black Ice*. Rydalmere, Australia: Hodder, 1997.
Svendsen, Mark. *Poison under Their Lips*. Port Melbourne: Lothian, 2001.
Tucker, Alan. *The Bombing of Darwin: The Diary of Tom Taylor*. Lindfield, Australia: Scholastic, 2002.
Walker, Sarah. *Water Colours*. Sydney: Hodder, 2000.
Walters, Celeste. *The Glass Mountain*. St Lucia: U of Queensland P, 2003.
Westerfeld, Scott. *Peeps*. New York: Penguin, 2005.
Whitcomb, Laura. *A Certain Slant of Light*. Boston: Graphia, 2005.
Zevin, Gabrielle. *Elsewhere*. London: Bloomsbury, 2006.

Critical Works

Aaron, Michele. "Introduction." *The Body's Perilous Pleasures: Dangerous Desires and Contemporary Culture*. Ed. Michele Aaron. Edinburgh: Edinburgh UP, 1999. 1–10.
———. "'Til Death Us Do Part." *The Body's Perilous Pleasures: Dangerous Desires and Contemporary Culture*. Ed. Michele Aaron. Edinburgh: Edinburgh UP, 1999. 67–84.

Agee, Jane M. "Mothers and Daughters: Gender-Role Socialisation in Two Newbery Award Books." *Children's Literature in Education* 24.3 (1993): 165–83.

Alderman, Belle. "Rites of Passage: Adolescent Literature." *Give Them Wings: The Experience of Children's Literature*. Eds. Maurice Saxby and Gordon Winch. 2nd ed. South Melbourne: Macmillan, 1987. 290–307.

"ANZAC Day". *Australian Government Culture and Recreation Portal*. 23 Oct. 2003. http://www.cultureandrecreation.gov.au/articles/ANZAC/index.htm.

"The ANZAC Day Tradition". *Australian War Memorial*. 23 Oct. 2003. http://www.awm.gov.au/commemoration/ANZAC/ANZAC_tradition.htm.

Ariès, Philippe. *The Hour of Our Death*. Trans. Helen Weaver. New York: Oxford UP, 1991.

———. *Images of Man and Death*. Trans. Janet Lloyd. Cambridge: Harvard UP, 1985.

———. *Western Attitudes toward Death: From the Middle Ages to the Present*. Trans. Patricia M. Ranum. Baltimore: Johns Hopkins UP, 1974.

Armitt, Lucie. *Theorising the Fantastic*. London: Hodder, 1996.

Astbury, Leigh. "Death and Eroticism in the ANZAC Legend." *Art and Australia* 30.1 (1992): 67–73.

Atterby, Brian. *Strategies of Fantasy*. Bloomington: Indiana UP, 1992.

Baccolini, Raffaella. "'A Useful Knowledge of the Present Is Rooted in the Past': Memory and Historical Reconciliation in Ursula K. Le Guin's *The Telling*." *Dark Horizons: Science Fiction and the Dystopian Imagination*. Eds. Raffaella Baccolini and Tom Moylan. New York: Routledge, 2003. 113–34.

Baccolini, Raffaella and Tom Moylan. "Dystopia and Histories." *Dark Horizons: Science Fiction and the Dystopian Imagination*. Eds. Raffaella Baccolini and Tom Moylan. New York: Routledge, 2003. 1–12.

Baker, A. W. *Death Is a Good Solution: The Convict Experience in Early Australia*. St Lucia: U of Queensland P, 1984.

Bakhtin, Mikhail. *Rabelais and His World*. Trans. Hélène Iswolsky. Cambridge: MIT P, 1968.

Barreca, Regina, ed. *Sex and Death in Victorian Literature*. Bloomington: Indiana UP, 1990.

———. "Writing as Voodoo: Sorcery, Hysteria, and Art." *Death and Representation*. Eds. Sarah Webster Goodwin and Elisabeth Bronfen. Baltimore: Johns Hopkins UP, 1993. 174–91.

Barry, Peter. *Beginning Theory: An Introduction to Literary and Cultural Theory*. Manchester: Manchester UP, 1995.

Bartkowski, Frances. *Feminist Utopias*. Lincoln: U of Nebraska P, 1989.

Bassein, Beth Ann. *Women and Death: Linkages in Western Thought and Literature*. Westport, CT: Greenwood, 1984.

Bataille, Georges. *Erotism: Death and Sensuality*. Trans. Mary Dalwood. San Francisco: City Lights, 1986.

Bateson, Catherine. "Making Maps: Catherine Bateson Talks About the Making of *Painted Love Letters*." *Magpies: Talking About Books for Children* 17.3 (2002): 12–13.

Baudrillard, Jean. *Symbolic Exchange and Death*. Trans. Iain Hamilton Grant. London: Sage, 1993.

Bauman, Zygmunt. *Mortality, Immortality and Other Life Strategies*. Cambridge, UK: Polity, 1992.

Beere, Diana. "Representations of the 'Absent Mother' in Australian Adolescent Fiction." *Papers: Explorations into Children's Literature* 8.3 (1998): 16–24.

Belsey, Catherine. *Critical Practice*. 2nd ed. London: Routledge, 2002.

———. *Desire: Love Stories in Western Culture*. Oxford: Blackwell, 1994.

Berger, James. *After the End: Representations of Post-Apocalypse*. Minneapolis: U of Minnesota P, 1999.

Berkhofer, Robert. *Beyond the Great Story: History as Text and Discourse*. Cambridge: Belknap P of Harvard UP, 1995.

Bertrand, Ina. "New Histories of the Kelly Gang: Gregor Jordan's *Ned Kelly*". *Senses of Cinema*. 26 (2003). 28 Jan. 2004. http://www.sensesofcinema.com/contents/03/26/ned_kelly.html.

Blanchot, Maurice. *The Space of Literature*. Trans. Ann Smock. Lincoln: U of Nebraska P, 1982.

Bloom, Clive. "Horror Fiction: In Search of a Definition." *A Companion to the Gothic*. Ed. David Punter. Oxford: Blackwell, 2000. 155–66.

Booker, M. Keith. *The Dystopian Impulse in Modern Literature: Fiction as Social Criticism*. Westport, CT: Greenwood, 1994.

———. *Dystopian Literature: A Theory and Research Guide*. Westport, CT: Greenwood, 1994.

Botting, Fred. *Gothic*. London: Routledge, 1996.

Brabander, Jennifer M. "Review: Francesca Lia Block, *Wasteland*." *The Horn Book Magazine* 79.6 (2003): 739–41.

Bradford, Clare. "Centre and Edges: Postcolonial Literary Theory and Australian Picture Books." *Writing the Australian Child: Texts and Contexts in Fictions for Children*. Ed. Clare Bradford. Nedlands: U of Western Australia P, 1996. 92–110.

———. "Embodied Subjectivities: Female-Authored Texts and Female Friendships." *Something to Crow About: New Perspectives in Literature for Young People*. Eds. Susan Clancy and David Gilbey. Wagga Wagga: Centre for Information Studies, Charles Sturt U, 1998. 109–17.

———. "Memory, History, Dystopia: *No Such Country* and *Secrets of Walden Rising*." 5th International Conference of the Utopian Studies Society, U of Porto, Portugal, 7–11 July 2004.

———. "Possessed by the Beast: Subjectivity and Agency in *Pictures in the Dark* and *Foxspell*." *Mystery in Children's Literature: From the Rational to the Supernatural*. Eds. Adrienne E. Gavin and Christopher Routledge. Houndmills, UK: Palgrave, 2001. 149–164.

———. *Reading Race: Aboriginality in Australian Children's Literature*. Melbourne: Melbourne UP, 2001.

———. *Unsettling Narratives: Postcolonial Readings of Children's Literature*. Waterloo, ON: Wilfrid Laurier UP, 2007.

Braithwaite, Elizabeth. "Young Adult Post-Disaster Fiction: Exploration of a Genre." Diss. U of Melbourne, 2006.

Brennan, Geraldine. "The Game Called Death: Frightening Fictions by David Almond, Philip Gross and Lesley Howarth." *Frightening Fiction*. Eds. Kimberley Reynolds, Kevin McCarron, and Geraldine Brennan. London: Continuum, 2001. 92–107.

Bronfen, Elisabeth. *Over Her Dead Body: Death, Femininity and the Aesthetic*. Manchester: Manchester UP, 1992.

———. "Risky Resemblances: On Repetition, Mourning, and Representation." *Death and Representation*. Eds. Sarah Webster Goodwin and Elisabeth Bronfen. Baltimore: Johns Hopkins UP, 1993. 103–29.

Bronfen, Elisabeth and Sarah Webster Goodwin. "Introduction." *Death and Representation*. Eds. Sarah Webster Goodwin and Elisabeth Bronfen. Baltimore: Johns Hopkins UP, 1993. 3–25.

Buchbinder, David. "Unruly Age: Representing the Aging Male Body." *Manning the Next Millennium: Studies in Masculinities*. Eds. Sharyn Pearce and Vivienne Muller. Bentley, Australia: Black Swan, 2002. 11–28.

Bull, Geoff. "Morning Comes Whether You Set the Alarm or Not: Science Fiction, a Genre for the Future." *Orana* 31.3 (1995): 159–69.

Bullen, Elizabeth and Elizabeth Parsons. "Risk and Resilience, Knowledge and Imagination: The Enlightenment of David Almond's *Skellig*." *Children's Literature* 35 (2007): 127–44.

Burke, Kenneth. "Thanatopsis for Critics: A Brief Thesaurus of Deaths and Dyings." *Essays in Criticism* 2.4 (1952): 369–75.

Butler, Judith. *The Psychic Life of Power: Theories in Subjection*. Stanford: Stanford UP, 1997.

Caesar, Adrian. "Invasions of the Mind: John Marsden and the Threat from Asia." *Overland* 157 (1999): 46–49.

Carden-Coyne, Anna Alexandra. "Classical Heroism and Modern Life: Bodybuilding and Masculinity in the Early Twentieth Century." *Journal of Australian Studies* 63 (1999): 138–49.

Carey, Peter. *True History of the Kelly Gang*. St Lucia: U of Queensland P, 2000.

Chamberlain, Lindy. *Through My Eyes*. Richmond, Australia: Heinemann, 1990.

Charmaz, Kathy, Glennys Howarth, and Allan Kellehear. "Preface." *The Unknown Country: Death in Australia, Britain and the USA*. Eds. Kathy Charmaz, Glennys Howarth, and Allan Kellehear. Houndmills, UK: Macmillan, 1997. vii–x.

Choron, Jacques. *Death and Western Thought*. New York: Collier, 1963.

———. *Modern Man and Mortality*. New York: Macmillan, 1964.

Christian-Smith, Linda. "Chills and Thrills: Childhood, Boys and Popular Horror Fiction." *Crossing the Boundaries*. Eds. Geoff Bull and Michèle Anstey. Frenchs Forest, Australia: Pearson, 2002. 161–74.

Clarke, Marcus. *For the Term of His Natural Life*. London: Macmillan, 1920.

Clover, Carol J. *Men, Women, and Chain Saws: Gender in the Modern Horror Film*. Princeton: Princeton UP, 1992.

Cockshut, A. O. J. "Children's Death in Dickens: A Chapter in the History of Taste." *Representations of Childhood Death*. Eds. Gillian Avery and Kimberley Reynolds. London: Macmillan, 2000. 133–53.

Connolly, Angela. "Psychoanalytic Theory in Times of Terror." *Journal of Analytical Psychology* 48 (2003): 407–31.

Conrad, Joseph. *Heart of Darkness*. Harmondsworth, UK: Penguin, 1973.

Cosslett, Tess. "Transformations of Pastoral and Gothic in Children's Fiction." *Signal* 98 (2002): 91–101.

Crawford, Neta C. "Feminist Futures: Science Fiction, Utopia, and the Art of Possibilities in World Politics." *To Seek out New Worlds: Science Fiction and World Politics*. Ed. Jutta Weldes. New York: Palgrave, 2003. 195–220.

Creed, Barbara. "Horror and the Monstrous Feminine: An Imaginary Abjection." *Feminist Film Theory: A Reader*. Ed. Sue Thornham. New York: New York UP, 1999. 251–66.

———. *The Monstrous Feminine: Film, Feminism, Psychoanalysis*. London: Routledge, 1993.

Critchley, Simon. *Very Little. Almost Nothing: Death, Philosophy, Literature*. London: Routledge, 1997.

Danaher, Geoff, Tony Schirato, and Jen Webb. *Understanding Foucault*. St Leonards, Australia: Allen, 2000.

Darian-Smith, Kate and Paula Hamilton. "Introduction." *Memory and History in Twentieth-Century Australia*. Eds. Kate Darian-Smith and Paula Hamilton. Melbourne: Oxford UP, 1994.

Davidson, Harriet. "Improper Desire: Reading *The Waste Land*." *The Cambridge Companion to T. S. Eliot*. Ed. A. D. Moody. Cambridge: Cambridge UP, 1994. 121–31.

Dawson, Graham. *Soldier Heroes: British Adventure, Empire and the Imagining of Masculinities*. London: Routledge, 1994.

Dever, Carolyn. *Death and the Mother from Dickens to Freud: Victorian Fiction and the Anxiety of Origins*. Cambridge: Cambridge UP, 1998.

Dixon, Robert. *Writing the Colonial Adventure: Race, Gender and Nation in Anglo-Australian Popular Fiction, 1875–1914*. Cambridge: Cambridge UP, 1995.

Doane, Mary Ann. *Femmes Fatales: Feminism, Film Theory, Psychoanalysis*. New York: Routledge, 1991.

Doherty, Gerald. "Death and the Rhetoric of Representation in D. H. Lawrence's *Women in Love*." *Mosaic* 27.1 (1994): 55–72.

Dollimore, Jonathan. *Death, Desire and Loss in Western Culture*. New York: Routledge, 1998.

Dusevic, Tom and Fiona Carruthers. "Aboriginal Areas Suffer Worst Death Rates." *The Australian* 27 July 1994: 3.

Eagleton, Terry. *Literary Theory: An Introduction*. 2nd ed. Oxford: Blackwell, 1996.

Edwards, Deborah. "Race, Death and Gender in the ANZAC Memorial." *Art and Australia* 28.4 (1991): 476–81.

Evans, Raymond and Bill Thorpe. "Commanding Men: Masculinities and the Convict System." *Journal of Australian Studies* 56 (1998): 17–34.

Fiske, John, Bob Hodge, and Graeme Turner. *Myths of Oz: Reading Australian Popular Culture*. Australian Cultural Studies. Ed. John Tulloch. North Sydney: Allen, 1987.

Fitting, Peter. "You're History, Buddy: Postapocalyptic Visions in Recent Science Fiction Film." *Fights of Fancy: Armed Conflict in Science Fiction and Fantasy*. Eds. George Slusser and Eric S. Rabkin. Athens: The U of Georgia P, 1993. 114–31.

FitzGerald, Frances. "The Influence of Anxiety: What's the Problem with Young Adult Novels?" *Harper's Magazine* Sept. 2004: 62–70.

Fitzpatrick, Lesley. "Secular, Savage and Solitary: Death in Australian Painting." *The Unknown Country: Death in Australia, Britain and the USA*. Eds. Kathy Charmaz, Glennys Howarth, and Allan Kellehear. Houndmills, UK: Macmillan, 1997. 15–30.

Flanagan, Victoria. "Reframing Masculinity: Female-to-Male Cross-Dressing." *Ways of Being Male: Representing Masculinities in Children's Literature and Film*. Ed. John Stephens. New York: Routledge, 2002. 78–95.

Foucault, Michel. *The Archaeology of Knowledge*. Trans. A. M. Sheridan Smith. London: Tavistock, 1972.

———. *Discipline and Punish: The Birth of the Prison*. Trans. Alan Sheridan. New York: Pantheon, 1977.

———. *The History of Sexuality*. Trans. Robert Hurley. Vol. 1. New York: Pantheon, 1978.

Freud, Sigmund. *Civilization and Its Discontents*. Trans. James Strachey. New York: Norton, 1989.

———. "The Ego and the Id." *The Standard Edition of the Complete Psychological Works of Sigmund Freud*. Ed. and trans. James Strachey. Vol. 19. London: Vintage, 2001. 12–63.

———. "The 'Uncanny'." *The Standard Edition of the Complete Psychological Works of Sigmund Freud*. Ed. and trans. James Strachey. Vol. 17. London: Vintage, 2001. 217–56.

Gaile, Andreas. "Re-Mythologizing an Australian Legend: Peter Carey's *True History of the Kelly Gang*." *Antipodes* 15.1 (2001): 37–39.

Gandhi, Leela. *Postcolonial Theory: A Critical Introduction.* Sydney: Allen, 1998.

Garton, Stephen. "War and Masculinity in Twentieth Century Australia." *Journal of Australian Studies* 56 (1998): 86–95.

Gibson, Lois Rauch and Laura M. Zaidman. "Death in Children's Literature: Taboo or Not Taboo?" *Children's Literature Association Quarterly* 16.4 (1991): 232–34.

Gilbert, Sandra M. and Susan Gubar. *The Madwoman in the Attic: The Woman Writer and the Nineteenth-Century Literary Imagination.* New Haven: Yale UP, 1979.

Gillis, Stacy. "The (Post)Feminist Politics of Cyberpunk." *Gothic Studies* 9.2 (2007): 7–19.

Gilman, Sander L. "'Who Kills Whores?' 'I Do,' Says Jack: Race and Gender in Victorian London." *Death and Representation.* Eds. Sarah Webster Goodwin and Elisabeth Bronfen. Baltimore: Johns Hopkins UP, 1993. 263–84.

Goodwin, Sarah Webster. "Romanticism and the Ghost of Prostitution: Freud, Maria, and 'Alice Fell.'" *Death and Representation.* Eds. Sarah Webster Goodwin and Elisabeth Bronfen. Baltimore: Johns Hopkins UP, 1993. 152–73.

Gray, Paul. " Carnage: An Open Book." *Time* 142.5 (1993): 54.

Griffiths, Tom. "The Language of Conflict." *Frontier Conflict.* Eds. B. Attwood and S. G. Foster. Canberra: Natl. Museum of Australia, 2003. 133–49.

Grosz, Elizabeth. "The Body of Signification." *Abjection, Melancholia, and Love: The Work of Julia Kristeva.* Eds. John Fletcher and Andrew Benjamin. London: Routledge, 1990. 80–103.

———. *Volatile Bodies: Toward a Corporeal Feminism.* Crows Nest, Australia: Allen, 1994.

Guthke, Karl Siegfried. *The Gender of Death: A Cultural History in Art and Literature.* Cambridge: Cambridge UP, 1999.

Hacking, Ian. *The Taming of Chance.* New York: Cambridge UP, 1990.

Halberstam, Judith. *Skin Shows: Gothic Horror and the Technology of Monsters.* Durham: Duke UP, 1995.

Hall, Stuart. "Editorial." *Soundings* 3 (1996): 116–18.

———. "The Work of Representation." *Representation: Cultural Representations and Signifying Practices.* Ed. Stuart Hall. London: Sage and Open U, 1997. 13–64.

Hamer, Michelle. "Truth and Dare". *The Age.* 11 Jan. 2004. 21 Apr. 2004. http://www.theage.com.au/articles/2004/01/07/1073437341741.html.

Hanzl, Anne. "*Painted Love Letters.*" *Magpies: Talking About Books for Children* 17.1 (2002): 38.

Harris, Joanna. "Good Girls Don't: Gender Ideologies in *Touching Earth Lightly* and *Wolf.*" *Papers: Explorations into Children's Literature* 9.1 (1999): 41–50.

Hawkins, Anne Hunsaker. "Constructing Death: Three Pathographies About Dying." *Omega* 22.4 (1991): 301–17.

Hegarty, Paul. *Georges Bataille: Core Cultural Theorist.* London: Sage, 2000.

Heidegger, Martin. *Being and Time.* Trans. John Macquarie and Edward Robinson. New York: Harper, 1962.

Hendershot, Cyndy. *The Animal Within: Masculinity and the Gothic.* Ann Arbor: U of Michigan P, 1998.

Herd, Kate. "Quest for the Anglo-Australian Adolescent 'Self'." Diss. Deakin U, 2002.

Hergenhan, Laurie. *Unnatural Lives: Studies in Australian Convict Fiction.* 2nd ed. St Lucia: U of Queensland P, 1993.

Higonnet, Margaret. "Frames of Female Suicide." *Studies in the Novel* 32.2 (2000): 229–42.

Hintz, Carrie. "Monica Hughes, Lois Lowry, and Young Adult Dystopias." *The Lion and the Unicorn* 26.2 (2002): 254–64.

Hintz, Carrie and Elaine Ostry. "Introduction." *Utopian and Dystopian Writing for Children and Young Adults.* Eds. Carrie Hintz and Elaine Ostry. New York: Routledge, 2003. 1–20.

Hodge, Bob and Vijay Mishra. *Dark Side of the Dream: Australian Literature and the Postcolonial Mind.* North Sydney: Allen, 1990.

Hollindale, Peter. "The Adolescent Novel of Ideas." *Children's Literature in Education* 26.1 (1995): 83–95.

Hollinger, Veronica. "Apocalypse Coma." *Edging into the Future: Science Fiction and Contemporary Cultural Transformation.* Eds. Veronica Hollinger and Joan Gordon. Philadelphia: U of Pennsylvania P, 2002. 159–73.

Holmlund, Christine. "A Decade of Deadly Dolls: Hollywood and the Woman Killer." *Moving Targets: Women, Murder and Representation.* Ed. Helen Birch. Berkeley: U of California P, 1994. 127–51.

Hooper, F. C. *Prison Boys of Port Arthur: A Study of the Point Puer Boys' Establishment, Van Diemen's Land, 1834 to 1850.* Melbourne: Cheshire, 1967.

Hourihan, Margery. *Deconstructing the Hero: Literary Theory and Children's Literature*. London: Routledge, 1997.

———. "Versions of the Past: The Historical Novel in Children's Literature." *Give Them Wings: The Experience of Children's Literature*. Eds. Maurice Saxby and Gordon Winch. 2nd ed. South Melbourne: Macmillan, 1987. 163–76.

Hughes, J. M., P. A. Michell, and W. S. Ramson, eds. *The Australian Concise Oxford Dictionary*. 2nd ed. Melbourne: Oxford UP, 1992.

Hughes, Monica. "The Struggle between Utopia and Dystopia in Writing for Children and Young Adults." *Utopian and Dystopian Writing for Children and Young Adults*. Eds. Carrie Hintz and Elaine Ostry. New York: Routledge, 2003. 156–60.

Hume, Kathryn. *Fantasy and Mimesis*. New York: Methuen, 1984.

Hunt, Peter. "Introduction." *Alternative Worlds in Fantasy Fiction*. Eds. Peter Hunt and Millicent Lenz. London: Continuum, 2001. 1–41.

———. *An Introduction to Children's Literature*. Oxford: Oxford UP, 1994.

Hutcheon, Linda. "'The Pastime of Past Time': Fiction, History, Historiographical Metafiction." *Essentials of the Theory of Fiction*. Eds. Michael Hoffman and Patrick Murphy. 2nd ed. Durham: Duke UP, 1996. 473–95.

Innes, Lyn. "Resurrecting Ned Kelly." *Sydney Studies in English* 29 (2003): 69–78.

Inness, Sherrie A. *Tough Girls: Women Warriors and Wonder Women in Popular Culture*. Philadelphia: U of Pennsylvania P, 1999.

"Interview 1: *Sabriel*". *Garth Nix*. 11 Dec. 2007. http://www.garthnix.co.uk/sabriel.

Jackson, Rosemary. *Fantasy: The Literature of Subversion*. London: Methuen, 1981.

Jones, Dudley and Tony Watkins. "Introduction." *A Necessary Fantasy: The Heroic Figure in Children's Popular Culture*. Eds. Dudley Jones and Tony Watkins. New York: Garland, 2000. 1–19.

———, eds. *A Necessary Fantasy: The Heroic Figure in Children's Popular Culture*. New York: Garland, 2000.

Kearl, Michael. *Endings: A Sociology of Death and Dying*. New York: Oxford UP, 1989.

———. "Images across Cultures and Time". *Kearl's Guide to the Sociology of Death: Death across Time and Space*. 6 Dec. 2007. http://www.trinity.edu/~mkearl/death-1.html#ar.

———. "You Never Have to Die! On Mormons, NDEs, Cryonics, and the American Immortalist Ethos." *The Unknown Country: Death in Australia, Britain and the USA*. Eds. Kathy Charmaz, Glennys Howarth, and Allan Kellehear. Houndmills, UK: Macmillan, 1997. 184–97.

Kellehear, Allan. "The Australian Way of Death: Formative Social and Historical Influences." *Death and Dying in Australia*. Ed. Allan Kellehear. South Melbourne: Oxford UP, 2000. 1–13.

Kellehear, Allan and Ian Anderson. "Death in the Country of Matilda." *The Unknown Country: Death in Australia, Britain and the USA*. Eds. Kathy Charmaz, Glennys Howarth, and Allan Kellehear. Houndmills, UK: Macmillan, 1997. 1–14.

Kellner, Hans. "Language and Historical Representation." *The Postmodern History Reader*. Ed. Keith Jenkins. London: Routledge, 1997. 127–38.

Kortenhaus, Carole M. and Jack Demarest. "Gender Role Stereotyping in Children's Literature: An Update." *Sex Roles: A Journal of Research* 28.3–4 (1993): 219–32.

Kristeva, Julia. *Powers of Horror: An Essay on Abjection*. Trans. Leon S. Roudiez. New York: Columbia UP, 1982.

Krzywinska, Tanya. "*Cicciolina* and the Dynamics of Transgression and Abjection in Explicit Sex Films." *The Body's Perilous Pleasures: Dangerous Desires and Contemporary Culture*. Ed. Michele Aaron. Edinburgh: Edinburgh UP, 1999. 188–209.

Kübler-Ross, Elizabeth. *On Death and Dying*. New York: Macmillan, 1969.

Lassén-Seger, Maria. *Adventures into Otherness: Child Metamorphs in Late Twentieth-Century Literature*. Diss. Åbo Akademi U, 2006. Turku: Åbo Akademi UP, 2006.

———. "Child-Power? Adventures into the Animal Kingdom—The Animorphs Series." *Children's Literature as Communication: The ChiLPA Project*. Ed. Roger D. Sell. Amsterdam: Benjamins, 2002. 159–76.

Latham, Don. "The Cultural Work of Magical Realism in Three Young Adult Novels." *Children's Literature in Education* 38.1 (2007): 59–70.

Lenz, Millicent. *Nuclear Age Literature for Youth: The Quest for a Life-Affirming Ethic*. Chicago: American Library Assn., 1990.

———. "Philip Pullman." *Alternative Worlds in Fantasy Fiction*. Eds. Peter Hunt and Millicent Lenz. London: Continuum, 2001. 122–69.

Lucas, Rose. "Dragging It Out: Tales of Masculinity in Australian Cinema, from *Crocodile Dundee* to *Priscilla, Queen of the Desert." Journal of Australian Studies* 56 (1998): 138–46.

Mallan, Kerry. "Challenging the Phallic Fantasy in Young Adult Fiction." *Ways of Being Male: Representing Masculinities in Children's Literature and Film*. Ed. John Stephens. New York: Routledge, 2002. 150–63.

———. "Fatal Attractions: Death, Femininity and Children's Literature." *Crossing the Boundaries*. Eds. Geoff Bull and Michèle Anstey. Frenchs Forest, Australia: Pearson, 2002. 175–90.

———. "Feeling a Little Queer? Performing Lesbian Desire and Identity in Youth Texts." *Seriously Playful: Genre, Performance, and Text*. Eds. Sharyn Pearce and Kerry Mallan. Flaxton, Australia: Post Pressed, 2004. 113–21.

———. "Hitting Below the Belt: Action Femininity and Representations of Female Subjectivity." *Youth Cultures: Texts, Images, and Identities*. Eds. Kerry Mallan and Sharyn Pearce. Westport, CT: Praeger, 2003. 139–53.

———. "Just Looking? The Body, the Gaze and the Male Artist." *Manning the Next Millennium: Studies in Masculinities*. Eds. Sharyn Pearce and Vivienne Muller. Bentley, Australia: Black Swan, 2002. 41–52.

———. "New World Orders and the Dystopian Turn: Transforming Visions of Territoriality and Belonging in *Red Heart*." 5th International Conference of the Utopian Studies Society, U of Porto, Portugal, 7–11 July 2004.

Mallan, Kerry and Sharyn Pearce. "Introduction: Tales of Youth in Postmodern Culture." *Youth Cultures: Texts, Images, and Identities*. Eds. Kerry Mallan and Sharyn Pearce. Westport, CT: Praeger, 2003. ix–xix.

Martin, Susan K. "Good Girls Die, Bad Girls Don't: The Uses of the Dying Virgin in Nineteenth-Century Australian Fiction." *The Unknown Country: Death in Australia, Britain and the USA*. Eds. Kathy Charmaz, Glennys Howarth, and Allan Kellehear. Houndmills, UK: Macmillan, 1997. 31–44.

Mason, Fran. "Loving the Technological Undead: Cyborg Sex and Necrophilia in Richard Calder's *Dead Trilogy." The Body's Perilous Pleasures: Dangerous Desires and Contemporary Culture*. Ed. Michele Aaron. Edinburgh: Edinburgh UP, 1999. 108–25

McCallum, Robyn. *Ideologies of Identity in Adolescent Fiction: The Dialogic Construction of Subjectivity*. New York: Garland, 1999.

McCallum, Robyn and John Stephens. "Unbronzing the Aussie: Heroes and Snags in Fiction and Television for Australian Adolescents." *A Necessary Fantasy: The Heroic Figure in Children's Popular Culture*. Eds. Dudley Jones and Tony Watkins. New York: Garland, 2000. 343–363.

McCarron, Kevin. "Dead Rite: Adolescent Horror Fiction and Death." *Representations of Childhood Death*. Eds. Gillian Avery and Kimberley Reynolds. London: Macmillan, 2000. 189–203.

McHoul, Alec and Wendy Grace. *A Foucault Primer: Discourse, Power and the Subject*. Ed. Ken Ruthven. Carlton South: Melbourne UP, 1993.

McInally, Kate. "Reading Girls' Desire in *Touching Earth Lightly*." Conference of the Australasian Children's Literature Association for Research, U of Technology, Sydney, 16–17 July 2004.

McKenna, Brendan and Sharyn Pearce. *Strange Journeys: The Works of Gary Crew*. Sydney: Hodder, 1999.

McKenzie, John. "The Representation of Suicide in Adolescent Literature as a Site of 'Crossing Boundaries'." *Crossing the Boundaries*. Eds. Geoff Bull and Michèle Anstey. Frenchs Forest, Australia: Pearson, 2002. 191–219.

McNay, Lois. *Foucault: A Critical Introduction*. Cambridge, UK: Polity, 1994.

McPherson, Joanne. "The Abject and the Oedipal in Sonya Hartnett's *Sleeping Dogs." Papers: Explorations into Children's Literature* 9.3 (1999): 15–22.

Meaney, Neville. "The 'Yellow Peril', Invasion Scare Novels and Australian Political Culture." *The 1890s: Australian Literature and Literary Culture*. Ed. Ken Stewart. St Lucia: U of Queensland P, 1996. 228–63.

Meiklejohn, Annette Dale. "ANZAC Day." *The Literature Base* 13.1 (2002): 14–17.

Mellor, Philip A. "Death in High Modernity: The Contemporary Presence and Absence of Death." *The Sociology of Death: Theory, Culture, Practice*. Ed. David Clark. Oxford: Blackwell, 1993. 11–30.

Mellor, Philip A. and Chris Shilling. "Modernity, Self-Identity and the Sequestration of Death." *Sociology* 27.3 (1993): 411–31.

Mikkonen, Kai. "Theories of Metamorphosis: From Metatrope to Textual Revision." *Style* 30.2 (1996): 309–40.

Mills, Alice. "Fixity and Flow in Garth Nix's *Sabriel*." *Papers: Explorations into Children's Literature* 11.3 (2001): 15–23.

———. "Writing on the Edge: Gary Crew's Fiction." *Papers: Explorations into Children's Literature* 8.3 (1998): 25–35.

Misson, Ray. "Not Telling It Straight." *Crossing the Boundaries*. Eds. Geoff Bull and Michèle Anstey. Frenchs Forest, Australia: Pearson, 2002. 221–34.

Moody, A. David. *Thomas Stearns Eliot: Poet*. 2nd ed. Cambridge: Cambridge UP, 1994.

Moore, Clive. "Colonial Manhood and Masculinities." *Journal of Australian Studies* 56 (1998): 35–52.

Mordue, Mark. "The Secret Life of Us: Australia's Young Adult Literature." *Australian Author* 35.1 (2003): 8–16.

Morling, Trevor. *Report of the Commissioner the Hon. Mr Justice T.R. Morling*. Darwin: Govt. Printer of the Northern Territory, 1987.

Morrison, Toni. "Playing in the Dark." *Literary Theory: An Anthology*. Eds. Julie Rivkin and Michael Ryan. Malden, MA: Blackwell, 1998. 923–35.

Moylan, Tom. *Scraps of the Untainted Sky: Science Fiction, Utopia, Dystopia*. Boulder, CO: Westview, 2000.

Munslow, Alan. *Deconstructing History*. London: Routledge, 1997.

Murrie, Linzi. "The Australian Legend: Writing Australian Masculinity/Writing 'Australian' Masculine." *Journal of Australian Studies* 56 (1998): 68–77.

———. "Changing Masculinities: Disruption and Anxiety in Contemporary Australian Writing." *Journal of Australian Studies* 56 (1998): 169–79.

"Ned Kelly". *Australian Government Culture and Recreation Portal*. 28 Jan. 2004. http://www.cultureandrecreation.gov.au/articles/nedkelly/.

Newsinger, John. "Fantasy and Revolution: An Interview with China Miéville". *International Socialism Journal* 88 (2000). 6 Jul. 2005. http:/pubs.socialistreviewindex.org.uk/isj88/newsinger.htm.

Niall, Brenda. *Australia through the Looking Glass*. Carlton South: Melbourne UP, 1984.

Nieuwenhuizen, Agnes. "Picture Books or Patrick White?" *Viewpoint: On Books for Young Adults* 1.1 (1993): 3–5.

Nikolajeva, Maria. *From Mythic to Linear: Time in Children's Literature*. Lanham, MD: Scarecrow, 2000.

Nimon, Maureen. "Scales of Judgment—Justice for All or the Strange Case of Prophet and Pervert, John Marsden." *Orana* 35.3 (1999): 5–16.

Nimon, Maureen and John Foster. *The Adolescent Novel: Australian Perspectives*. Wagga Wagga: Ctr. for Information Studies, Charles Sturt U, 1997.

Nodelman, Perry. "Ordinary Monstrosity: The World of Goosebumps." *Children's Literature Association Quarterly* 22.3 (1997): 118–25.

———. "The Other: Orientalism, Colonialism and Children's Literature." *Children's Literature Association Quarterly* 17.1 (1992): 29–35.

O'Leary, Stephen D. *Arguing the Apocalypse: A Theory of Millennial Rhetoric*. New York: Oxford UP, 1994.

Ostry, Elaine. "'Is He Still Human? Are You?': Young Adult Science Fiction in the Posthuman Age." *The Lion and the Unicorn* 28.2 (2004): 222–46.

Owen, Mary. "Developing a Love of Reading: Why Young Adult Literature Is Important." *Orana* 39.1 (2003): 11–17.

Page, Sue. "Looking for Action—Women in Young Adult Fantasy." *Crossing the Boundaries*. Eds. Geoff Bull and Michèle Anstey. Frenchs Forest, Australia: Pearson, 2002. 125–44.

Palmer, Paulina. *Lesbian Gothic: Transgressive Fictions*. London: Cassell, 1999.

Pearce, Sharyn. "Growing up Gender-Wise: What We Give to Girls." *Magpies: Talking About Books for Children* 6.5 (1991): 10–14.

———. "Messages from the Inside? Multiculturalism in Contemporary Australian Children's Literature." *The Lion and the Unicorn* 27.2 (2003): 235–50.

Pearl, Monica B. "Symptoms of AIDS in Contemporary Film: Mortal Anxiety in an Age of Sexual Panic." *The Body's Perilous Pleasures: Dangerous Desires and Contemporary Culture*. Ed. Michele Aaron. Edinburgh: Edinburgh UP, 1999. 210–25.

Pierce, Peter. "Preying on the Past: Contexts of Some Recent Neo-Historical Fiction." *Australian Literary Studies* 15.4 (1992): 304–12.

Price, David. *History Made, History Imagined: Contemporary Literature, Poiesis, and the Past*. Urbana: U of Illinois P, 1999.

Prior, Lindsay. *The Social Organization of Death: Medical Discourse and Social Practices in Belfast.* New York: St. Martin's, 1989.

Punter, David. *Gothic Pathologies: The Text, the Body and the Law.* Houndmills, UK: Macmillan, 1998.

———. *The Literature of Terror: A History of Gothic Fictions from 1765 to the Present Day.* 2nd ed. Vol. 2. Harlow, UK: Longman, 1996.

Rajan, Rajeswari Sunder. "Representing Sati: Continuities and Discontinuities." *Death and Representation.* Eds. Sarah Webster Goodwin and Elisabeth Bronfen. Baltimore: Johns Hopkins UP, 1993. 285–311.

Reynolds, Kimberley. "Fatal Fantasies: The Death of Children in Victorian and Edwardian Fantasy Writing." *Representations of Childhood Death.* Eds. Gillian Avery and Kimberley Reynolds. London: Macmillan, 2000. 169–88.

Reynolds, Kimberley and Paul Yates. "Too Soon: Representations of Childhood Death in Literature for Children." *Children in Culture: Approaches to Childhood.* Ed. Karín Lesnik-Oberstein. Houndmills, UK: Macmillan, 1998. 151–77.

Richardson, Alan. "The Dangers of Sympathy: Sibling Incest in English Romantic Poetry." *Studies in English Literature* 25.4 (1985): 737–54.

———. "Rethinking Romantic Incest: Human Universals, Literary Representation, and the Biology of the Mind." *New Literary History* 31.3 (2000): 553–72.

Rivkin, Julie and Michael Ryan. "The Class of 1968—Post-Structuralism *par lui-même.*" *Literary Theory: An Anthology.* Eds. Julie Rivkin and Michael Ryan. Malden, MA: Blackwell, 1998. 333–57.

———. "The Politics of Culture." *Literary Theory: An Anthology.* Eds. Julie Rivkin and Michael Ryan. Malden, MA: Blackwell, 1998. 1025–27.

———. "Strangers to Ourselves: Psychoanalysis." *Literary Theory: An Anthology.* Eds. Julie Rivkin and Michael Ryan. Malden, MA: Blackwell, 1998. 119–227.

Robert, Hannah. "Disciplining the Female Aboriginal Body: Inter-Racial Sex and the Pretence of Separation." *Australian Feminist Studies* 16.34 (2001): 69–81.

Robinson, Sally. *Engendering the Subject: Gender and Self-Representation in Contemporary Women's Fiction.* Albany: State U of New York P, 1991.

Romøren, Rolf and John Stephens. "Representing Masculinities in Norwegian and Australian Young Adult Fiction." *Ways of Being Male: Representing Masculinities in Children's Literature and Film.* Ed. John Stephens. New York: Routledge, 2002. 216–33.

Rose, Deborah Bird. *Dingo Makes Us Human: Life and Land in an Australian Aboriginal Culture.* 2nd ed. Oakleigh, Australia: Cambridge UP, 2000.

———. *Nourishing Terrains: Australian Aboriginal Views of Landscape and Wilderness.* Canberra: Australian Heritage Comm., 1996.

———. *Reports from a Wild Country: Ethics for Decolonisation.* Sydney: U of New South Wales P, 2004.

Rutherford, Leonie. "'Lineaments of Gratified [Parental] Desire': Romance and Domestication in Some Recent Australian Children's Fiction." *Papers: Explorations into Children's Literature* 4.1 (1993): 3–13.

Sambell, Kay. "Carnivalizing the Future: A New Approach to Theorizing Childhood and Adulthood in Science Fiction for Young Readers." *The Lion and the Unicorn* 28.2 (2004): 247–67.

———. "Presenting the Case for Social Change: The Creative Dilemma of Dystopian Writing for Children." *Utopian and Dystopian Writing for Children and Young Adults.* Eds. Carrie Hintz and Elaine Ostry. New York: Routledge, 2003. 163–78.

Saunders, Corinne. "Epilogue: Into the Twenty-First Century." *A Companion to Romance: From Classical to Contemporary.* Ed. Corinne Saunders. Oxford: Blackwell, 2004. 539–41.

Saxby, Maurice. *The Proof of the Puddin': Australian Children's Literature, 1970–1990.* Gosford, Australia: Scholastic, 1993.

Scates, Bruce. "In Gallipoli's Shadow: Pilgrimage, Memory, Mourning and the Great War." *Australian Historical Studies* 33.119 (2002): 1–21.

Schaffer, Kay. *Women and the Bush: Forces of Desire in the Australian Cultural Tradition.* Cambridge: Cambridge UP, 1988.

Schleifer, Ronald. "Afterword—Walter Benjamin and the Crisis of Representation: Multiplicity, Meaning, and Athematic Death." *Death and Representation.* Eds. Sarah Webster Goodwin and Elisabeth Bronfen. Baltimore: Johns Hopkins UP, 1993. 312–33.

———. *Rhetoric and Death: The Language of Postmodernism and Postmodern Discourse Theory.* Urbana: U of Illinois P, 1990.

Schober, Adrian. "The Lost and Possessed Child in Henry James's *The Turn of the Screw*, William Friedkin & William Peter Blatty's *The Exorcist* and Victor Kelleher's *Del-Del*." *Papers: Explorations into Children's Literature* 9.2 (1999): 40–48.

Schopenhauer, Arthur. *The World as Will and Idea*. Trans. R. B. Haldane and J. Kemp. 7th ed. Vol. 3. London: Paul, n.d.

Schwenger, Peter. "Corpsing the Image." *Critical Inquiry* 26.3 (2000): 395–413.

Scutter, Heather. *Displaced Fictions: Contemporary Australian Fiction for Teenagers and Young Adults*. Carlton South: Melbourne UP, 1999.

Seale, Clive. *Constructing Death: The Sociology of Dying and Bereavement*. Cambridge: Cambridge UP, 1998.

Searsmith, Kelly. "News from Somewhere: A Case for Romance-Tradition Fantasy's Reformist Poetic." *The Utopian Fantastic: Selected Essays from the Twentieth International Conference on the Fantastic in the Arts*. Ed. Martha Bartter. Westport, CT: Praeger, 2004. 137–49.

Shilling, Chris. *The Body and Social Theory*. London: Sage, 1993.

Singer, Linda. *Erotic Welfare: Sexual Theory and Politics in the Age of Epidemic*. New York: Routledge, 1993.

Smith, Andrew and Diana Wallace. "The Female Gothic: Then and Now." *Gothic Studies* 6.1 (2004): 1–7.

Spargo, Tamsin. "Introduction: Past, Present and Future Pasts." *Reading the Past: Literature and History*. Ed. Tamsin Spargo. Houndmills, UK: Palgrave, 2000. 1–11.

The Spirit of ANZAC. n.p.: Parliament New South Wales, Australia, 2004. N. pag.

Stephen, Kylie. "Sexualised Bodies." *Real Bodies: A Sociological Introduction*. Eds. Mary Evans and Ellie Lee. Houndmills, UK: Palgrave, 2002. 29–45.

Stephens, John. "Constructions of Female Selves in Adolescent Fiction: Makeovers as Metonym." *Papers: Explorations into Children's Literature* 9.1 (1999): 5–13.

———. "Editor's Introduction: Always Facing the Issues—Preoccupations in Australian Children's Literature." *The Lion and the Unicorn* 27.2 (2003): v–xvii.

———. "Gender, Genre and Children's Literature." *Signal* 79 (1996): 17–30.

———. "'I'll Never Be the Same after That Summer': From Abjection to Subjective Agency in Teen Films." *Youth Cultures: Texts, Images, and Identities*. Eds. Kerry Mallan and Sharyn Pearce. Westport, CT: Praeger, 2003. 123–37.

———. "'Is This the Promised End.?' *Fin de Siécle* Mentality and Children's Literature." *Reflections of Change: Children's Literature since 1945*. Ed. Sandra L. Beckett. Westport, CT: Greenwood, 1997. 99–106.

———. *Language and Ideology in Children's Fiction*. New York: Addison, 1992.

———. "Post-Disaster Fiction: The Problematics of a Genre." *Papers: Explorations into Children's Literature* 3.3 (1992): 126–30.

Stephens, John and Robyn McCallum. *Retelling Stories, Framing Culture: Traditional Story and Metanarratives in Children's Literature*. New York: Garland, 1998.

———. "'There Are Worse Things Than Ghosts': Reworking Horror Chronotopes in Australian Children's Fiction." *Mystery in Children's Literature: From the Rational to the Supernatural*. Eds. Adrienne E. Gavin and Christopher Routledge. Houndmills, UK: Palgrave, 2001. 165–83.

Stewart, Garrett. *Death Sentences: Styles of Dying in British Fiction*. Cambridge: Harvard UP, 1984.

———. "A Valediction for Bidding Mourning: Death and the Narratee in Brontë's *Villette*." *Death and Representation*. Eds. Sarah Webster Goodwin and Elisabeth Bronfen. Baltimore: Johns Hopkins UP, 1993. 51–79.

Stir. Dir. Stephen Wallace. Hoyts, 1980.

Tanner, Laura E. *Lost Bodies: Inhabiting the Borders of Life and Death*. Ithaca: Cornell UP, 2006.

Taylor, Sandra. "Transforming the Texts: Towards a Feminist Classroom Practice." *Texts of Desire: Essays on Fiction, Femininity, and Schooling*. Ed. Linda K. Christian-Smith. London: Falmer, 1993. 126–44.

The Terminator. Dir. James Cameron. Orion Pictures, 1984.

Terminator 2: Judgment Day. Dir. James Cameron. TriStar Pictures, 1991.

Tong, Rosemarie Putnam. *Feminist Thought: A More Comprehensive Introduction*. 2nd ed. St Leonards, Australia: Allen, 1998.

Trites, Roberta Seelinger. *Disturbing the Universe: Power and Repression in Adolescent Literature*. Iowa: U of Iowa P, 2000.

———. "Theories and Possibilities of Adolescent Literature." *Children's Literature Association Quarterly* 21 (1996): 2–3.

Tseëlon, Efrat. *The Masque of Femininity*. London: Sage, 1995.

Tumarkin, Maria. "'Wishing You Weren't Here.' Thinking About Trauma, Place and the Port Arthur Massacre." *Journal of Australian Studies* 67 (2001): 196–205.

Turner, Bryan S. *The Body and Society: Explorations in Social Theory*. 2nd ed. London: Sage, 1996.

Turner, Graeme. *National Fictions: Literature, Film and the Construction of Australian Narrative*. 2nd ed. St Leonards, Australia: Allen, 1993.

Twitchell, James B. *Dreadful Pleasures: An Anatomy of Modern Horror*. New York: Oxford UP, 1985.

Walker, David. "The Getting of Manhood." *Australian Popular Culture*. Eds. Peter Spearritt and David Walker. Sydney: Allen, 1979. 121–44.

Walter, Tony. *The Revival of Death*. London: Routledge, 1994.

———. "Sociologists Never Die: British Sociology and Death." *The Sociology of Death: Theory, Culture, Practice*. Ed. David Clark. Oxford: Blackwell, 1993. 264–95.

———. "The Sociology of Death." *Sociology Compass* 2.1 (2008): 317–36. 7 Feb. 2008 http:// www.blackwell-synergy.com/doi/pdf/10.1111/j.1751–9020.2007.00069.x.

Watkins, Tony. "Homelands: Landscape and Identity in Children's Literature." *Landscape and Identity: Perspectives from Australia*. Proceedings of the Conference of the Centre for Children's Literature, U of South Australia, Adelaide, 25–27 February, 1994. Eds. Wendy Parsons and Robert Goodwin. Adelaide: Auslib, 1994. 3–20.

Wetherell, Margaret. "Romantic Discourse and Feminist Analysis: Interrogating Investment, Power and Desire." *Feminism and Discourse: Psychological Perspectives*. Eds. Sue Wilkinson and Celia Kitzinger. London: Sage, 1995. 128–44.

Wilson, Kim. "Abjection in Contemporary Australian Young Adult Fiction." *Papers: Explorations into Children's Literature* 11.3 (2001): 24–31.

Wolmark, Jenny. "Staying with the Body: Narratives of the Posthuman in Contemporary Science Fiction." *Edging into the Future: Science Fiction and Contemporary Cultural Transformation*. Eds. Veronica Hollinger and Joan Gordon. Philadelphia: U of Pennsylvania P, 2002. 76–89.

Index